The DOCTRINE OF GOD

The MOSLEM CHRIST

Two classic books by

SAMUEL M. ZWEMER

The Apostle to Islam

The MOSLEM DOCTRINE OF GOD
Original ©1905

The MOSLEM CHRIST
Original ©1912

ISBN: 978-0-9715346-4-3 Paperback

Published by:

ANM
publishers

Advancing Native Missions
P.O. Box 5303
Charlottesville, VA 22905
www.Adnamis.org

FOREWORD

The book that you hold in your hand contains two publications birthed from missionary experience and the cry of a heart on fire for God. *The Moslem Doctrine of God* (1905) and *The Moslem Christ* (1912) were two of the earliest of Samuel M. Zwemer's many published works. The son of Dutch immigrants to America, Zwemer was a fervent evangelical minister with the Dutch Reformed Church in America (now the Reformed Church in America) and one of the founders of the Arabian Mission.

Known in his lifetime as the "Apostle to Islam," missionary Samuel M. Zwemer (1867-1952), left a rich legacy and godly example, especially regarding how the Church should think about Islam and act towards Muslims.

Muslims are now a seemingly permanent fixture in the daily news, yet very few Christians have taken the time to even understand the basic facts of what they believe. Many Christians, when first learning about Islam, are often amazed at what appears to be a number of common beliefs between the two, especially as it relates to God and Jesus Christ. But is one to assume from these apparent similarities that the Koran, the holy book of Muslims, teaches the same thing as the Bible?

Are Islam and Christianity really compatible? Does use of the same terminology by Muslims necessitate equal definitions of those terms within Christianity? The author explores these questions and definitively answers them. Using original Islamic source materials in Arabic, coupled with personal experience, the author reveals what Muslims actually believe about God and Jesus Christ. By so doing, he sets forth a challenge to the Christian reader to take the Gospel to Muslims.

Khalil Ullah

بسم الله الرحمن الرحيم

A TALISMAN FROM A MOSLEM BOOK ON THE NAMES OF ALLAH.

Translation: "*In the name of Allah the Merciful, the Compassionate. Truly Thou wilt preserve the one who carries this writing of mine from the evil of all that might harm him and Thou wilt appoint over him its angels and servants and assistants who are entrusted with its service and guard him by day and by night. Mohammed is the Apostle of Allah and those with him are stronger than the unbelievers. Among them are merciful ones whom we see bowing and kneeling seeking kindness from Allah and favor. Their marks are on their faces, the effect of prostration, and that is their likeness in the Pentateuch and the Gospel.*"

THE MOSLEM
DOCTRINE OF GOD

An Essay on the Character
and Attributes of Allah
according to the Koran
and Orthodox Tradition

BY

SAMUEL M. ZWEMER

Author of "Arabia, the Cradle of Islam,"
"Raymund Lull," etc.

ANM
publishers

TO MY BELOVED FATHER

Adrian Zwemer.

"Yet most I thank thee, not for any deed,
But for the sense thy living self did breed
That Fatherhood is at the great world's core."

"Your God and our God are the same."—*The Koran.*

"Thou believest that there is one God; thou doest well, the devils also believe and tremble."—*James 2: 19.*

"Neither knoweth any man the Father save the Son and he to whomsoever the Son will reveal Him."—*Matt. 11: 27.*

PREFACE

JEWS, Christians and Mohammedans believe in one God and yet differ widely in their interpretation of this idea. Unless we know the Moslem's idea of God we cannot understand his creed nor judge his philosophy, nor intelligently communicate our idea of God to him. The strength of Islam is not in its ritual nor in its ethics, but in its tremendous and fanatical grasp on the one great truth —Monotheism.

Our purpose in these pages is to learn the extent and content of this idea; an idea which holds the Moslem world even more than they hold it. I have found no book in English, among the wealth of literature on Islam, that treats of this subject. In German there are two books on the theology of the Koran,[1] but both are rare and limited, as appears from their titles, to a consideration of what *the Koran* teaches.

For a fair interpretation, however, of Islam's idea of God we must go not only to the Koran, but also to orthodox tradition. The *Hadith* are the records of the authoritative sayings and doings of Moham-

[1]Haller's *Lehre von Gott aus dem Koran gezogen.* Altenburg, 1779. Dettinger's *Beitrage zu einer Theologie des Korans.* Tübingen Zeitschrift für Theologie, 1831, 3's Heft.

med and have exercised tremendous power on Moslem
thought since the early days of Islam; not only by
supplementing but by interpreting the Koran. The
Hadith are accepted by every Moslem sect, in some
form or other, and are indispensable to Islam. For
proof of these statements we refer to Sprenger and
Muir. The Koran-text quoted is from Palmer's
translation, together with references to the three
standard commentaries of Beidhawi, Zamakhshari
and Jellalain. For orthodox tradition I have used
the collection known as *Mishkat-ul-Misabih,* because
it is short, authoritative, and because an English
translation of this collection exists. (Captain Matthew's *Mishcat-ul-Masabih,* or a collection of the
most authentic traditions regarding the actions and
sayings of Mohammed; exhibiting the origin of the
manners and customs, the civil, religious and mili-
tary policy of the Musselmans. Translated from the
original Arabic. Calcutta, 1809; 2 folio volumes.)
This collection, originally the work of *Bagäwi*
(516 A.H.) and based on the classical works of
Buchari and *Muslim,* was edited and issued in its
present form by *Abdullah-al-Khatib* (737 A.H.);
and Brockelmann in his history of Arabic literature
calls it "the most correct and practical book of Moslem traditions." I had no access to the translation
and all references are to the Arabic edition printed
in Delhi.

The frontispiece is from the celebrated *Shems-ul-*

Ma'arif of *Mŭhyee-ed-Din-al-Buni,* This book treats of the names of God and their use in amulets, healing, recovering lost property, etc. I am aware that in some parts of the Mohammedan world disintegration of religious ideas is in progress and t.at the *theology* as well as the ethics of Islam is being modified by contact with Western civilization, Protestant missions, and Christian morals. My idea, however, was not to sketch the theological views of Moslems in Liverpool nor of the reformers of Islam in India, but of the vast orthodox majority of the people both learned and illiterate.

In the comparative study of any religion the idea of God is fundamental, and if these pages give a clearer idea of what Mohammed taught and what his followers believe concerning Allah, the Christian missionary will the more earnestly preach to Moslems the Gospel of our Saviour, who said, "He that hath seen Me hath seen the Father."

S. M. ZWEMER.

BAHREIN, ARABIA,
February, 1905.

The MOSLEM DOCTRINE OF GOD

CONTENTS

"Historically, a pure theism is all but impotent. There is only one example of it on a large scale in the world, and that is a kind of bastard Christianity—Mohammedanism; and we all know what good that is as a religion. There are plenty of people who call themselves Theists and not Christians. Well, I venture to say that is a phase that will not last. There is little substance in it. The God whom men know outside of Jesus Christ is a poor nebulous thing; an idea and not a reality. You will have to get something more substantial than the far-off god of an unchristian Theism if you mean to sway the world and to satisfy men's hearts."—*Alexander Maclaren* (in sermon on John 14:1).

ANALYSIS OF ISLAM AS A SYSTEM

"There is no god but Allah, and Mohammed is His Apostle."

THE DOCTRINE OF GOD "Pantheism of Force."

1. Negative (*Nafi*) "There is no god"—

2. Positive (*Athbat*) "but Allah."

THE DOCTRINE OF REVELATION:

(Mohammed, the Apostle of God, is the sole channel of revelation and abrogates former revelations.)

Orthodox Moslems acknowledge two kinds of revelation and one authority beside them:

1. By the KORAN

(*Wahi el Matlu*)

Verbal revelation, which teaches the two-fold demands of Islam:—

(The Book)

A. FAITH:

(what to believe)

"Iman"
[The six *articles* of faith]

1. In God
2. Angels { angels / jinn / devils }
3. Books—
5. Last Day (Judgment)
6. Predestination
4. Prophets:—

B. PRACTICE:

(what to do)

"Din"

[*the five pillars*]

1. Repetition of Creed
2. *Prayer* (five times daily) including:—
3 Fasting (month of Ramadhan)
4. Alms-giving (about 1-40 of income)
5. Pilgrimage . . .

II. By TRADITION
(*Wahi gheir el Matlu*)
Revelation by example of the perfect prophet
(The Man)

1. Records of what Mohammed *did* (Sunnat-el-fa'il) (example)
2. Records of what Mohammed *enjoined* (Sunnat-el-kaul) (precept)
3. Records of what Mohammed *allowed* (Sunnat-et-takrir) (license)

III. Other Authority

a. Among the *Sunnites*:

b. Among the *Shiahs*:

DEVELOPED FROM ITS CREED

His names . . . . { of the *essence, Allah* (*the absolute unit*)
{ of the attributes,—*ninety-nine names.*

His attributes . . . { The physical emphasized above the *moral.*
{ Deification of *absolute force.*

His nature . . . . { Expressed by a series of *negations* "He is
{ *not.*"

Moslems believe that 104 "books" were sent from
heaven in the following order:

To Adam — ten books
" Seth—fifty   "   } these are utterly lost.
" Enoch—thirty "
" Abraham²—ten "
" Moses—the TORAH   } These are highly spoken of in the Koran but are now
" David—the ZABOOR   { in corrupted condition and have been abrogated by
" Jesus—the INJIL   { the final book.
" Mohammed—the KORAN   { eternal in origin; complete and miraculous in
{ character; supreme in beauty and authority.

A. The
Greater:
{ Adam—"Chosen of God"
{ Noah—"Preacher of God"
{ Abraham—"Friend of God"
{ Moses—"Spokesman of God"
{ Jesus—called "Word of God" and
{   "Spirit of God"
{ MOHAMMED, (*who has 201 names and*
{   *titles*)

{ Enoch, Hud, Salih,
{ Ishmael, Isaac,
{ Jacob, Joseph, Lot,
{ Aaron, Shuaib,
{ Zakariah, John,
{ David, Solomon,
{ Elias, Job, Jonah,
{ Ezra, Lukman,
{ Zu-el-kifl,
{ Alexander the Great,
{ Elisha,

B. *The* Of these there have been thousands.
Less Twenty-two are mentioned in the Koran, viz.—

1. Purification { washing various parts of the body
{ three times according to fourteen
{ rules.

2. Posture(prostrations){ facing the Kiblah (Mecca)
{ prostrations
{ genuflections

3. Petition { Declarat'n
{ the Fatihah or first Surah.
{ Praise and Confession—the Salaam.

. . . { *Mecca* (incumbent)
{ Medina (meritorious but voluntary)
{ Kerbela (Meshed Ali, etc.), (Shiahs)

Verbally handed
down from
mouth to mouth
and finally *sifted*
and recorded by
both sects:

A. The Sunnite Traditions:
(collected and recorded by the
following six authorities)

B. The Shiah Traditions:
(five authorities)

1. Buchari	A.H.	256[1]
2. Muslim	"	261[1]
3. Tirmizi	"	279[1]
4. Abu Daood	"	275[1]
5. An-Nasaee	"	303[1]
6. Ibn Majah	"	273[1]
1. Kafi	A.H.	329
2. Sheikh Ali	"	381
3. "Tahzib"	"	466[2]
4. "Istibsar"	"	466[2]
5. Ar-Razi	"	406

IJMA'A or unanimous consent of the leading companions of Mohammed concerning Source I., i.e., the Koran.
KIYAS or the deductions of orthodox teachers from Sources I. and II.

The doctrine of the twelve IMAMS (beginning with *Ali*), who interpret I. and II.

[1]Not one of them flourished until *three centuries* after Mohammed.   ² By Abu Jaafer.

I

THERE IS NO GOD BUT ALLAH

"One God the Arabian prophet preached to man;
  One God the Orient still
Adores through many a realm of mighty span—
  A God of power and will.

"A power that at his pleasure doth create
  To save or to destroy,
And to eternal pain predestinate
  As to eternal joy."
                              —*Lord Houghton.*

AMONG all the religions of the world there is
none that has a shorter creed than Islam;
none whose creed is so well known and so often repeated. The whole system of Mohammedan theology
and philosophy and religious life is summed up in
seven words: *La ilaha illa Allah, Mohammed rasul
Allah.* "There is no god but Allah and Mohammed
is Allah's apostle"—on these two phrases hang all
the laws and teaching and morals of Islam. The
logical development of Islam took place after the
death of Mohammed in two ways: by the interpretation of the Koran and by the collection (or inven-

tion) of a mass of so-called tradition. The former is what Allah revealed by means of a book; the latter is what Allah revealed by means of a man, Mohammed. Both revelations have well-nigh equal authority and both rest their authority on the *kalimet* or creed of seven words. The accompanying analysis shows this relation.[1]

Gibbon characterizes the first part of the Moslem's creed as "an eternal truth" and the second part as a "necessary fiction."[2] Concerning the latter statement there is no dispute, but whether we can admit the former depends altogether on the character of the Being of whom it is affirmed that He displaces all other gods. If Allah's nature and attributes are in any way distorted or are unworthy of Deity, then even the first clause of the briefest of all creeds is false. "Because Mohammed taught the unity of God it has been too hastily concluded that he was a great social and moral reformer as well. But there is no charm in the abstract doctrine of the unity of God to elevate humanity. The essential point is the character attributed to this one God."[3] It is, therefore, not superfluous to inquire both from the Koran and from orthodox Tradition what Moslems mean by asserting God's unity and what character they ascribe to their only, true God. For there is no doubt

[1]Revised and reprinted from *Arabia, the Cradle of Islam.*
[2]*Decline and Fall of the Roman Empire,* Vol. III., pp. 488.
[3]Osborne's *Islam under the Khalifs of Bagdad,* p. vii.

that they themselves emphasize nothing so much as this part of their system. It is the motto-text of the Moslem's home-life, the baptismal formula to welcome the infant as a believer, the final message to whisper in the ears of the dying, *La ilaha illa Allah*. These words they chant when carrying a burden or a bier; these words they inscribe on their banners and their door-posts; they appear on all the early coins of the caliphs and have been the great battle-cry of Islam for thirteen centuries. By repeating these words, the infidel turns Moslem and the renegade is welcomed back to a spiritual brotherhood. By this creed the faithful are called to prayer five times daily, from Morocco to the Philippines, and this is the platform on which all the warring sects of Islam can unite, for it is the foundation and criterion of their religion. According to a traditional saying of Mohammed, "God said to Moses, if you were to put the whole universe on one side of the scale-pans and the words *La ilaha illa Allah* on the other this would outweigh that."[1] Orthodox tradition also relates that the prophet one day was passing by a dry and withered tree and as soon as he struck it with his staff the leaves fell off; then the prophet said, Verily, the words *La ilaha illa Allah* shake off the believer's sins as my staff shook off the leaves from this tree.[2]

[1] *Mishkat el Misabih*, Delhi edition, Book X., p. 201.
[2] *Ibid.*, p. 202.

The Koran is never weary of reiterating the formula which expresses God's unity, and the one hundred and twelfth Surah, specially devoted to this subject, is, so Moslems say, equal in value to one-third of the whole book. It is related by Zamakhshari in his commentary that Mohammed said, "The seven heavens and the seven earths are built on this Surah and whoever reads it enters paradise."

Now in spite of the emphasis thus put on the doctrine of God's unity by Moslems, and in spite of the fact that it is *this* part of their creed which is their glory and boast, there has been a strange neglect on the part of most writers who have described the religion of Mohammed to study Mohammed's idea of God. It is so easy to be misled by a name or by etymologies. Nearly all writers take for granted that the God of the Koran is the same being and has like attributes as Jehovah or as the Godhead of the New Testament. Especially is this true of the rationalistic students of Islam in Germany and England. Is this view correct? The answer, whether affirmative or negative, has important bearing not only on missions to Moslems but on a true philosophical attitude toward this greatest of all false faiths. If we have to deal with "an eternal truth" linked to "a necessary fiction" our simple task is to sever the link and let the eternal truth stand to make men free. On the other hand, if the necessary fiction is put as the foundation of a distorted truth, there can be no compromise; both clauses of the creed fall together.

To the etymologist, Zeus-Pater, Jupiter and Heavenly Father mean the same thing; but these words express widely different ideas to the student of comparative religions. Many people have a better knowledge of Jupiter, Brahma or Thor as deities than of *Allah;* and it is so because in the former case they go to mythology and in the latter case to etymology for the sum of their ideas. The word *Allah* is used for God not only by all Moslems, but by all Arabic-speaking Jews and Christians in the Orient. But this does not necessarily mean that the *idea* expressed by the word is the same in each case. The ideas of Mohammed regarding God's existence, character and attributes came to him from three sources. First he undoubtedly had a knowledge of God from nature, and the passages of the Koran which set forth this natural theology are some of them the most beautiful and poetic in the whole book. Then, by his heredity and environment he could not free himself from the pagan ideas of Deity current among the Arabs. Lastly, he learned something of the God of Abraham and of the teachings of the New Testament from the Jews and Christians of Arabia and Abyssinia. From these three sources Mohammed obtained his theology, and to each source we can trace some of the ideas he sets forth in the Koran and in his table-talk concerning Allah. What was the re-

sult? This question we will try to answer in what
follows. It remains to quote a few authoritative
testimonies to show at the outset that the verdict
is not unanimous regarding the ethical value
and the philosophic truth of Mohammedan Monotheism.

Frederick Perry Noble, an authority on Islam in
Africa, writes:[1] "The crowning benefit bestowed
upon the benighted negro by Islam, its advocate exclaims, is the belief in the one true God. Is not this
an advance, an immense advance, upon fetichism
and idolatry? This depends on the content and effect
of the idea of God in Islam and in African paganism.
If the two members of the religious equation prove
of equal value, the answer must be: $x = y$ and the
gain is zero." This is very strong language. In the
following paragraphs of that chapter of his book the
author puts Allah in the balances against an African
fetich and the scales hang nearly even! How different is this testimony from that of Canon Taylor, and
Dr. Blyden and Bosworth Smith regarding Islam's
blessing to dark Africa.[2] Major Osborne, in sketch-
ing the history of religion under the Khalifs of Bagdad, concludes: "The God of the Moslem is not a
righteous God, but an arbitrary sovereign. I know
that passages in the Koran can be produced wherein

[1] *The Redemption of Africa*, Vol. I., p. 73.
[2] See, for example, Blyden's *Christianity, Islam and the
Negro Race*, pp. 7, 28, 199-215, 277-299. London, 1888.

the righteousness of God is strongly insisted upon. But such passages have failed to mould to any great extent the practical religion of Islam, because (as I have already observed) the Koran is a book without moral gradations. Every institution and every precept stands upon the same ground—the will of God. A chain is no stronger than its weakest link; and it is the veneration paid to a black stone, not to the One God, which denotes the high-water mark of the moral and intellectual life of the Moslem world."[1]   Johannes Hauri, in his classical study of Islam, voices a similar sentiment and gives the clue to the favorable judgment of so many other writers.   He says:[2] "What Mohammed tells us of God's omnipotence, omniscience, justice, goodness and mercy sounds, for the most part, very well indeed, and might easily awaken the idea that there is no real difference between his God and the God of Christianity. But Mohammed's monotheism was just as much a departure from true monotheism as the polytheistic ideas prevalent in the corrupt Oriental churches.   Mohammed's idea of God is out and out deistic. God and the world are in exclusive, external and eternal opposition. Of an entrance of God into the world or of any sort of human fellowship with God he knows nothing.   This is the reason Islam

[1] *Islam under the Khalifs*, pp. viii. and 138.
[2] *Der Islam in seinem Einfluss auf das Leben seiner Bekenner.* Leiden, 1882, pp. 44, 45.

received the warm sympathies of English deists and German rationalists; they found in its idea of God flesh of their flesh and bone of their bone." The following chapters will show whether this statement is overdrawn and whether Noble's indictment of Allah will stand.

II

ALLAH, THE DIVINE ESSENCE

> "The interpretation of God consists of two distinct yet complementary parts—a doctrine of God and of the Godhead. God is deity conceived in relation, over against the universe, its cause or ground, its law and end; but the Godhead is deity conceived according to His own nature as He is from within and for Himself."—*Principal Fairbairn.*

CONCERNING the real significance of the Arabic word *Allah* there has been much speculation and endless discussion among Moslem exegetes and lexicographers. The author of the Muheet-el-Muheet dictionary, a Christian, says: "Allah is the name of necessary Being. There are twenty different views as to the derivation of this name of the Supreme; the most probable is that its root is *iläh,* the past participle form, on the measure *fï'äl,* from the verb *ilaho* = to worship, to which the article was prefixed to indicate the supreme object of worship." When we open the pages of Ferozabadi, Beidhawi or Zamakhshari and read some of these *twenty* other derivations we find ourselves at the outset before an unknown God. The intellectual difficulty was a real one to the Moslem exegete, as he must discover some root and some theory of derivation that is not in conflict with *his* accepted idea of God. Beidhawi, for example, suggests that *Allah* is derived "from an [invented] root *ilaha* = to be in perplexity, because the mind is perplexed when it tries to form the idea of the Infinite!" Yet more fanciful are the other derivations given and the Arabic student can satisfy his curiosity in Beidhawi, Vol. I., pp. 5 and 6.

According to the opinion of some Moslem theologians, it is infidelity (*kufr*) to hold that the word has any derivation whatever! This is the opinion of the learned in Eastern Arabia. They say "God is not begotten," and so His name cannot be derived. He is the first, and had an Arabic name before the creation of the worlds. Allah is an eternal combination of letters written on the throne in Arabic and each stroke and curve has mystical meaning. Mohammed, they teach, received the revelation of this name and was the first to preach the divine unity among the Arabs by declaring it. This kind of argument is of one piece with all that Moslems tell of "the days of ignorance" before the prophet. But history establishes beyond the shadow of a doubt that even the pagan Arabs, before Mohammed's time, knew their chief god by the name of *Allah* and even, in a sense, proclaimed His unity. In pre-Islamic literature, Christian or pagan, *ilah* is used for any god and *Al-ilah* (contracted to *Allah*), *i.e.,* ὁ θεός, *the god,* was the name of the Supreme. Among the pagan Arabs this term denoted the chief god of their pantheon, the Kaaba, with its three hundred and sixty idols. Herodotus informs us (Lib. III., cap. viii.) that in his day the Arabs had two principal deities, *Orotal* and *Alilat.* The former is doubtless a corruption of *Allah Taál,* God most high, a term very common in the Moslem vocabulary; the latter is *Al Lat,* mentioned as a pagan goddess in the Koran. Two of the pagan poets of Arabia, Nabiga and Labid,[1] use the word *Allah* repeatedly in the sense of a supreme deity. Nabiga says (Diwan, poem I., verses 23, 24) : *"Allah* has given them a kindness and grace which others have not. Their abode is *the* God (Al-ilah) Himself and their religion is strong," etc.

Labid says : "Neither those who divine by striking stones or watching birds, know what *Allah* has just created."[2]

Ash-Shahristani says of the pagan Arabs that some

---

[1] Brockelman in his *Geschichte der Arab. Literatur* remarks, Vol. I , p. 30, "Auch bei an-Nabiga und Lebid finden sich manche specifisch christliche Gedanken die uns beweisen dass das Christentum an der durch die Poesie repräsentierten geistigen Bildung seinen stillen Anteil hatte " Cheikho claims that Lebid was a Christian poet. Nabiga died before the Hegira.

[2] Quoted by Dr. St. Clair Tisdall, in the *Journal of the Victoria Institute*, Vol. XXV., p. 149. He gives the Arabic text of both Nabiga and Lebid's stanzas.

of them "believed in a Creator and a creation, but denied Allah's prophets and worshipped false gods, concerning whom they believed that in the next world they would become mediators between themselves and Allah." And Ibn Hisham, the earliest biographer of Mohammed whose work is extant, admits that the tribes of Kinanah and Koreish used the following words when performing the pre-Islamic ceremony of *ihlal:*[1] "We are present in thy service, O God. Thou hast no partner except the partner of thy dread. Thou ownest him and whatsoever he owneth."

As final proof, we have the fact that centuries before Mohammed the Arabian Kaaba, or temple at Mecca, was called *Beit-Allah,* the house of *God,* and not *Beit-el-Alihet,* the house of idols or gods. Now if even the *pagan* Arabs acknowledged Allah as supreme, surely the Hanifs (that band of religious reformers at Mecca which rejected all polytheism and sought freedom from sin by resignation to God's will) were not far from the idea of the Unity of God. It was henotheism[2] in the days of paganism; and the Hanifs led the way for Mohammed to preach absolute monotheism. The Koran often calls Abraham a Hanif and stoutly affirms that he was not a Jew or a Christian (Surahs 2:129; 3:60, 89; 6:162; 16:121, etc.). Among the Hanifs of Mohammed's

[1] *Sirat,* Part II., p. 27.
[2] "The adoration of one god above others as the specific tribal god."—C. P. Tiele.

time were Waraka, the prophet's cousin, and Zaid bin 'Amr, surnamed the Inquirer. Both exerted decided influence on Islam and its teaching.

Nöldeke thinks Mohammed was in doubt as to which name he would select for the supreme being and that he thought of adopting *Er-Rahman,* the merciful, as the proper name of God in place of Allah, because that was already used by the heathen. *Rahmana* was a favorite Hebrew name for God in the Talmudic period and in use among the Jews of Arabia.[1] On the Christian monuments found by Dr. Edward Glaser in Yemen, Allah is also mentioned. The Sirwah inscription (A.D. 542) opens with the words: "In the power of the All-merciful and His Messiah and the Holy Ghost,"[2] which shows that, at least in Yemen, Arabian Christians were not in error regarding the persons of the Trinity. One other term often used for *Allah* we will have occasion to study later. It is the word *Es-Samad* [the Eternal], and seems to come from the same root as *Samood,* the name of an idol of the tribe of 'Ad and mentioned in the poem of Yezid bin Sa'ad.[3] Hobal, the chief god of the Kaaba (and whom Dozy identifies with

---

[1]*Encyclop. Brit.*, Ninth edition, Vol. XVI., p. 549

[2]*Recent Research in Bible Lands*, by Hilprecht, p. 149. Does not this Christian introductory formula show whence Mohammed borrowed his *Bismillahi-er Rahman-er-Rahim?*

[3]*Taj-el-Aroos Dictionary*, Vol. II., p. 402. See note at the end of the chapter.

Baal),[1] is, strange to say, not mentioned in the Koran. Perhaps he was at this period already identified by the Meccans with Allah. This would explain Mohammed's silence on the subject.

We thus are led back to the sources from which the Arabian prophet drew his ideas of Allah; namely (as for all his other teaching), from Arabian paganism, Talmudic Judaism and Oriental Christianity. Islam is not original, not a ripe fruit, but rather a wild offshoot of foreign soil grafted on Judaism. It will not surprise us, therefore, if its ideas of God are immature and incomplete.

The passages of the Koran that teach the existence and unity of God (Allah) are either those that refer for proof of His unity to creation (Surahs 6: 96-100; 16:3-22; 21:31-36; 27:60-65, etc.), or state that polytheism and atheism are contrary to reason (Surah 23:119), or that dualism is self-destructive (Surah 21:22), or bring in the witness of former prophets (Surahs 30:29; 21:25; 39:65; 51:50-52). The dogma of absolute monotheism is held forth first against the pagan Arabs as, *e.g.,* in Surah 71:23, where Noah and Mohammed agree in condemning the idols of antediluvian polytheists. "Said Noah, My Lord, verily they have rebelled against me and followed him whose wealth and children have but

[1]See his book, *De Israeliten te Mekka* van David's tijd tot op de vijfde eeuw, etc., Haarlem, 1864, pp. 83-85, and also Pocock's *Spec. Hist. Arab.,* p. 98, ed. White.

added to his loss and they have plotted a great plot and said, Ye shall surely not leave your gods; ye shall surely neither leave *Wadd* nor *Suwah* nor *Yaghuth* nor *Ya'ook* nor *Nasr*,[1] and they led them astray," etc. But this dogma is no less aimed at the Jews whom the Koran accuses of deifying Ezra (Surah 9:30) and Christians who believe in the Trinity. This Trinity Mohammed misunderstood or misrepresented as consisting of Allah, *Jesus* and the Virgin Mary.[2] The deity of Christ is utterly rejected (Surahs 19:35, 36; 3:51, 52; 43:57-65; 5:19, etc.), and His incarnation and crucifixion denied, although not His miraculous birth (Surahs 19:22-24; 3:37-43, 47-50; 4:155, 156).

The word *Allah* is called by Moslem theologians *Ism-ul-That*, the name of the essence, or of the Being of God. All other titles, even that of *Rabb* (Lord) being considered *Isma-ul-Sifat, i.e.,* names of the attributes. In this first name, therefore, we have (barren though it be) the Moslem idea of the nature of God apart from His attributes and creation (in accordance with the motto at the head of this chapter), although at the same time in sharp contrast with Christian ideas of the Godhead.

As is evident from the very form of the Moslem creed their fundamental conception of Allah is nega-

---

[1] Of course these were *Arabian* idols, but the Koran is full of such strange anachronisms.

[2] See Chapter VI.

tive. God is unique, as well as a unit, and has no
relations to any creature that partake of resemblance.
The statement in Genesis that man was created in
the divine image is to the Moslem blasphemy. Allah
is defined by a series of negations. As popular song
has it—

> "Whatsoever your mind can conceive,
> That Allah is not you may well believe."

Mohammed, outside of the Koran, was silent regarding the nature of God's being. "For while traditions have been handed down in abundance which
give the responses of the Prophet to inquiries concerning prayer, almsgiving, fasting and pilgrimage
there is not one having reference to the being [and
attributes] of God. This is a fact acknowledged by
all those most profoundly versed in Traditional
lore."[1] The great Imams are agreed regarding the
danger and impiety of studying or discussing the
nature of the being of God. They, therefore, when
speaking of Allah's being, fall back on negations.

The idea of absolute sovereignty and ruthless omnipotence (borrowed, as we shall see, from the nature
of Allah's attributes) are at the basis. For the rest
his character is impersonal—that of an infinite, eternal, vast nomad. God is not a body. God is not a

---

[1] *The Khalifs of Bagdad*, p. 136. I have put his words "and
attributes" in brackets. Osborne's statement is too strong.
There are traditions, although not many, on Allah's attributes.

spirit. Neither has God a body nor has he a spirit. The Imam El-Ghazzali says: "Allah is not a body endued with form nor a substance circumscribed with limits or determined by measure. Neither does He resemble bodies, as they are capable of being measured or divided. Neither is He a substance, nor do substances exist in Him; neither is He an accident, nor do accidents exist in Him. Neither is He like to anything that exists; neither is anything like Him. His nearness is not like the nearness of bodies nor is His essence like the essence of bodies. *Neither does He exist in anything nor does anything exist in Him.*"[1]

The words "There is no God but Allah" occur in Surah Mohammed, verse 21, but the Surah which Moslems call the Surah of the Unity of God is the 112th. According to Tradition, this chapter is Mohammed's definition of Allah. Beidhawi says: "Mohammed (on him be prayers and peace) was asked concerning his Lord and then this Surah came down." Zamakhshari says: "Ibn Abbas related that the Koreish said, O Mohammed, describe to us your Lord whom you invite us to worship; then this Surah was revealed." As a specimen of Moslem exegesis, here is the Surah with the comments first of Beidhawi and then of Zamakhshari; the words of

[1] See *El Maksadu-l-asna* by this famous Moslem scholastic. An extract is found in Ockley's *History of the Saracens* and quoted in Hughes' *Dict. of Islam.*

the Koran are put in italics and the translation is literal:[1]

"*Say, He is God, One.* God is the predicate of He is, and One is in apposition to it or is a second predicate. *God is 'eternal'* (*Samad*), that is, God is He to whom men betake themselves for their needs. *He does not beget,* because of the impossibility of His homogeneousness. *And is not begotten,* because of the impossibility of anything happening concerning Him. *And there is not to Him a single equal, i.e.,* equivalent or similar one. The expression 'to Him' is joined to the word 'equal' and precedes it because the chief purpose of the pronouns is to express the denial. And the reason for putting the word 'single' last, although it is the subject of the verb, is that it may stand separate from 'to Him.' " The idea of Beidhawi seems to be that even in the grammatical order of the words there must be entire and absolute separation between Allah and creation!

Zamakhshari interprets likewise as follows: "*God is one,* unified (unique?) in His divinity, in which no one shares, and He is the one whom all seek since they need Him and He needs nobody. *He does not beget,* because He has none of His own genus, and so possesses no female companion of His own kind, and

---

[1] Beidhawi, the most celebrated of all Sunni exegetes, died at Tabriz in 685 A.H. Zamakhshari died 538 A.H., and spent most of his life at Mecca. He was for a time a free-thinker, but his commentary is held equal to that of Beidhawi.

consequently the two of them propagate. This is indicated by God's saying, 'How can there be off-spring to Him and He has no female companion.[1] *And He is not begotten.* Because everything born is an occurrence and a (material) body. God, however, is ancient, there is no beginning to His existence and He is not a body. *And He has no equal, i.e.,* no like-ness or resemblance. It is allowed to explain this of companionship in marriage and to deny a female con-sort."[2]

This, then, is the definition of the Essence of God, according to the Koran and the best commentaries. How far such negations come short of the sublime statements of revelation: God is a Spirit; God is light; God is love.

[1] I have purposely used the word *God* for Allah in my trans-lation and capitalized *He* to show how shocking such ideas seem to the Christian consciousness.

[2] On the word *Samad* (Eternal) there is a curious note in the biography of Mohammed known as *Insan-el Ayoon* (Vol. I., p. 372), margin: "*Samad* means that which has no insides or inside organs and was the name given by Mohammed to God in reply to the Nejran Christians who affirmed that Jesus ate food; for God needs no food and has no organs of digestion!" The same explanation of the word is given by Ibn Abbas, Mujahid, and Ibn Zobeir. According to Al Shôbi, it means one who neither eats nor drinks. Others say it means one who has no successor. Al Suddi explains it to be one who is sought after for favors and presents. (See further Dr. Hartwig Hirschfeld's *New Researches into the Composition and Exe-gesis of the Quran,* p. 42, note. London, 1902; Royal Asiatic Society.)

III

THE NINETY-NINE BEAUTIFUL NAMES OF ALLAH

"I make but little of Mohammed's praises of
Allah, which many praise; they are borrowed, I
suppose, mainly from the Hebrew, at least they
are far surpassed there. But the eye that flashes
direct into the heart of things and sees the truth
of them; this to me is a deeply interesting object.
Great Nature's own gift."—*Carlyle, in "Hero
Worship."*

THE attributes of God are called by Moslems
Ismā-ul-Sifat and are also called in the Koran
Isma-ul-Husna, the excellent names. We read in
Surah 7:179: "But God's are the excellent names;
call on Him then thereby and leave those who pervert
His names." The number of these names or attributes
of Allah is given by Tradition as ninety-nine. Abu
Huraira relates that Mohammed said, "Verily, there
are ninety-nine names of God and whoever recites
them shall enter Paradise." In the same tradition
these names are mentioned, but the number is arbitrary and the lists of the names differ in various Mos-

lem books.[1] It is the custom of many pious Moslems
to employ in their devotions a rosary of ninety-nine
beads to represent these names, and the repetition of
them is called *Thikr,* or remembrance. The latter
is the chief religious exercise among the various
schools of dervishes.

We will now give these names in order with the
place where they occur in the Koran and brief comment where necessary. Edwin Arnold has made so
much of these *Pearls of the Faith* in his poem that
we need to get back to the *Moslem* idea of these attributes. His *Pearls of the Faith* is as one-sided
a presentation of Islam as his *Light of Asia* is of
Buddhism.

1. *Er-Rahman*—The Merciful. (Surah 1:1,
etc.)

2. *Er-Rahim*—The Compassionate. Both of these
names are from the same root and are very frequently used in the Koran. They occur as the opening formula, "In the name of Allah, the Merciful,
the Compassionate," before every Surah of the
Koran except the ninth. Beidhawi says that *Er-
Rahman* is a more exalted attribute than *Er-Rahim,*
because it not only contains five letters in Arabic,

[1]Compare the lists as given in *Mishkat-el Misabih, Al Mus-
tatraf,* Hughes' *Dict. of Islam,* Nofel's *Sinajet el Tarb.,* Arnold's
Pearls of the Faith, etc.; Ahmed bin Ali el Bûni's *Shems-ul
Múarif* is one of many books on the ninety-nine names of God.
In this book these names are written in talismanic form, and
one of these talismans is given in our frontispiece.

while Rahim only has four, but it expresses that universal attribute of mercy which the Almighty extends to all men, the wicked and the good, believers and unbelievers. This is a noble thought.

3. *El Malik*—The King, or the Possessor, used often in the Koran as in the first Surah, "King of the day of judgment." In Surah 43:77, however, the same word is used for the angel who presides over hell. Is this latter use of the word allied to Molech, the fire-god of Syria?

4. *El Kuddūs*—The Holy. Only *once* used of Allah in the Koran (Surah 59:23), "He is God beside whom there is no deity, the King, the Holy." The Taj-el-Aroos dictionary instead of defining this important attribute discusses the various readings of its vowel-points! (See the next chapter.) The Holy Spirit is a term frequently used in the Koran, but is in no case applied to Deity.[1]

5. *Es-Salam*—The Peace, or the Peace-maker. The latter significance is given by Zamakhshari. Beidhawi again explains it *by a negation,* "He who is free from all loss and harm." Used only in Surah 59:20.

6. *El-Mu'min*—The Faithful. (Surah 59:28.)

[1]Nine times the word Spirit or Holy Spirit is said to refer to the Angel Gabriel (Surahs 2 : 81; 2 : 254; 5 : 109; 16 : 2; 16 : 104; 26 : 193; 70 : 4; 97 : 4; 19 : 17); three times to Jesus Christ (4 : 169; 21 : 91; 66 : 12), in this case without the epithet holy; the other cases are left in doubt by the commentators. In none of them does even "Spirit" apply to deity.

7. *El-Muhaimin*—The   Protector.   (S u r a h
59:23.)

8. *El-Aziz*—The Mighty One. Very frequently
used; *e.g.,* Surahs 42:2, 3, 18; 46:1, etc. It is one
of the dozen or more names that express Allah's
power.

9. *El-Jabbār*—The   All-Compelling.   (Surah
59:23.) The word is also translated, The Giant or
the Absolute ruler. What Moslems think the word
means is evident from the teachings of the sect, which
denies all free agency to man, and who call themselves after this name, *Jabariyah.* (See Hughes'
Dict. of Islam in loco.)

10. *El-Mutakabbir*—The   Proud.   This   word
when used of a human being always implies haughti-
ness, and Zamakhshari defines it (Surah 59:23),
"Supreme in pride and greatness or the One who is
haughty above the wickedness of His slaves."

11. *El-Khālik*—The Creator.

12. *El-Bari*—The Maker.

13. *El-Musawwir*—The Fashioner. These three
are used in succession for Allah as creator in Surah
59:23. The commentators take pains to explain
away any *nearness* of the Creator to the creature in
the last term used.

14. *El-Ghāfer*—The Forgiver, sometimes given
as Al Ghaffār. Both have the same significance, but
the latter, as well as *Al Ghafūr,* are intensive. (Surah
2:225.) All are frequently used.

15. *El-Kahār*—The Dominant. (Surah 13: 17.)

16. *El-Wahāb*—The Bestower. (Surah 3:6, etc.) This name is commonly used with *Abd* as a surname among the Arabs, "Slave of the Bountiful."

17. *Er-Razzak*—The Provider.   Once used in Surah 51:58.

18. *El-Fattah*—The Opener. (Surah 34:25.) This name is inscribed over gates and doors, on the title-pages of books and is used as the first copy-book lesson for boys at school.

19. *El-'Alim*—The Knowing One. (Surah 35:43.) Frequently used in nearly every long Surah of the Koran.

20. *El-Kabidh*—The Grasper, the Restrainer.

21. *El-Bāsit*—The Spreader or Uncloser of the hand. These two names are complementary. The former occurs not in the Koran as a noun, but was put in the list in reference to a passage in the Surah of the Cow. The latter is found in Surah 13:15, and there means He who dispenses riches.

22. *El-Khafidh*—The Abaser. (Surah ?)

23. *Er-Rafia'*—The Exalter. (Surah 3:48.) In reference to the translation of Jesus Christ.

24. *El-Mu'izz*—The Strengthener. The word does not occur in the Koran, but the idea is referred to in Surah 3:25: "Thou strengthenest whom Thou pleasest."

25. *El-Mŭthill*—The One-who-l e a d s-a s t r a y. (Surahs 4: 90; 4: 142; 17: 99; 18: 6, and fre-

quently elsewhere.) "God misleadeth whom He pleaseth," is a common phrase in the Koran.

26. *Es Samia*—The Hearer. (Surah 40:21, etc.)

27. *El-Basir*—The Seer. (Surah 40:21 and frequently elsewhere.) According to Surah 31, Allah has present vision of five secret things: the day of judgment, and the times of rain, the child hid in the womb, what happens to-morrow, and where every mortal dies.

28. *El Hakîm*—The Wise, the Only Wise. Very often used, as in Surah 2:123, *e.g.,* "Thou art the mighty and the wise." It is used in every-day Arabic for a philosopher or a physician.

29. *El 'Adl*—The Just. It is remarkable and very significant that this title does not occur in the Koran, but is put in the list by Tradition. The word *'Adl,* Justice, occurs twelve times only, and is never used of the righteous *acts* of God and only once (Surah 5: 115) of His words. In every other case it refers to human equity or faithfulness (as in 4: 128) toward one's wives in their marriage rights, etc.

30. *El-Latif*—The Subtle. (Surah 6:103.) Edwin Arnold translates this word "Gracious One" and hangs to this invention a verse or two of Christian thought on God's grace to sinners. Zamakhshari gives the Moslem idea of this word when he says: "He is too subtle (too ethereal) for eyes to see Him." (El Kishaf in loco.)

31. *El-Khabîr*—The Cognizant. (Surah 6:103.)

32. *El-Halîm*—The Clement. (Surah 2:225.) "He will not catch you up for a casual word in your oaths, but He will catch you up for what your hearts have earned; but God is forgiving and *clement.*" Mohammed's idea of clemency!

33. *El-ʾAdhim*—The Grand. (Surah 2:257.)

34. *El-Ghafūr*—The Forgiving. (S u r a h 35:27.)

35. *Esh-Shakŭr*—"The A c k n o w l e d g e r of Thanksgiving." This is more correct than to translate The Grateful. (Surah 35:27.) "That He may pay them their hire. . . . Verily He is Forgiving and Grateful."

36. *El-ʾAli*—The Exalted. (Surah 2:257.)

37. *El-Kabîr*—The Great. (Surah 34:22.) This is never used by Arabic-speaking Christians as a title for the Godhead, since it really means big in size or station. Zamakhshari says (Vol. II., p. 231): "Al-Kabir means the possessor of pride."

38. *El-Hafîdh*—The Guardian. (Surah 86:3.) This name is often put over house-doors.

39. *El-Mukît*—The Feeder, the Maintainer. (Surah 4:88.)

40. *El-Hasîb*—The Reckoner. Occurs three times. (Surahs 4: 7, 88; 33: 39.) Arnold's comment here is thoroughly Mohammedan:

> "Laud Him as Reckoner casting up th' account
> And making little merits largely mount."

41. *El-Jalîl*—The Majestic. (Surah 55:25.)

42. *El-Karîm*—The Generous. (Surah 96:3. "He is the most generous.")

43. *Er-Rakîb*—The Watchful. (Surah 4: 1.)

44. *El-Mujîb*—The Answerer (of prayer). (Surah 11:64.) Compare comment of Zamakhshari in loco.

45. *El-Wasia*—The Capacious. (Surah 2:248.)

46. *El-Hākim*—The Judge. "The most just of judges (or rulers)." (Surahs 95: 8 and 7: 85.)

47. *El-Wadŭd*—The Affectionate. Occurs only *twice* in the Koran. (Surahs 11: 92 and 85: 14.)

48. *El-Majîd*—The Glorious. (Surah 11:76 and elsewhere.)

49. *El-Ba'ith*—The Awakener or Raiser; used frequently in the verbal form in regard to the resurrection of the body. (Surah 22: 7 by inference.)

50. *Esh-Shahîd*—The Witness. Frequently used. (Surah 3: 93.)

51. *El-Hak*—The Truth. (Surah 22:62.) According to orthodox Tradition, a lie is justifiable in three cases: "To reconcile those who quarrel, to satisfy one's wife and in case of war." (*El Hidayah,* Vol. IV., p. 81.) And Abu Hanifah alleges that if a man should swear "by the *truth* of God" this does not constitute an oath. Imam Mohammed agrees with him. (Oaths, Hughes' *Dict.,* p. 438.) Of absolute truth in Deity or in ethics the Moslem mind has very

distorted ideas and Tradition affords a thousand examples of Moslem teaching in this regard.

52. *El-Wakîl*—The Agent. (Surah 4:83.)

53. *El-Kawi*—The Strong. (Surah 11:69.) Used of physical strength.

54. *El-Mutîn*—The Firm; in the sense of a fortress. Used in Surah 51:58: "God is the provider. . . . The Firm."

55. *El-Walî*—The Helper. (Surah 22: last verse.) By implication. I cannot find it elsewhere.

56. *El-Hamid*—The L a u d a b l e.   Frequent. (Surah 11:76.)

57. *El-Muhsi*—The Counter. Only by reference to Surah 36:11, which speaks of God "reckoning up."

58. *El-Mubdi*—The Beginner. Reference to Surah 85:13.

59. *El-Mŭeed*—The Restorer. Reference to Surah 85:13.

60. *El-Muhyi*—The Quickener or Life-giver.

61. *El-Mumît*—The Slayer. These two names are in a pair and occur together in Surah 2:26 in a verbal form. The former also occurs, Surahs 30: 49 and 41:39, in both cases referring to quickening the soil after rain as proof of the resurrection.

62. *El-Hai*—The Living. (Surah 3:1.) Very frequent.

63. *El-Kayŭm*—The Self-Subsisting. (Surah 3:1.) Beidhawi and Zamakhshari both speak of the

latter term in a purely *physical* way. "He who always stands up," *i.e.,* does not need rest or sleep. Compare the same words as used in the verse of the Throne, Surah 2d, and the commentaries.

64. *El-Wâjid*—The Inventor or Maker. The word does not occur in the Koran.

65. *El-Mugheeth*—The Refuge or the Helper. The word does not occur in the Koran.

66. *El-Wāhid*—The One. (Frequently, as in 2:158.)

67. *Es-Samad*—The Eternal. (Surah 112.) According to the dictionaries and some commentaries, the word means "One to whom one repairs in exigencies," and hence the Lord, the Eternal One.

68. *El-Kadîr*—The Powerful. (Surah 2:19, and in many other places.) The word is from the same root as *Kadr,* fate, predestination; and Zamakhshari, in commenting on Surah 2:19, leaves no doubt that the term used means to him "The One-who-predestines-all."

69. *El-Muktadir*—The Prevailer or Overcomer. Used three times in the Koran. (Surahs 18:43; 54:42; 5:55.)

70. *El-Mukaddim*—The Approacher or Bringer forward.

71. *El-Muākhir*—The Deferrer. This pair of titles does not occur in the Koran.

72. *El-Awwal*—The First.

73. *El-Akhir*—The Last.

74. *El-Dhahir*—The Substance.

75. *El-Bātin*—The Essence. These four divine titles are known by the technical appellation of "The mothers of the attributes," being regarded as fundamental and all-comprehensive. All four occur together in Surah 57:3. This verse is a great favorite among the Mystics of Islam.

76. *El-Wali*—The Governor. (Surah 13:12.)

77. *El-Muta'ali*—The Lofty One; better, He-who-tries-to-be-the-Highest. (Surah 13:10.)

78. *El-Bărr*—The Beneficent. (Surah 52:27.) The word used for *Righteous* is *El Bār* and does not occur in the Koran. Once only is this name used.

79. *Et-Tawwāb*—The Relenting—one who turns frequently. Used four times in Surah 2d and twice in the 9th Surah. Also, beautifully, in Surah 4:119: "He has also turned in mercy unto the three who were left behind, so that the earth, spacious as it is, became too strait for them; and their souls became so straitened within them that there was no refuge from God, but unto Himself. Then was He turned to them that they might turn to Him. Verily, God is He that turneth (*At-Tawwāb*) the merciful."

80. *El-Muntakim*—The Avenger. (S u r a h 32:22.) Also Surahs 43:40 and 44:15.

81. *El-Afuw*—The Pardoner. Literally, the Eraser or Cancellor. (Surah 4:51.)

82. *Er-Ra'oof*—The Kind or Indulgent. Frequently used. (Surah 2:138.)

83. *Malik-ul-Mulk*—Ruler of the Kingdom. (Surah 3:25.)

84. *Dhu-al-Jilal*—Possessor of Majesty. (Surah 55:78.)

85. *El-Müksit*—The Equitable. It does not occur in the Koran, but in Tradition.

86. *El-Jāmia'*—The Gatherer. (Surah 4:139.)

87. *El-Ghani*—The Rich. (Surah 60:6.)

88. *El-Müghni*—The Enricher. (Surah 4:129.)

89. *El-Mu'ti*—The Giver. (Referred to Surah 108:1.)

90. *El-Mānia'*—The Withholder. Not in the Koran.

91. *Edh-Dhür*—The Harmful. Not in the Koran.

92. *En-Nāfia'*—The Profiter. Not in the Koran. Although these names, and others, are not found in the Koran they belong to Allah's attributes on authority of the Prophet and are used especially in invocations and incantations.

93. *En-Nur*—The Light. Used only in the remarkable 35th verse of the 24th Surah. Quoted elsewhere with comment. The idea seems borrowed from the Old Testament and the golden candlestick.

94. *El-Hādi*—The Guide. (From Surah 1:5, etc.)

95. *El-Azili*—The Eternal-in-the-Past. Arabic speech has another word, *Abadi,* for eternal future, and a third, *Sarmadi,* to include both.

96.   *El-Baki*—The Enduring.   (Surah 28: last verse by inference.)

97.   *El-Warith*—The Inheritor of all things. Not in the Koran, but implied in various passages.

98.   *Er-Roshîd*—The Director.   It occurs only once in the Koran, and is not there applied to God. (Surah 11:80.)   "Is there not among you one who can rightly direct?"   The word is still in common use as a proper name among the Arabs.

99.   *Es-Sabŭr*—The Patient.   (Surah 3:15?)

The word *Rabb,* Lord (although it is also an attribute, according to the Moslem ideas of the Unity), is not mentioned among the ninety-nine names. It is, however, used most frequently of all the divine titles and is combined with other words in Moslem theology, such as: Lord of Glory, Lord of the Universe, Lord of Lords, Lord of Slaves (*i.e.,* His servants).   It is not without significance to note that later many of these divine titles were applied to Mohammed himself by the pious, and in the list of his two hundred and one titles there are a score of the ninety-nine beautiful names![1]

[1] See *Mishkat-el-Misabih* and any book of Moslem prayers or devotions for proof.   (*Ismâ-en-Nebi.*)

IV

ALLAH'S ATTRIBUTES ANALYZED AND EXAMINED

"And the thunder proclaimeth His perfection, with His praise; the angels likewise fear Him. And He sendeth the thunderbolts and striketh with them whom He pleaseth whilst they dispute concerning God; for He is mighty in power."— *The Koran* (Surah 13: 13).

"There is none of all that are in the heavens and the earth but he shall come unto the Compassionate as a slave."—*The Koran* (Surah 19 : 94).

THESE verses from the Koran are a fit introduction to the study of Allah's attributes; they express the effect those attributes are intended to have and do have on His worshippers and explain in a measure the reason for the usual Moslem classification of God's ninety-nine names. Through fear of death and terror of Allah's mighty power the pious Moslem is all his life subject to bondage.

By some the attributes are divided into three classes (as their rosary is into three sections), *i.e.*, the attributes of wisdom, of power and of goodness.

But the more common division is into two: *Isma-ul-Jalaliyah* and *Isma-ul-Jemaliyah,* terrible attributes and glorious attributes. The former are more numerous and more emphasized than the latter, not only in the Koran but in Tradition and in daily life. If we try to classify the names given in the last chapter we find the following result: Seven of the names (*viz.,* 66, 67, 72, 73, 74, 75 and 86) describe Allah's unity and Absolute being. Five speak of Him as Creator or Originator of all nature (*viz.,* 11, 12, 13, 62 and 63). There are twenty-four titles which characterize Allah as merciful and gracious (to believers) (*viz.,* 1, 2, 5, 6, 14, 16, 17, 32, 34, 35, 38, 42, 47, 56, 60, 78, 79, 81, 82, 89, 92, 94, 98, 99) and we are glad to acknowledge that these are indeed *beautiful* names and that they are used often and beautifully in the Koran. On the other hand, there are *thirty-six* names to describe Mohammed's idea of Allah's power and pride and absolute sovereignty (*viz.,* 3, 7, 8, 9, 10, 15, 20, 21, 23, 24, 28, 33, 36, 37, 39, 41, 45, 48, 49, 53, 54, 58, 59, 61, 65, 68, 69, 76, 77, 83, 84, 87, 88, 95, 96 and 97). And in addition to these "terrible attributes" there are five which describe Allah as hurting and avenging (*viz.,* 22, 25, 80, 90, 91). He is a God who abases, leads astray, avenges, withholds His mercies, and works harm. In all these doings He is independent and all-powerful.

Finally, there are *four* terms used, which may be said in a special sense to refer to the *moral* or *forensic*

in deity (*viz.*, 4, 29, 51 and 85); although we admit
that the merciful attributes are in a sense *moral* attributes. Of these only two occur in the Koran, and
both are of doubtful significance in Moslem theology!
While we find that the "terrible" attributes of God's
power occur again and again in the Koran, the net
total of the moral attributes is found in *two* verses,
which mention that Allah is Holy and Truthful, *i.e.*,
in the Moslem sense of those words. What a contrast
to the Bible! The Koran shows and Tradition illus-
trates that Mohammed had in a measure a correct
idea of the *physical* attributes (I use the word in the
theological sense) of Deity; but he had a false conception of His moral attributes or no conception at
all. He saw God's power in nature, but never had a
glimpse of His holiness and justice. The reason is
plain. Mohammed had no true idea of the nature of
sin and its consequences. There is perfect unity in
this respect between the prophet's book and his life.
Arnold says (*Der Islam,* p. 70): "Das Attribut der
Heiligkeit wird im Koran durchaus ignorirt; alles
was über die unnahbare Reinheit und Heiligkeit des-
sen der in der Bibel als der Dreimal Heilige darge-
stellt wird, gesagt ist läszt sich von jedem ehrenhaften
menschen sagen." The attribute of holiness is ignored in the Koran; everything put forward concerning the unapproachable purity and holiness of Him
who is represented as Thrice Holy in the Bible can
be applied to any respectable man. The Koran is

silent on the nature of sin not only, but tells next to nothing about its origin, result and remedy. In this respect the latest Sacred Book of the East stands in marked contrast with all the other sacred books of the heathen and the Word of God in the Old and New Testaments. This was noticed as early as the days of the Reformation; for Melancthon says in an introduction to a Latin Koran that he thinks Mohammed "was inspired by Satan, because he does not explain what sin is and sheweth not the reason of human misery."[1]

The passages of the Koran that treat of sin are the few following: Surahs 4:30; 2:80; 4:46; 14:39; also Surahs 2:284-286; 9:116; 69:35; 86:9; 70:19-25, and 47:2, 3.

The nearest approach to a definition that can be gathered from these passages is that sin is a wilful violation of known law or, as Wherry puts it: "Sin, according to most Moslem authorities, is a conscious act committed against known law; wherefore sins of ignorance are not numbered in the catalogue of crimes." This idea of sin gives rise to the later Judæic distinction of sins great and small (Matt. 22:36, cf. Surah 4:30, etc.) on which are based endless speculations of Moslem commentators. Some say there are seven great sins: idolatry, murder, false charge of adultery, wasting the substance of

[1] Quoted in *Literary Remains of Emanuel Deutsch*, London, 1874, p. 62.

orphans, usury, desertion from *Jihad,* and disobedience to parents. Others say there are seventeen, still others catalogue seven hundred! Without entering into the fruitless discussion of what constitutes a sin, great or small, it is to be noted that to the Moslem all sins except the *Kebira,* "great sins," are regarded with utter carelessness and no qualm of conscience. Lying, deception, anger, lust and such like are all smaller and lighter offences; all these will be "forgiven easily" if only men keep clear from great sins.

Another important distinction between the scriptural doctrine of sin and Moslem teaching and which has direct bearing on our interpretation of Allah's attributes is the terms used. The most common word used in the Koran for sin is *thanib,*[1] although other terms are used, especially *harām* (forbidden).

The words "permitted" and "forbidden" have superseded the use of "guilt" and "transgression;" the reason for this is found in the Koran itself. Nothing is right or wrong by nature, but becomes such by the fiat of the Almighty. What Allah forbids is sin, even should he forbid what seems to the human conscience right and lawful. What Allah allows is not sin and cannot be sin *at the time he allows it,* though it may have been before or after. One has

---

[1]This word is used for Mohammed's sins and those of other "prophets," and yet nearly all Moslems hold that all of the prophets, including Mohammed, are sinless!

only to argue the matter of polygamy with any Moslem mullah to have the above statements confirmed. To the common mind there is, indeed, no distinction whatever between the ceremonial law and the moral; nor is it easy to find such a distinction even implied in the Koran. It is as great an offence to pray with unwashen hands as to tell a lie, and "pious" Moslems who nightly break the seventh commandment (according to their own lax interpretation of it) will shrink from a tin of English meat for fear they be defiled with swine's flesh. As regards the moral code Islam is phariseeism translated into Arabic.

The lack of all distinction between the ceremonial and moral law comes out most of all in the traditional sayings of the prophet. These sayings, we must remember, have nearly equal authority with the Koran itself. Take two examples: "The prophet, upon whom be prayers and peace, said, One dirhem of usury which a man eats, knowing it to be so, is more grievous than thirty-six fornications; and whosoever has been so nourished is worthy of hell-fire." "The taking of interest has seventy parts of guilt, the least of which is as if a man commits incest with his mother." "The trousers of a man must be to the middle of his leg . . . but whatever is below that is in hell-fire."[1]

To understand the great lack of the moral element

[1] *Mishkat-el-Misabih* in loco, and Osborn's *Islam under the Khalifs of Bagdad*, p. 63.

in the attributes of Allah we must go still further. In the Moslem system and according to the Koran, fortified by Tradition, *all sin is, after all, a matter of minor importance.* It is the repetition of the creed that counts, and not the reformation of character. To repeat the *kilimah,* "There is no god but Allah and Mohammed is Allah's prophet," *ipso facto* constitutes one a true believer. All other considerations are of less import. So confidently is this asserted by Moslem teachers that they say, even if one should repeat the *kilimah* accidentally or by compulsion, it would make him a Moslem. In a fanatic company, I was told, it would be decidedly dangerous for a non-Moslem to say "the creed" even casually in conversation because, so they said, they would "then take the Nasrani by force and circumcise him." Repeating the creed is the door into the religion of Mohammed.

The Koran teaches that the first sinner was Adam (Surah 2:35), and yet the general belief of Moslems to-day is that all the prophets, including Adam, *were without sin.* Especially is the latter asserted in regard to Mohammed, the seal of the prophets; Koran, Tradition, and history to the contrary notwithstanding. The portion of unrepentant sinners is hell-fire (Surahs 18:51; 19:89 and 20:76); the punishment is eternal (43:74-78) and there is then no repentance possible (26:91-105). All the wealth of Arabic vocabulary is exhausted in Mohammed's fearful and particularized descriptions of the awful torments of the doomed.

And for deeper tints in the horrible picture one has only to read the commentators, who also delight in describing the situation of the unbelievers. Hell has seven divisions, each with special terrors and purpose and name. *Jahannum* is the Moslem's purgatory; *Laza* blazes for Christians; *El Hatumah* is hot for the Jews; *Sa'eer* for the Sabeans; *Sakar* scorches the Magi; *El Jahim* is the huge, hot fire for idolaters, and *Hawiyah* the bottomless pit for hypocrites. So say the commentaries, but the Koran only gives the names and says that "each portal has his party."

It is remarkable that nearly all the references to hell-punishment are in the Medinah Surahs, and therefore belong to the latter period of the prophet's life. The allusions to hell in the Mecca Surahs are very brief and "are in every case directed against unbelievers in the prophet's mission and not against sin." (Hughes' *Dictionary of Islam,* p. 171.)

The conclusion we come to, both from the study of the Koran and of Tradition, is that *Allah does not appear bound by any standard of justice.* For example, the worship of the creature is heinous to the Moslem mind and yet Allah punished Satan for not being willing to worship Adam. (Surah 2:28-31.) Allah is merciful in winking at the sins of His favorites, such as the prophets and those who fight in His bat-

tles, but is the quick avenger of all infidels and idolaters. He reveals truth to His prophets, but also
abrogates it, changes the message, or makes them
forget it. (Surah 2:105.) The whole teaching of
Moslem exegetes on the subject of *Nasikh* and *Man-
sookh*, or the Abrogated verses of the Koran, is
utterly opposed to the idea of God's immutability
and truth. There are twenty cases given in which
one revelation superseded, contradicted or abrogated
a previous revelation to Mohammed.[1] Allah's moral
law changes, like His ceremonial law, according to
times and circumstances. He is the Clement. Moslem teachers have in my presence utterly denied that
Allah is subject to an absolute standard of moral
rectitude. He can do what He pleases. The Koran
often asserts this. Not only physically, but morally,
He is *almighty*, in the Moslem sense of the word.
Allah, the Koran says, is the best plotter. Allah
mocks and deceives. Allah "makes it easy" for those
who accept the prophet's message. (Surahs 8:29;
3:53; 27:51; 86:15; 16:4; 14:15; 9:51.)

Al-Ghazzali says: "Allah's justice is not to be
compared with the justice of men. For a man may
be supposed to act unjustly by invading the possession of another, but no injustice can be conceived
on the part of God. It is in His power to pour down
upon men torments, and if He were to do it, His jus-

[1]See Hughes' *Dict. of Islam*, p. 520. Jalalu-Din in his *Itkan*
gives the list of passages.

tice could not be arraigned.   Yet He rewards those
that worship Him for their obedience on account of
His promise and beneficence, not of their merit or of
necessity, *since there is nothing which He can be tied
to perform;* nor can any injustice be supposed in
Him nor can He be under any obligation to any person whatsoever."[1]   According to one tradition, the
seven chief attributes of Deity are: Life, knowledge,
purpose, power, hearing, sight and speech.[2]   Even
granted that these are used in a superlative sense
they would still describe only *an Intelligent Giant.*
Muhammed-al-Burkawi in his book on these seven
chief attributes uses language that leaves no doubt
of *his* idea of what the Koran teaches.   He says:
"Allah can annihilate the universe if it seems good
to Him and recreate it in an instant.   He receives
neither profit nor loss from whatever happens.   If
all the infidels became believers and all the wicked
pious He would gain nothing.   And if all believers
became infidels it would not cause Him loss.   He can
annihilate even heaven itself.   He sees all things,
*even the steps of a black ant on a black rock in a dark
night."*   This last expression shows how the idea of
God's omniscience remains purely *physical,* even in
its highest aspect.   How much loftier is the thought
of God's omniscience in the 139th Psalm than in any

[1]Al Maksad-ul-Asna, quoted in Ockley's *Hist. of the Saracens.*
[2]Hughes' *Dict. of Islam,* p. 27.

verse of the Koran or any passage of the Traditions. In the Koran, God's eye is a big microscope by which He examines His creatures. In the Bible, His eye is a flame of fire laying bare the deepest thoughts and intents of the heart. The Koran has no word for conscience. It is the same when we go to the Koran, or to Tradition, for a description of God's *power*. The wonderful "Verse of the Throne," which is often quoted as proof of Mohammed's noble ideas, is an instance in point. The verse reads: "God there is no god but He, the living, the self-subsistent. Slumber takes Him not nor sleep. His is what is in the heavens and what is in the earth. Who is it that intercedes with Him save by His permission? He knows what is before them and what behind them, and they comprehend not aught of His knowledge but of what He pleases. His throne extends over the heavens and the earth and it tires Him not to guard them both, for He is the high and the grand." Zamakhshari, after explaining on this passage why Allah does not need physical sleep, tells the following Tradition: "The children of Israel asked Moses why God did not slumber or sleep or take rest?[1] In reply to their question God told Moses to remain awake for three days and nights and at the end of that time

---

[1]Moslems are often offended at the verses in Genesis and in Exodus which speak of God "resting" the seventh day and tell our Bible colporteurs that such statements are "kŭfr," *i.e.*, infidelity. God never rests, never needs rest.

to hold two glass bottles in his hands. He did so, and, overcome with drowsiness, smashed the one against the other. Tell your people, said Allah, that I hold in one hand the seven heavens and in the other the seven worlds; if my eyes should slumber, verily the universe would smash as did Moses' bottles."

What must have been Mohammed's idea of the character of God when he named Him The Proud, The All-compelling, The Slayer, The Deferrer, The Indulgent and The Harmful?

Nor can the mind reconcile such attributes with those of goodness and compassion without doing violence to the text of the Koran itself. Some Moslem theologians, therefore, teach that all the good attributes are exercised toward believers and the terrible ones toward unbelievers, making of Allah a sort of two-faced Janus. In the Moslem doctrine of the Unity all real unity is absent. The attributes of Allah can no more be made to agree than the Surahs which he sent down to Mohammed; but in neither case does this lack of agreement, according to Moslems, reflect on Allah's character.

When God is once called The Holy in the Koran (Surah 59), the term does not signify *moral* purity or perfection, as is evident from the exegetes and from any *Mohammedan* Arabic lexicon.

Beidhawi's comment on the word is: "Holy means the complete absence of anything that would make

Him less than He is."[1]   All the commentaries I have
seen *leave out* the idea of moral purity and use at the
most the word *tahir* as a synonym; this means cere-
monially clean, circumcised, etc.   In the dictionaries,
too, the idea of holiness, for *kŭddŭs,* in the Old Testament sense, is absent.   The *Taj-el-Aroos* and the
Muheet-el-Muheet dictionaries tell us *kŭddŭs* is pure
(*tahir*); but when our hopes were awakened to find
a   spiritual   idea,   the   next   definition   reads:
"*kaddŭs,* a vessel used to wash the parts of the body
in the bath; this is the special name for such a vessel
in Hejaz."   El   Hejaz   was   Mohammed's   native
country.

It is no better if we study the Koran use of the
word *tahir.*   That, too, has only reference to outward
purity of the body.   As, for example, in the Koran
text which states "None shall touch it but the purified."   This is generally applied to circumcision or
to lustrations as incumbent on all who handle the
"holy-book" of Mohammed.

One who was for many years an English missionary in Egypt writes: "Some years ago I was anxious
to see what the Koran teaches with regard to the
necessity of man's being holy inwardly.   I closely
examined all the verses having any reference to this
subject and did not find a single passage pointing

---

[1]The Arabic expression is *"Al baligh fi'l nazăhet ámma
yŭjib naksănahŭ,"* which means anything or nothing!   Again
a definition by negation.

out the necessity of man's being holy or becoming
sanctified in his heart, mind or thoughts. I remember finding *one* passage which seemed likely to point
somewhat more to inward purity, but when I read
the commentary showing under what circumstances
the verse was revealed, I found a long story explaining that Mohammed having addressed a series of
questions to certain people in order to find out
whether they were true believers ultimately declared
them to be *mutahiroon,* "purified" (sanctified?) because he had ascertained that they performed their
purifications in the proper manner, with three clean
stones! It is a hopeless case to look for the doctrine
of the holiness of God and the necessity of purity of
heart in the Koran." The whole idea of moral
purity and utter separation from sin is unknown to
the Koran vocabulary.

One further thought we get by study of the Moslem
idea of God's attributes; it is the key to what Palgrave calls "the Pantheism of Force."

The seventy-second, seventy-third, seventy-fourth
and seventy-fifth names on the list of attributes are
called "mothers of the attributes," *i.e.,* they are the
fundamental ideas in the conception of God. *"Essence* and *Substance,* the *First* and the *Last."* This
is to Moslems—

> "The verse which all the names of Allah holdeth
> As in one sky the silver stars all sit."

Whether Mohammed himself intended to teach the

ideas of pantheism or had any idea of the import of
these terms does not alter the fact that they spell
pantheism to many of his followers. If pantheism
is the doctrine of one substance, it is taught here.
God is the inside and the outside of everything. He
is the phenomena (*Dhahir*) and the power behind the
phenomena (*Bātin*). It is this verse that is the delight of the Sufîs and the mystics. On this revelation of God they built their philosophy after the
Vedanta school of the Hindus. How far this teaching was carried is best seen in the celebrated *Masnavi*
of Jalal-u-din-ar-Rumi, translated into English by
E. H. Whinfield.[1] He puts these words as emanating
from Deity:—

"I am the Gospel, the Psalter, the Koran;
I am Uzza and Lat—Bel and the Dragon.
Into three and seventy sects is the world divided,
Yet only One God; the faithful who believed in Him am I.
Lies and truth, good, bad, hard and soft
Knowledge, solitude, virtue, faith,
The deepest ground of hell, the highest torment of the flames,
The highest paradise,
The earth and what is therein,
The angels and the devils, Spirit and man, Am I.
What is the goal of speech, O tell it, Shems Tabrîzi?
The goal of sense? This—The World Soul Am I."

Not only are there thousands of Moslems who are

[1]*Masnavi-i-Mánavi*, the Spiritual Couplets of Jalalu-din Moh.
Rumi, translated by E. H. Whinfield, M.A., London, 1898,
Trübner & Co.

pantheists of the Sufi-school, but there is not a Moslem sect which does not go to extremes in its erroneous conception and misconstruction of the doctrine of God.   The Wahabîs are accused, and not without reason, of being gross anthropomorphists. As a revolt from the rationalism of the Mutazilite school many, in the days of the Abbasids, held anthropomorphic views of Deity and materialistic ideas in regard to the soul. "The soul, for example, was conceived of by them as corporeal or as an accident of the body and the Divine Essence was imagined as a human body.   The religious teaching and art of the Moslems were greatly averse to the symbolical God-Father of the Christians, but there was an abundance of absurd speculations about the form of Allah.   Some went so far as to ascribe to Him all the bodily members together, with the exception of the beard and other privileges of Oriental manhood."[1]

The *Salabiyah* hold that "God is indifferent to the actions of men, just as though He were in a state of sleep."   The *Muztariyah* hold that good and evil are both directly from God and that man is entirely irresponsible.   The *Nazamiah* hold that it is lawful to speak of the Almighty as "The Thing."

Some schools hold that the attributes are eternal and others deny it to save their idea of pure and absolute monism in Deity.   For, they argue, if any of

[1]*The History of Philosophy in Islam,* by Dr. T. J. de Boer, London, 1903, p. 44.

the attributes are eternal, or all of them, there is more than one Eternal; and two Eternals is infidelity!

One sect, the *Mutarabisiyah,* chose an impossible, although golden, mean by teaching that Allah with all His attributes, save three, is eternal; but His power, knowledge and purpose were created. What Allah could have been before He had power, knowledge or purpose they do not say.

In only one passage of the Koran, Allah is described as seemingly *dependent* on or indebted to something outside of Himself; the verse represents Allah as the Light of the World, but the commentaries cast no light on its peculiar and evidently mystical teaching; "God is the light of the heavens and the earth; His light is as a niche in which is a lamp, and the lamp is in a glass, the glass is as though it were a glittering star; *it is lit from a blessed tree, an olive, neither of the east nor of the west, the oil of which would well-nigh give light though no fire touched it. Light upon Light."* (Surah 24:35.)

Is this one of the many distorted reflections of ideas which Mohammed borrowed from the Jews and does he refer to the Golden Candlestick?

V

THE RELATION OF ALLAH TO HIS WORLD

"We may well believe that heathen religions so far from having arisen, as some have vainly imagined, out of the soil of lofty aspiration after a God unknown, are devices more or less elaborate for shutting out the thought of God as He is from the minds and hearts of men. The Gospel meets its greatest triumphs not among those who have the most finished, but among those who have the crudest systems of religion. Elaborateness, completeness, finish, here seem to be elaborateness, completeness, finish of escape from the consciousness of God."—*Rev. E. N. Harris* (of Burma).

"Whoever desires an introduction to Allah—Islam's absentee landlord, who, jealous of man, wound the clock of the universe and went away forever — is referred to Palgrave." — *Frederick Perry Noble.*

MOHAMMED'S doctrine of the Unity of God is at the same time his doctrine of Providence and his philosophy of life. The existence and character of God, not only, but His relation past, present, and future to the universe are latent in the words *La ilaha illa Allah,* There is no god but God.

It was not a theologian nor a philosopher who first called attention to this fundamental idea in Islam as the key to a proper understanding of the Moslem mind, but the Arabian traveller, William Gifford Palgrave, who knew Islam not from books as much as from long and close contact with the Arabs themselves. Whatever may be the opinion concerning Palgrave's accuracy as a geographer, there is no doubt that he was a capital observer of the *people,* their manners and religion. It is, therefore, without apology for the length of the quotation that we give here Palgrave's famous characterization of Allah.[1]

"There is no god but God—are words simply tantamount in English to the negation of any deity save one alone; and thus much they certainly mean in Arabic, but they imply much more also. Their full sense is not only to deny absolutely and unreservedly all plurality whether of nature or of person in the Supreme Being, not only to establish the unity of the Unbegetting and the Unbegot, in all its simple and uncommunicable Oneness, but besides this the words in Arabic and among Arabs imply that this one Supreme Being is also the only Agent, the only Force, the only Act existing throughout the universe and leaves us to all beings else, matter or spirit, instinct or intelligence, physical or moral, nothing but pure unconditional passiveness, alike in movement

[1] *Narrative of a Year's Journey through Central and Eastern Arabia,* 1862-63, by W. S. Palgrave, Vol. I., pp. 365-367.

or in quiescence, in action or in capacity. The sole
power, the sole motor, movement, energy and deed is
God; the rest is downright inertia and mere instrumentality, from the highest archangel down to the
simplest atom of creation. Hence in this one sen-
tence, 'La ilaha illa Allah,' is summed up a system
which, for want of a better name, I may be permitted
to call the Pantheism of Force, or of Act, thus exclusively assigned to God, who absorbs it all, exercises
it all, and to Whom alone it can be ascribed, whether
for preserving or for destroying, for relative evil or
for equally relative good. I say *relative* because it
is clear that in such a theology no place is left for
absolute good or evil, reason or extravagance; all is
abridged in the autocratical will of the one great
Agent: 'sic volo, sic jubeo, stet pro ratione voluntas;'
or more significantly still, in Arabic, *'Kama yesha,'*
'as He wills it,' to quote the constantly recurring expression of the Koran.

"Thus immeasurably and eternally exalted above,
and dissimilar from, all creatures which lie levelled
before Him on one common plane of instrumentality
and inertness, God is One in the totality of omnipo-
tent and omnipresent action, which acknowledges no
rule, standard or limit, save His own sole and absolute will. He communicates nothing to His
creatures; for their seeming power and act ever remain His alone, and in return He receives nothing
from them; for whatever they may be, that they are

in Him, by Him and from Him only.[1] And secondly, no superiority, no distinction, no preëminence can be lawfully claimed by one creature over another in the utter equalization of their unexceptional servitude and abasement; all are alike tools of the one solitary Force, which employs them to crush or to benefit, to truth or to error, to honor or shame, to happiness or misery, quite independently of their individual fitness, deserts or advantage and simply because He will it and as He wills it.

"One might at first sight think that this tremendous Autocrat, this uncontrolled and unsympathizing Power would be far above anything like passions, desires or inclinations. Yet such is not the case, for He has with respect to His creatures one main feeling and source of action, namely, jealousy of them, lest they should perchance attribute to themselves something of what is His alone, and thus encroach on His all-engrossing kingdom. Hence He is ever more ready to punish than to reward, to inflict pain than to bestow pleasure, to ruin than to build. It is His singular satisfaction to make created beings continually feel that they are nothing else than His

---

[1]Note the distinction between this and the New Testament phrase: *"Of Him, and through Him and to Him are all things."* The fact that a Moslem never thanks the giver, but only God, for alms or kindness is a capital illustration of what Palgrave asserts. There is much thanksgiving to God, but no *gratitude to man,* in Moslem lands.

slaves, His tools, and contemptible tools also, that
thus they may the better acknowledge His superiority, and know His power to be above their power,
His cunning above their cunning, His will above
their will, His pride above their pride; or rather,
that there is no power, cunning, will or pride save
His own. But He Himself, sterile in His inaccessi-
ble height, neither loving nor enjoying aught save
His own and self-measured decree, without son, companion or counsellor, is no less barren for Himself
than for His creatures; and His own barrenness and
lone egoism in Himself is the cause and rule of His
indifferent and unregarding despotism around. *The
first note is the key of the whole tune, and the primal
idea of God runs through and modifies the whole
system and creed that centres in Him.*

"That the notion here given of the Deity, monstrous and blasphemous as it may appear, is exactly
and literally that which the Koran conveys or intends
to convey, I at present take for granted. But that it
indeed is so, no one who has attentively perused and
thought over the Arabic text (for mere cursory reading, especially in a translation, will not suffice) can
hesitate to allow. In fact, every phrase of the preceding sentences, every touch in this odious portrait
has been taken to the best of my ability, word for
word, or at least meaning for meaning, from 'the
Book,' the truest mirror of the mind and scope of its
writer. And that such was in reality Mahomet's

mind and idea is fully confirmed by the witness-tongue of contemporary tradition. Of this we have many authentic samples: the Saheeh, the commentaries of Beidhawi, the Mishkat-el-Misabih and fifty similar works afford ample testimony on this point."

The only criticism which the student of Islam can offer on this masterpiece of word-painting on the Moslem idea of God is that it applies more particularly to the Wahabi sect than to other sects of Islam. But this criticism only adds force to Palgrave's argument, for the Wahabi revival was nothing else than an attempt to return to primitive Islam and to go back to Mohammed's own teaching. After living in Arabia for over thirteen years, I have no hesitation in saying that, to my mind, the Wahabi sect is more orthodox (*i.e.*, closer to the Koran and earliest tradition) than any other sect of Islam both in their creed and their practice.[1] What Palgrave states regarding Allah's relation to His creatures can be best proved and illustrated by treating first the Moslem doctrine of Creation and then that of Providence. We will find in this study that orthodox Islam is at once deistic and pantheistic. Theologians and philosophers have pantheistic views of Allah, making Him the sole force in the universe; but the popular thought of Him (owing to the iron-weight of the doctrine of fatalism) is deistic. God stands aloof from

[1]See a paper on the Wahabis in the *Journal of the Victoria Institute*, Vol. XXXIII., pp. 311-333. London, 1901.

creation; only His power is felt; men are like the pieces on a chess-board and He is the only player.

Creation itself was not intended so much for the manifestation of God's glory or the outburst of His love, as for a sample of His power. The following are the Koran texts that speak of creation (Surah 50:37): "Of old we created the heavens and the earth and all that is between them in *six* days, and no weariness touched us." (Surah 41:8.) "Do ye indeed disbelieve in Him who in *two* days created the earth? Do ye assign Him equals? The Lord of the world is He. And He hath placed on the earth the firm mountains which tower above it, and He hath blessed it and distributed its nourishments throughout it (for the cravings of all alike) in *four* days. Then He applied Himself [went] to the heaven which was but smoke; and to it and to the earth He said, 'Come ye in obedience or against your will?' And they both said, 'We come obedient.' And He completed them as seven heavens in *two* days and in each heaven made known its office; and He furnished the lower heavens with lights and guardian angels. This is the disposition of the Almighty, the all-knowing One." Again in Surah 16:3: "He created the heavens and the earth to set forth His truth. High let Him be exalted above the gods they join with Him. Man hath He created out of a moist germ, etc." Surah 13:2: "It is God who hath reared the heavens without pillars, thou canst behold; then seated Himself upon His throne and ('compelled to service') imposed laws on the sun and moon; each travelleth to its appointed goal.   He ordereth all things."   Surah 35:12: "God created you out of dust, then of the germs of life, then made you two sexes."

The first thing that strikes one is the evident contradiction in these texts regarding the number of the days of creation.   (Cf. Surahs 50:37 and 41:8.) But such disagreement of statement is common in the Koran.   Beidhawi's commentary tries hard to reconcile the discrepancy, but finally gives it up.   On Surah 41st he remarks: "Allah did not command the heavens and the earth to come in order to prove their obedience, but only to manifest His power." He explains the *two* days of creation thus: "He created the heavens on Thursday and the sun, moon and stars on Friday."   According to the table-talk of the prophet (Mishkat-el-Misabih 24:1, part 3) God created the earth on Saturday, the hills on Sunday, the trees on Monday, *all unpleasant things on Tuesday,* the light on Wednesday, the beasts on Thursday, and Adam, who was the last creation, was created after the time of afternoon prayers on Friday.

In this orthodox tradition, Mohammed's idea that Allah is the author of evil crops out.   This idea occurs also in Surah 113:2: "I seek refuge in the Lord of the daybreak from the evil he did make." Zamakhshari comments thus: "The evil of His creation and of His creatures, both those who are responsible and those who are not responsible," etc. The common Moslem idea, undoubtedly taken from the Koran and Tradition, is that Allah created hell and created Satan such as they are. He is the creator of *evil Jinn* as well as of the *good Jinn;* and He made them evil in the same sense as He made the scorpion poisonous and arsenic deadly. Why did Allah create hell? To fill it with infidels. In describing creation Moslem theologians take pains to establish the fact that the universe is not infinite; God alone is that and to believe *two* infinites possible, is *shirk,* polytheism. A Persian Mullah, in recent years, offered to give an English traveller logical proof of the fact as follows: "Let us suppose that the Universe is infinite. Then from the centre of the earth draw two straight lines diverging at an angle of 60° and produce them to infinity. Join the terminal points by another straight line to form the base of a triangle. Since one of the angles is 60° and the two sides are equal, the remaining angles are 60° each and the triangle is equilateral. Therefore, since the sides are infinite, the base is also of infinite length. But the base is a straight line joining two points (*viz.,* the terminal points of the sides), that is to say, it is limited in both directions. Therefore, it is not infinite, neither are the sides infinite, and a straight line cannot be drawn to infinity. Therefore, the Universe is

finite."[1]   Such argument needs no comment; but it
is a sample of Mohammedan logic.

El Buchari gives the following tradition of the
prophet regarding the order of creation:[2] "The first
thing which God created was a pen, and He said to
it, Write.   It said, What shall I write?   And God
said, Write down the quantity of every individual
thing to be created.   And it wrote all that was and
that will be to eternity."   In Surah 13:2, *seq.*
(quoted above), there occurs an expression which has
given rise to much discussion among Moslems: "It is
God who hath reared the heavens without pillars,
then *seated* Himself upon His throne."   The word
used for *seated* (*istawa*)[3] has given rise to endless
disputations.   Even the last Mohammedan reform,
under Mohammed bin Abd-ul-Wahāb, made this
word the shibboleth of their theology.   Most commentaries interpret the word deistically, "Then He
made for the throne," i.e., left the world entirely and
absolutely.   Zamakhshari escapes the dilemma by
silence and Beidhawi says, "He betook Himself to
the throne, *i.e.,* to preserve and to direct."   Husaini,
the commentator, remarks on Surah 9:131: "The
throne of God has 8,000 pillars and the distance be-

[1]E. G. Browne's *A Year among the Persians,* p. 144.

[2]Hughes' *Dict. of Islam,* p. 472.

[3]From the root *sawa,* to intend, to be equal; VIII. conju-
gation *istawa,* to be equal, to ascend, intend, to sit firm and
square upon. See Penrice's *Dictionary of the Koran.*

tween each pillar is 3,000,000 miles." Others make
the throne more spiritual, but all are agreed that
Allah is now on the throne and that He rules the
world by means of angels and jinn and men, all subject to His will and decrees. One Moslem author
settled the matter of Allah's sitting in the famous
dogmatic phrase, often quoted, "That He sits is certain; how He sits only He knows; and why He sits
it is infidelity to ask."

Why He sits it is infidelity to ask—that is the orthodox Moslem reply to the questions that arise in
the human heart concerning the Divine government
of the world and the problem of evil. When the
Mu'tazilite sect (the only school of Moslem thought
that ever dared to give human reason a place of
authority) in Bagdad attempted to answer questions
they were gagged by the orthodox party. Renan
says:

"Science and philosophy flourished on Musalman soil during the first half of the middle ages; but it was not by reason
of Islam, it was in spite of Islam. Not a Musalman philosopher or scholar escaped persecution. During the period just
specified persecution is less powerful than the instinct of free
enquiry, and the rationalistic tradition is kept alive; then intolerance and fanaticism win the day. It is true that the
Christian Church also cast great difficulties in the way of science in the middle ages; but she did not strangle it outright,
as did the Musalman theology. To give Islam the credit of
Averroes and of so many other illustrious thinkers, who passed
half their life in prison, in forced hiding, in disgrace, whose
books were burned and whose writings almost suppressed by

theological authority, is as if one were to ascribe to the Inquisition the discoveries of Galileo, and a whole scientific development which it was not able to prevent."[1]

The relation of Allah to the world is such that all free-will not only but all freedom in the exercise of the intellect is preposterous. God is so great and the character of His greatness is so pantheistically absolute that there is no room for the human. All good and all evil come directly from Allah. In twenty passages of the Koran, Allah is said "to lead men astray." (See Sir William Muir's *Selections from the Coran,* p. 52.) Still worse, God is said to have created a multitude of spirits and of men expressly for torture in such a hell as only the Koran and Tradition can paint. (Surahs 16: 180 and 32: 13.) "The word must be fulfilled. Verily, I will most surely fill up hell with jinns and men together." Even for the true believer there is no sure hope. One celebrated verse in the Koran (Surah Miriam, vs. 72) says that every one of the *believers* must enter hell, too! Hope perishes under the weight of this iron-bondage and pessimism becomes the popular philosophy. Islam saw only one side of a many-sided truth. As Clarke puts it, "Islam saw God, but not man; saw the claims of Deity, but not the rights of humanity; saw authority, but failed to see freedom—therefore, hardened into despotism, stiffened into

formalism, and sank into death."[1]   Elsewhere the
same author calls Mohammedanism "the worst form
of monotheism in that it makes of God pure will—
will divorced from reason and love." Islam, instead
of being a progressive and completed idea, goes to a
lower level than the religions it claims to supplant.
"Mohammed teaches a God above us; Moses teaches
a God above us and yet *with us;* Jesus Christ teaches
God above us, God with us and God in us." God
above us, not as an Oriental despot, but as a Heavenly Father. God with us, Emmanuel, in the mystery of His Incarnation, which is the stumbling
block to the Moslem. God in us through His Spirit
renewing the heart and controlling the will into a
true *Islam,* or obedient subjection by a living faith.

[1]James Freeman Clarke's *Ten Great Religions,* Vol. II., p. 68.
Although he is a Unitarian, he has no praise for Mohammedan
monotheism.

VI

MOHAMMEDAN IDEAS OF THE TRINITY

"They say the Merciful has taken to Himself a
son—ye have brought a monstrous thing! The
heavens well-nigh burst asunder thereat, and the
earth is riven and the mountains fall down
broken, that they attribute to the Merciful a
son! But it becomes not the Merciful to take to
Himself a son."—*Surah Miriam, vs. 91-93.*

"Praise belongs to God who has not taken to
Himself a son and has not had a partner in His
kingdom, nor had a patron against such abasement."—*The Night Journey, vs. 112.*

THE Moslem idea of God consists not only in
what is asserted of Deity, but also, and more
emphatically, in what is denied. James Freeman
Clarke, in his study of the Ten Great Religions, calls
attention to this fact in regard to all false faiths in
these pregnant words: "Of all the systems of belief
which have had a widespread hold on mankind this
may be posited, that they are commonly true in what
they affirm, false in what they deny. The error in
every theory is usually found in its denials, that is,

its limitations. What it sees is substantial and real; what it does not see is a mark only of its limited vision."[1]

The Mohammedan controversy with Christians has ever had two great centres; and although the form of the ellipse has changed since the days of Raymund Lull, or even since the time of Henry Martyn, the foci remain the same. The integrity of Scripture and the reasonableness of the doctrine of the Trinity are the two points in Christianity against which Islam emphatically testifies. At the same time these two ideas are fundamental in the Christian system. The doctrine of the Trinity is not only fundamental but essential to the very existence of Christianity. Dr. Baur of the Tübingen school acknowledges this when he says that "in the battle between Arius and Athanasius the existence of Christianity was at stake." In some form the doctrine of the Trinity has always been confessed by the Church and all who opposed it were thrown off from its fellowship. "When this doctrine was abandoned, other articles of faith, such as the atonement, regeneration, etc., have almost always followed, by logical necessity, as when one draws the wire from a necklace of gems, the gems all fall asunder." (Henry B. Smith.) The doctrine of the Trinity, in its widest sense, includes that of the Incarnation and of the Holy Spirit. In studying what the Koran teaches on this subject,

[1] *Ten Great Religions,* Vol. II., p. 62.

therefore, we must examine not only what it tells of the Trinity, but also those passages that speak of the nature of Jesus Christ and of the Holy Spirit.

The following order will be observed in our study: (*a*) the Koran passages that speak directly of the Trinity; (*b*) those that refer to the subject indirectly; (*c*) the Christology of the Koran as it bears on this doctrine; (*d*) the passages that speak of the Holy Spirit.

(*a*) The direct references to the Trinity are not many in the Koran and all occur in *two* Surahs, composed by Mohammed toward the close of his career at Medina. Surah 4:167-170 reads: "O ye people of the Book do not exceed in your religion nor say against God aught save the truth. The Messiah, Jesus, the son of Mary, is but the apostle of God and His Word which He cast into Mary and a spirit from Him; believe, then, in God and His apostles, and say not, Three. Have done! It were better for you. God is only one God, celebrated be His praise from that He should beget a son!" Again Surah 5:77: "They misbelieve who say, Verily, God is the third of three; for there is no God but one, and if they do not desist from what they say there shall touch those who misbelieve among them grievous woe. Will they not turn again towards God and ask pardon of Him? for God is forgiving and merciful." The third passage, and that most often used as a proof-text by

Moslems against Christians, is in the same Surah
(5:116): "And when God said, O Jesus, son of
Mary! Is it thou who didst say to men, take me and
my mother for two gods beside God? He said,
I celebrate Thy praise, what ails me that I should
say what I have no right to? If I had said
it Thou wouldst have known it; Thou knowest
what is in my soul, but I know not what is in
Thy soul; verily, Thou art one who knoweth the
unseen."

These passages leave no doubt that Mohammed
denied the doctrine of the Trinity and that he conceived it to be, *or affirmed it to be,* a species of
tritheism, consisting of God, Mary and Jesus Christ.
[Whether Mohammed had a correct idea of the Trinity and deliberately put forth this travesty of the
Christian idea, we will consider later.] The commentaries interpret the Koran as follows: Zamakhshari on
4:169 remarks, "The story received among Christians is that God is one in essence and three persons,
(*akanîm*) the person of the Father, the person of the
Son and the person of the Holy Spirit. And they
verily mean by the person of the Father, the Being,
and by the person of the Son, knowledge, and by the
person of the Holy Spirit, life. And this supposes
that God is the third of three, or, if not, that there
are three gods. And that which the Koran here refers to is the clear statement of theirs, that God and
Christ and Mary are three gods and that the Christ

is a child (*walad*) of God from Mary." For proof
he then quotes Surah 5:116, and adds: "And it is
universally known concerning Christians that they
hold the deity and humanity of Christ as regards his
father and mother." From this it is evident that
Zamakhshari had a more correct idea of the doctrine
of the Trinity than did Mohammed and that after
offering a modal trinity as the creed of Christians
he covers up the Koran mistake by asserting, without proof, that the trinity was a triad of Father, Son
and Mother. (Vol. I. of the *Kishaf,* p. 241.)
Beidhawi (on 4:169) remarks: "Jesus is called the
Spirit of God because He makes the dead to live or
quickens hearts." On the following verse he is doubtful; "Either God is the third of three gods or is a
triad of Father, Son and Holy Spirit." (Vol. I.,
p. 319.) He, too, avoids a real explanation of the
gross misstatement in the Koran that Mary is one
of the persons of the Trinity. The *Jilalain* (Vol. I.,
p. 278) prove that Jesus cannot be God, "because
He has a spirit and everything possessed of a spirit
is compounded (*murakkib*), and God is absolutely
without compounding, arrangement (*tarkib*), *i.e.,*
simple." He says the Trinity consists of "Allah and
Jesus and His mother."

It is interesting to note here that the earliest of
these three exegetes is most correct in his ideas and
the latest one entirely ignores the apparently well-
known facts as given by Zamakhshari and admitted

by Beidhawi. The dates of their commentaries were: Zamakhshari, 604 A.H.; Beidhawi, 685 A.H., and Jilalain, 864-911 A.H. On the other passages of the Koran quoted above these commentaries offer no new explanations or ideas.

(*b*)   Let us turn to other Koran texts that have a bearing on this false trinity, or the tritheism of which Christians are accused. By *shirk* the Koran and Moslems mean ascribing companions or plurality to Deity; and according to the Wahabi writers, it is of four kinds: 1. *Shirk-ul-Ilm* is to ascribe knowledge to others than God. Jesus knows no secret thing and does not share in what God knows. 2. *Shirk-ut-Tassarŭf* is to ascribe power-to-act-independently, to any one else than to God. All are His slaves. No one can intercede except by God's permission.[1] To say that Christ intercedes by His own power or merit is *shirk,* polytheism. 3. *Shirk-ul-Abāda* is to ascribe a partner to God who can be worshipped, or worshipping the created instead of the Creator, as Christians are said to do when they worship Christ or adore Mary. 4. *Shirk-ul-'Adat* is to perform ceremonies or follow superstitions which indicate reliance or trust on anything or any one save God. There is no doubt that this fourfold classification by the Wahabi sect has its ground in the Koran, and it is on these four items that Christians are called *mushrikŭn,* or polytheists, by Moslems to-day, although that word is

[1]Surahs 2:256; 19:90; 20:108; 34:22; 39:45; 78:38,

specially used for the Meccan idolaters in the Koran.[1] Logically the use of this term for Christians is perfectly natural and correct from a Moslem point of view, for we certainly hold that the Son of God is omniscient, independent of the creature, has power as an intercessor and is worthy of worship. Practically, therefore, all the passages in the Koran that speak against idolatry and assert God's unity are used by Moslems as testimony against the doctrine of the Trinity. These texts have already been considered in Chapter II. and are too numerous to mention.

(c) The Christology of the Koran includes the apocryphal account of Jesus' birth and life among men, His translation into heaven and the ideas regarding His second advent; but what more especially concerns us is to know what Islam teaches regarding the *person* of Christ. For a full and generally fair treatment of this subject the reader is referred to Gerock's Christologie des Koran;[2] much of what the Koran teaches concerning Christ is not germane to our topic, although of curious interest.

Regarding the birth of Jesus Christ, the Koran

[1] Al Bagawi says (on 98 : 1) that the term *Ahl-ul-Kitab*, people of the book, is always used for the Jews and Christians and *Mushrikūn* for those who worship idols. Cf. Hughes' *Dict. of Islam*, pp. 579, 580.

[2] *Versuch einer Darstellung der Christologie des Koran*, von C. F. Gerock, Professor der Geschichte am Gymnasium zu Buchsweiler im Elfasz. Hamburg, 1839.

and Tradition agree that it was miraculous, but they
equally deny an incarnation of Deity in the Christian sense. Surah 3:37-43: "And when the angels
said, O Mary, verily God has chosen thee and has
purified thee and has chosen thee above the women
of the world. O Mary! be devout unto thy Lord and
adore and bow down with those who bow. . . . O
Mary, verily God gives thee the glad tidings of a
Word from Him his name shall be Messiah Jesus,
the son of Mary, regarded in this world and the next,
and of those whose place is nigh to God. And He
shall speak to people in his cradle and when grown
up, and shall be among the righteous. She said, Lord,
how can I have a son when man has not yet touched
me ? He said, Thus God creates what He pleaseth.
When He decrees a matter He only says, Be and it
is. . . ." Surah 19:16-21: "And mention in the
book, Mary; when she retired from her family into
an eastern place; and she took a veil to screen herself
from them; and we sent unto her our spirit, and he
took for her the semblance of a well-made man. Said
she, Verily, I take refuge in the Merciful One from
thee, if thou art pious. Said he, I am only a messenger of thy Lord to bestow on thee a pure
boy." . . . Zamakhshari comments on this
verse in the usual coarse, materialistic way by saying
that the virgin conceived "when the angel Gabriel
blew up her garment." (Vol. II., p. 4.) It is impossible to translate the gross and utterly sensual

ideas of Moslem commentators on the miraculous birth of Jesus Christ. The above verses from the Koran, however, will indicate to the thoughtful reader how far off even Mohammed was from a *spiritual* conception of God's power as creator, though he believed Christ to be merely human. The Moslem mind to-day is too carnal to understand what the Christian Church means by its doctrine of the Incarnation. Husain, the commentator, *e.g.*, says: "When she went eastward, *i.e.*, out of her house in an eastward direction to perform her ablutions, Gabriel appeared to her." And Zamakhshari suggests that this accounts for the eastward position in prayer on the part of Christians!

The Koran denies the Divinity and the eternal Sonship of Christ. He is a creature like Adam. God could destroy Jesus and His mother without loss to Himself. Surah 19:35, 36: "God could not take to Himself any son. . . . When He decrees a matter He only says to it 'Be,' and it is." Surah 3:51: "Verily, the likeness of Jesus with God is as the likeness of Adam. He created him from the earth, then He said to him Be, and he was." Surah 9:30: "The Jews say Ezra is the son of God;[1] and the Christians say that the Messiah is the son of God; that is what they say with their mouths imi-

---

[1]There is no Jewish tradition whatever in support of this accusation of Mohammed and it was probably a malicious invention. Cf. Palmer's note and the Commentaries.

tating the sayings of those who misbelieved before. God fight them! How they lie." Surah 5:19: "Infidels are they who say, Verily, God is the Messiah, the son of Mary. Say, who has any hold on God if He wished to destroy the Messiah, the son of Mary, and his mother and those who are on the earth together ?"

Although the Koran and Tradition give Jesus Christ a high place among the prophets, and affirm His sinlessness[1] and power to work miracles,[2] *all this does not distinguish His person in any way as to its nature from other prophets who came before Him.* The pre-existence of the Word of God is denied. While Tradition is full of stories about the *Nŭr-Mohammed* or "Light of Mohammed which was created before all things made by God." Specially is it to be noted that the Koran denies the atonement and the crucifixion of Jesus Christ. (Surahs 3: 47-50; 4: 155, 156.) Wakidi relates that Mohammed had such repugnance to the sign of the cross that he destroyed everything brought to his house with that figure upon it. Even in Moslem Tradition regarding the second coming of Jesus this hatred of the cross comes out. Abu Huraira relates that the prophet

---

[1]See *Mishkat-ul-Misabih*, Book XXIII., ch. xii. In the same book the sinlessness of Mary, as well as of Jesus, is asserted (Bk. I., ch. iii., pt. 1). Hughes' *Dict. of Islam*, p. 205.

[2]Surahs 3 : 43-46; 5 : 112-115. Cf. Beidhawi's *Commentary* on the latter passage.

said: "I swear by God it is near when Jesus, son of Mary, will descend from heaven upon your people a just king, and he will break the crucifix and will kill the swine and will remove the poll-tax from the unenfranchised." (Mishkat 23:6.) The hatred toward the sign of the cross as emblem of the atonement is widespread among Moslems; Doughty, the Arabian traveller, tells how in the heart of Nejd, away from all Christian influences or offences, the children draw a cross on the desert sand and defile it to show that they are true Moslems.[1] On the other hand, the sign of the cross is used in amulets and on property because of its sinister power; the frontispiece gives an illustration of such use. All Moslems are agreed that Jesus is now alive and in heaven, but they disagree as to the degree of his exaltation. According to Tradition, Mohammed said that "he saw Jesus and John in the second heaven on the night of his *Mi'raj,* or celestial journey."[2] In the commentary known as *Jamia'-l-Bayyan* it is said that Christ is in the third region of bliss; while some say He is in the fourth heaven.[3] In the tradition of this *Mi'raj,* Mohammed ascends to the seventh heaven, where he finds Abraham; Moses is in the sixth. These statements indicate that Christ occupies no *supreme* place in heaven according to the

[1]*Arabia Deserta,* Vol. I., p. 156.
[2]*Mishkat-ul-Misabih,* Book XXIV., ch. vii.
[3]*Dict. of Islam,* articles on the Mi'raj and on Jesus Christ.

Prophet. In considering the character and content of Moslem monotheism, a Christian can never forget that Jesus Christ has no place in the Moslem idea of God, and that the portrait of our Saviour as given in the Koran and in Tradition is a sad caricature.

(*d*) The third person of the Trinity, the Holy Spirit, is mentioned by that name three times in the Koran. Surah 16:104 speaks of Him as the inspiring agent of the Koran: "Say the Holy Spirit brought it down from thy Lord in truth;" and twice in the 2d Surah, vs. 81 and 254, we read: "We strengthened him (*i.e.*, Jesus) with the Holy Spirit." *But all Moslem commentators are agreed that the Holy Spirit in these passages means the angel Gabriel.* Why Mohammed confounded Gabriel with the Holy Spirit is far from clear. The only distinct assertion that Gabriel was the channel of Mohammed's revelation occurs in a Medina Surah (2:91), and Gabriel is mentioned only once besides (66:4). Was this a misapprehension or a misrepresentation on the part of the Koran and the commentators? We have already seen that the commentators at least were not in ignorance of the fact that the Holy Spirit is the third person of the Trinity among Christians. Was Mohammed ignorant of the true doctrine of the Trinity as held by Christians? The common idea is that he was; and this idea finds its support in the old story of the Collyridian sect in

Arabia.[1] The assertion is that Mohammed got his idea of the Trinity from this heretical sect, "who invested the Virgin Mary with the name and honours of a goddess," and offered to her cylindrical cakes (κολλύριδες), hence their name. Let us see what basis there is for this view. The only authority we have to prove even the *existence* of this female sect is the history of heresies by Epiphanius;[2] what others tell is quoted from his chapter. Gerock says: "Epiphanius does not relate anything definite concerning the sect, and the long chapter devoted to this heresy contains next to nothing save controversy, in which the author seems to delight. Even had such a sect existed at the time of Epiphanius in Arabia, it is far from probable that, consisting only of women, it would have continued for three centuries until the time of Mohammed and become so extended and strong that Mohammed could mistake it for the Christian religion."[3] Mohammed came in contact

[1]Gibbon, Vol. III., p. 488. Hottinger, *Hist. Orient*, p. 225, and copied in most of the later accounts of the history of Moslem teaching, *e.g.*, Sale's *Prelim. Discourse to the Koran.*

[2]"Epiphanius," says Dr. Schaff (*Hist. of Christian Church*, Vol. III., p. 169), "was lacking in knowledge of the world and of men, in sound judgment and critical discernment. He was possessed of boundless credulity, now almost proverbial, causing innumerable errors and contradictions in his writings." Scaliger calls him "an ignorant man who committed the greatest blunders, told the greatest falsehoods, and knew next to nothing about either Hebrew or Greek."

[3]Gerock's *Christologie*, p. 75.

with Oriental Christianity from *three* quarters: the
Christians of Yemen visited Mecca, and Abraha
was turned back in defeat with his army, in the year
in which Mohammed was born; Mohammed had as
concubine a Christian Coptic woman, Miriam, the
mother of his son Ibrahim; Mohammed went once
and again to Syria with Khadijah's caravan of mer-
chandise. Early Christianity in Arabia was much
more extended and influential than is generally supposed.[1] Nearly all of Yeman and Nejran was per-
meated with the doctrines of Christianity and there
had been many martyrs. Concerning the view held
by all Yemen Christians regarding the Trinity, we
have unimpeachable evidence in the monuments
found by Glaser. (See remark in Chapter II.)
The Abyssinian Church of the fifth century was undoubtedly corrupt and paid high honors to the Virgin
Mary and the saints; but it is certain also that this
Church always held, as it does now, that the three
persons of the Trinity are the Father, the Son and
the Holy Spirit. The same is true as regards the
Nestorians, the Jacobites, the Armenians and the
Maronites; because the Monophysite controversy concerned itself not with the doctrine of the Trinity,
but with the Person of Christ.[2] Both Nestorians
and Monophysites accepted the Nicene Creed without the *Filioque*. Now how is it possible to imagine

[1] Wright's *Early Christianity in Arabia*, London, 1855; and
Arabia, the Cradle of Islam, pp. 300-314.
[2] See Schaff's *Creeds of Christendom*, Vol. I., pp. 79-82.

that Mohammed, who knew of Arabian Christianity, visited Syria and married a Coptic woman, who became his special favorite, and whose earliest converts took refuge in Abyssinia—how is it possible to imagine that he was ignorant of the persons of the Trinity?

In addition to the reasons given above we read in Ibn Hisham (quoted from Ibn Ishak) that the Christians of Nejran sent a large and learned deputation to Mohammed headed by a Bishop of the Emperor's faith, *i.e.*, of the orthodox Catholic Church. Now is it possible that a Bishop could have represented the Holy Trinity to consist of God, Christ and Mary (as Tradition says he did) after the whole Eastern world had been resounding for ages with the profound and sharply defined controversies concerning this fundamental doctrine?

In concluding our investigation of this subject, can we resist the conclusion of Koelle as given in his critical and classical book on Mohammed and Mohammedanism?[1] *"Not want of opportunity, but want of sympathy and compatibility kept him aloof from the religion of Christ. His first wife introduced him to her Christian cousin; one of his later wives had embraced Christianity in Abyssinia; and the most favored of his concubines was a Christian damsel from the Copts of Egypt. He was acquainted with ascetic monks and had dealings with learned*

[1] Koelle's *Mohammed and Mohammedanism*, p. 471. This is the best recent book on Islam and the life of Mohammed.

Bishops of the Orthodox Church. In those days the reading of the Holy Scriptures in the public services of the Catholic Church was already authoritatively enjoined and universally practised; if he had wished thoroughly to acquaint himself with them he could easily have done so. But having no adequate conception of the nature of sin and man's fallen•state, he also lacked the faculty of truly appreciating the remedy for it which was offered in the Gospel." And if Koelle is correct, as I believe he is, then Mohammed's idea of God includes a deliberate rejection of the Christian idea of the Godhead—the Father, the Son and the Holy Spirit.[1]

[1]The question whether Mohammed could read and write is important in this connection. On this point Moslems themselves are not agreed. Some Shiahs affirm he could, while the Sunnis deny it. Western scholars are also divided in their opinion on this question. The following hold that Mohammed could read and write and give good reasons for their opinion: M. Turpin in *Hist. de la Vie de Mahomet*, Vol. I., pp. 285-88; Wahl, *Intro. to the Koran*, p. 78; Sprenger, *Life of Moh.*, Vol. II., pp. 398-402; Weil, *Intro. to the Koran*, p. 39; H. Hirschfeld, *Jüdische Elemente im Koran*, p. 22. Others deny it, among them: Marraci, p. 535; Prideaux, p. 43; Ockley, *Hist. of the Saracens*, p. 11; Gerock's *Christologie d. Koran*, p. 9; Caussin de Perceval, Vol. I., p. 353; J. M. Arnold, p. 230; Palmer's *Quran*, p. 47, etc. Granted that Mohammed was unable to read or write, it is still plain from a thoughtful perusal of any biography of the prophet that he had abundant opportunity to learn from Christians by word of mouth first at Mecca and specially afterwards at Medina. We must remember that *all* the Koran teaching on the Trinity occurs in the *later* Surahs.

VII

PREDESTINATION VS. FATALISM

> "'Tis all a chequer-board of nights and days
> Where destiny with men for pieces plays;
> Hither and thither moves and mates and slays,
> And one by one back in the closet lays."
> —*Omar Khayyam.*

> "It is this dark fatalism which, whatever the
> Koran may teach on the subject, is the ruling
> principle in all Moslem countries. It is this
> which makes all Mohammedan nations decay."—
> *Sell's "Faith of Islam."*

THE sixth great point of faith in Islam[1] is Predestination, and it has important bearing on
the Moslem idea of God. It expresses God's relation
to the creature and to man as a moral agent. Although the terms used in describing predestination
by Moslems and Christians (especially Calvinists)
have much similarity the result of their reasoning is
far apart as the East from the West. It has often
been asserted that the Mohammedan belief in God's
eternal decrees and foreknowledge of good and evil
is a sort of Oriental Calvinism. This, as we hope to

[1] See the analysis of Islam in table, between pages 16
and 17.

show, is not the case. The word used by the Koran
and in the *Hadith* for predestination is *kadar;* in
theological works by Moslems the more technical
word is *takdir.* Both come from the same root, which
means "to measure out," "to order beforehand." The
Koran passages on this subject are many; the following are representative:

Surah 54:59: "All things have been created after
fixed decree."

Surah 3:139: "No one can die except by God's
permission according to the book that fixes the term
of life."

Surah 8:17: "God slew them, and those shafts
were God's, not thine."

Surah 9:51: "By no means can aught befall us
save what God has destined for us."

Surah 14:4: "God misleadeth whom He will and
whom He will He guideth." This occurs frequently.

Surah 37:94: "When God created you *and what
ye make.*"

And finally, the great proof-text, the Gibraltar in
many a hot controversy, Surah 76:29, 30: "This
truly is a warning; and whoso willeth taketh the way
of his Lord; *but will it ye shall not* unless God will
it, for God is knowing, wise."

Not to weary the reader with the commentaries,
we give the orthodox interpretation of the above text
in the words of Al Berkevi: "It is necessary to confess that good and evil take place by the predestina-

tion and predetermination of God; that all that has been and all that will be was decreed in eternity and written on the *preserved tablet;* that the faith of the believer, the piety of the pious and their good actions are foreseen, willed and predestined, decreed by the writing on the preserved tablet produced and approved by God; that the unbelief of the unbeliever, the impiety of the impious, and bad actions come to pass with the foreknowledge, will, predestination and decree of God, but not with His satisfaction or approval. Should any ask why God willeth and produceth evil, we can only reply that He may have wise ends in view which we cannot comprehend." Practically, all Sunnite orthodox Moslems believe this doctrine in such a way that "by the force of God's eternal decree man is constrained to act thus or thus." This view is undoubtedly in accordance with the traditional sayings of Mohammed. Some of these traditions have been given in Chapter V; those that follow are literally translated from the section on *Kadar* in Mishkat-ul-Misabih:

"God created Adam and touched his back with His right hand and brought forth from it a family. And God said to Adam, I have created this family for Paradise and their actions will be like unto those of the people of Paradise. Then God touched the back of Adam and brought forth another family and said, I have created this for hell and their actions will be like unto those of the people of hell. Then

said a man to the prophet, Of what use will deeds
of any kind be? He said, When God creates His
slave for Paradise his actions will be deserving of it
until he die, when he will enter therein; and when
God creates one for the fire his actions will be like
those of the people of hell till he die, when he will
enter therein."

"Adam and Moses were once disputing before
their Lord, and Moses said, 'Thou art Adam whom
God created with His hand and breathed into thee
of His spirit and angels worshipped thee and He
made thee dwell in Paradise and then thou didst
make men to fall down by thy sin to the earth.'
Adam replied, 'Thou art Moses whom God distinguished by sending with thee His message and His
book and He gave thee the tables on which all things
are recorded. Now tell me how many years before I
was created did God write the *Torat* (the Pentateuch)?' Moses replied, 'Forty years.' Said Adam,
'And did you find written there, Adam transgressed
against his Lord?' 'Yes,' said Moses. Said Adam,
'Then, why do you blame me for doing something
which God decreed before He created me by forty
years?' "

Another tradition relates that Mohammed one day
took up two handfuls of earth and scattered them.
So he said God "empties His hand of His slaves, a
portion for Paradise and a portion for the blaze"
(Mishkat, p. 21, bottom. Delhi edition). Another

form of the same tradition puts it still more coarsely:
"These are for Paradise and I care not; and these for
hell-fire and I care not."[1]

It is related that 'Aisha said: "The prophet was
invited to the funeral of a little child. And I said,
'O Apostle of God, Blessed be this little bird of the
birds of Paradise, it has not yet done evil nor been
overtaken by evil.' 'Not so, 'Aisha,' said the apostle,
'verily, God created a people for Paradise and they
were still in their father's loins, and a people for the
fire and they were yet in their father's loins.' "

According to these traditions, and the interpretation of them for more than ten centuries in the life of
Moslems, this kind of predestination should be called
fatalism and nothing else. For fatalism is the doctrine of an inevitable necessity and implies an om-
nipotent and arbitrary sovereign power. It is derived from the Latin *fatum,* what is spoken or decreed, and comes close to the Moslem phrase so often
on their lips, *"Allah katib,"* God wrote it. Among
the Greeks, as in Homer, Fate had a twofold force;
it is sometimes considered as superior and again as
inferior in power to Zeus. Nor does the Greek idea
of fate exclude guilt on the part of man.[2] In both
respects this idea of destiny is less fatalistic in its
results than the teaching of Mohammed. "The God

[1]*Kisas-ul-Anbiya,* Persian edition, p. 21.
[2]See article on Homer's Idea of Fate in McClintock and
Strong's *Encyclopedia,* Vol. III., p. 494.

of Islam is more terrible even than the Æschylean Zeus, inasmuch as of Him it cannot be asserted that He fears Fate or dreads the coming of one who shall drive Him from power. Nay, further, instead of being subject to Fate or Necessity, Allah's will *is* Fate."[1] With such attributes as Mohammed ascribed to Allah, these ideas of predestination, or, better, fatalism, are in perfect accord. Islam exalts the Divine in its doctrine of the eternal decrees, not to combine it with, but to oppose it to, the human. This not only leads to neglect of the ethical idea in God, but puts fatalism in place of responsibility, makes God the author of evil, and sears the conscience as with a hot iron. God not only decreed the fall of Adam, but created Adam weak and with sensuous appetites so that it was natural he should fall. (Compare the commentaries on the passage, Surah 4:32, "God wants to make it easy for you and man was created weak.") *"Allah katib,"* God decreed it, is the easy covering for many crimes. Moslem criminals often use it before their judge in a trial; and the judge, remembering Surah 4: 32, sometimes gives his verdict on the same basis.

We can see also what Moslems understand by predestination from their use of certain other religious expressions which are so very common in all Moslem communities. *Inshallah,* "if God wills," that daily cloak of comfort to Moslems, from Calcutta to Cairo,

[1] W. St. Clair Tisdall's *The Religion of the Crescent,* p. 65.

is an example.[1] This phrase is equivalent grammatically, not logically, to the Biblical "if God wills."
(James 4:15; Acts 18:21.) To the Moslem, God's
will is certain, arbitrary, irresistible and inevitable
before any event transpires. To the Christian God's
will is secret until He reveals it; when He does reveal it we feel the imperative of duty. The Christian prays, "Thy will be done." This prayer is little
less than blasphemy to a strict Mohammedan. Allah
only reveals His will in accomplishing it; man submits. Therefore, were a Moslem to pray to Allah,
"Thy will be done on earth as it is in heaven," he
would at the least be guilty of folly. An archangel
and a murderer, a devil and a gnat equally execute
the will and purpose of Allah every moment of their
existence. As He wills, and because He wills, they
are what they are and continue what they are.

The same difference appears when we study the
phrase, *El-Hamdu-lillah,* "the Praise is to God."
The Biblical phrase, "Praise ye the Lord," implies
personal responsibility, gratitude, activity; the Moslem phrase expresses submission, inevitableness, passivity, fatalism. Therefore, it is so often used in
circumstances that to the Christian seem incongruous.[2] The one phrase is the exponent of Islam, sub-

[1] Surah 18 : 23 and Tradition.

[2] It is true that the common people sometimes use the words
to express joyful satisfaction and gratitude to the Almighty.
But they use them continually in a fatalistic sense.

mission; the other of Christianity, joy and gratitude. The first never occurs in Scripture; the latter is absent from the Koran.

The Moslem theory of prayer, also, is in accordance with this doctrine of the decrees. Prayer is reduced to a gymnastic exercise and a mechanical act; any one who has lived with Moslems needs no proof for this statement. According to the Koran and Tradition, prayer *is* always regarded as a *duty* and never as a *privilege*. It is a task imposed on Moslems by Allah. Allah first imposed fifty prayers a day, but Mohammed begged off from this number, on Moses's advice, ten after ten, until he returned triumphant with only five daily prayers on his list.[1] Moslem daily prayer consists in worship rather than in petition; very few Moslems admit that prayer has objective power as well as subjective.

Mohammedan Fatalism is distinguished, still more radically, from even ultra-Calvinistic views of predestination, when we consider in each case the *source* of the decrees and their ultimate *object*. IN ISLAM THERE IS NO FATHERHOOD OF GOD AND NO PURPOSE OF REDEMPTION TO SOFTEN THE DOCTRINE OF THE DECREES.

1. The attribute of love is absent from Allah. We have already indicated this in our discussion of the attributes. The Love of God in a Christian sense

[1] *Mishkat-ul-Misabih* and other books of Tradition in the section on prayer give this story in detail.

means either God's love to us or our love to Him. Both ideas are strange to Islam. An inter-communion of such tender regard between God and the creature is seldom or never spoken of in the Koran. In Surah 2:160 we read: "Yet there are some among men who take to themselves idols other than God; they love them *as God's love.*" But orthodox exegesis explains the last words by saying, *i.e.,* "as His greatness and the impulse to obedience which He causes." (Beidhawi, Vol. I., p. 95.) In Surah 5:59 there is another reference to the love of God on the part of men similarly explained. How strong is the contrast between these *two* or three exceptional passages and the abundant and plain teaching of the Old and New Testament regarding the love which God requires of man and which flows out from God to man!

In like manner God's love to man when it is referred to in the Koran is rather a love for his good qualities than for the man himself. Dr. Otto Pautz, who has collected all the passages that in any way bear on this subject, comes to the conclusion that *"in no case is there any reference to an inner personal relation"* when the Koran even hints at this subject of which the Bible is so full.[1] Umbreit says: "The God of Mohammed is in the wind, and in the earthquake, and in the fire, but not in the still small voice of

[1] Otto Pautz's *Muhammed's Lehre von der Offenbarung quellenmassig untersucht,* Leipzig, 1898, pp. 142, 143.

love."[1] The mystic love of the Sufis (*widespread and weighty though it be in its influence*) is not a characteristic of orthodox Islam, but arose in rebellion to it.

The Fatherhood of God and the repeated declarations of Scripture that God loves the world, loves the sinner, loves mankind—that God is love—all this has had its influence on Christian speculation regarding the problem of God's decrees. *In like manner the character of Allah has been the key to the same problem among Moslems.* Islam, as we have seen, reduces God to the category of the will. He is at heart a despot, an Oriental despot. He stands at abysmal heights above humanity. He cares nothing for character, but only for submission. The only affair of men is to obey His decrees.

2. The Moslem doctrine of hell is in accordance with their coarse beliefs regarding Predestination and Mohammed's utter want of conception of the spiritual. According to the Koran and Tradition, Hell *must be filled,* and so God creates infidels.[2] Of all religions in the world, Islam is the most severe in its conception of the capacity and the torments of hell. "On that day We will say to hell, Art thou full? and it will say, Are there any more?" (Surah 50:29.) The conception of hell is brutal, cruel and to the last degree barbarous. The whole picture, as

[1]*Theol. Studien,* 14 Jahrgang, p. 240.
[2]Surahs 32 : 13; 97 : 5; 4 : 11; 9 : 69. Cf. Commentaries.

given in the Koran and commented on by Tradition, is horribly revolting. "Hell shall be a place of snares, the home of transgressors, to abide therein for ages. No coolness shall they taste nor any drink, save boiling water and liquid pus. Meet recompense!" (Surahs 88:1-7; 2:38; 3:197; 14:20; 43:74-78, etc., etc.) The word *Jehannum* occurs thirty times; fire (*nar*) is still more frequently used; there are six other words used for the place of torment. One cannot read the traditions which give what Mohammed said on this subject without feeling how heartless and loveless is the creed of Islam.[1] Yet it is in connection with such ideas of God that the Moslems believe in Predestination.

It is not difficult to surmise whence Mohammed got his ideas of a Predestination after the pattern of fatalism. Like so much of his other teaching, it seems that the doctrine of *kādār* comes from the Talmud. Rabbi Geiger has shown how Mohammed borrowed from' Judaism not only words, conceptions, legal rules and stories, but also doctrinal views.[2] The Scribes and Pharisees differed even at the time of Christ in their view of Predestination. The latter more and more followed a fatalistic idea of God's

[1] Read Chapter X. on the Hell of Islam in Stanley Lane-Poole's *Studies in a Mosque*, pp. 311-326.

[2] See *Judaism and Islam*, a Prize Essay by Rabbi Geiger, translated from the German. Madras, 1898. Also the original work. Wiesbaden, 1833.

decrees. Josephus writes as if, according to the
Pharisees, the chief part in every good action de-
pended on fate. (Jewish Wars 2:8.)   And Edersheim grants that the Pharisees carried their ac-
centuation of the Divine to the verge of fatalism.
Their ideas, he shows, were in every respect similar
to the present Moslem ideas.   "Adam had been
shown all the generations that were to spring from
him. Every incident in the history of Israel had been
foreordained and the actors in it, for good or for evil,
were only instruments for carrying out the Divine
Will. . . . It was because man was predestined to die that the serpent came to seduce our
first parents."[1]   The stories told in the Talmud
about predestination of a man's bride, and his position and the place and time of his death, find their
duplicates almost verbatim in the Moslem traditions.[2]
Wheresoever a man was destined to die thither would
his feet carry him, says the Talmud.   "On one occasion, King Solomon when attended by his two scribes
suddenly perceived the Angel of Death. As he looked
so sad, Solomon ascertained as its reason that the
two scribes had been demanded at his hands. On this
Solomon transported them by magic into the land of
Luz, where, according to legend, no man ever died.
Next morning Solomon again perceived the Angel of
Death, but this time laughing, because, as he said,

[1]Edersheim's *Life of Jesus the Messiah*, Vol. I., p. 317.
[2]See the References in Edersheim to the Talmudic tractates.

Solomon had sent these men to the very place whence
he had been ordered to fetch them." (Talmudic
Tractate. *Sukkah*, 53 *a.*) This same story is told
by Moslems, according to traditions of the Prophet.[1]

There have been heterodox views on the subject
of predestination. But no one who has read the history of Moslem sects can doubt that the account given
in this chapter is the orthodox side of the question.
The three views to which the multitude of sects can
be reduced on this knotty problem are: The *Jabariyun,* or extreme fatalists; the *Kadariyun,* who affirm
that man has free-agency (Moslem free-thinkers belong to this school); and the *'Asharians,* who are a
little more moderate than the first school.[2] "The
orthodox or Sunni belief is theoretically *'Ashárian,*
but practically the Sunnis are confirmed *Jabariyun."*
Other doctrines are considered quite heretical.

When we consider the deadening influence of this
doctrine of fatalism we must remember that generally speaking there have been two schools of Moslem
philosophy—the orthodox and the heretical. It is
only the latter school that added to the knowledge of
philosophy one iota. The attainments of the Arabs
in philosophy have been greatly overrated. They
were translators and transmitters of the Greek philosophy, and whatever was added to Plato and Aristotle

[1] See Commentaries on Surah 32 : 11 and margin of *Daka'ik
ul-Akhbar* and *Shammoos-ul-Anwar.*
[2] E. Sell's *Faith of Islam,* p. 173.

came not from the side of orthodoxy, but was entirely
the work of heretics, such as Averroës, Alfarabi and
Avicenna.[1]

The orthodox philosopher of Islam was Al-Ghazz-
zali, and the result of his work was the complete triumph of unphilosophical orthodoxy.[2]

So utterly barren of ideas and opposed to all reason did this orthodoxy become that Sprenger sarcas-
tically remarks concerning it: "The Moslem student
marvelled neither at the acuteness nor yet at the
audacity of his master; he marvelled rather at the
wisdom of God which could draw forth such mysteri-
ous interpretations. *Theology, in fact, had now
made such happy progress that men looked on common sense as a mere human attribute—the reverse
being that which they expected from Deity."* And
this was one of the results of Moslem speculation on
the Koran doctrine of predestination.[3]

[1]See Ueberweg's *Hist. of Philosophy* and Renan's *Hist. Lang.
Semit.*

[2]Ibid.

[3]A special study on the Moslem Idea of Predestination has
just appeared from the press by Rev. A. de Vlieger of the
Calioub Mission. It is entitled, *Kitab al Quadr*, Materiaux
pour servir à l'étude de la doct. de la predestination dans la
theologie musulmane. Leiden, 1902.

VIII

THE COMPLETED IDEA AND ITS INSUFFICIENCY

"If we regard God merely as the Absolute
Being and nothing more, we know Him only as
the general irresistible force, or, in other words,
as *the Lord*. Now it is true that the fear of the
Lord is the beginning of wisdom, but it is likewise true that it is *only* its beginning. In the
Mohammedan religion God is conceived only as
the Lord. Now although this conception of God
is an important and necessary step in the development of religious consciousness, it yet by no
means exhausts the depths of the Christian idea
of God."—*Hegel's Werke, Vol. VI., p. 226.*

WHAT is the result of our investigation of the
Moslem idea of God? Is the statement of
the Koran true, "Your God and our God is the
same?" In as far as Moslems are monotheists and
in as far as Allah has many of the attributes of
Jehovah we cannot put Him with the false gods.
But neither can there be any doubt that Mohammed's
conception of God is inadequate, incomplete, barren
and grievously distorted. It is vastly inferior to the

Christian idea of the Godhead and also inferior to the Old Testament idea of God. In the Book of Job alone there are more glorious descriptions of God's personality, unity, power and holiness than in all the chapters of the Koran. Carlyle in his praise of the Hero-prophet acknowledges this and says "he makes but little of Mohammed's praises of Allah, borrowed from the Hebrew and far surpassed there." Even the Fatherhood of God is clearly taught in the Old Testament, but it is wholly absent from the Koran.

In the comparative study of religious ideas there must be a standard of judgment, and a Christian can only judge other religions by the standard of the Gospel. Islam itself, through its prophet (who came, so he says, as the seal of all prophecy), and in its Book challenges comparison by this standard. We are not dealing with the monotheism of Greek philosophy, which arose in the Court of the Gentiles under Plato and Aristotle; but with a monotheism which arose six centuries after Christ and professes to be an improvement or at least a restatement of the Christian idea. (See Surahs 42: 1; 10: 37, 93; 5: 77, etc.) We accept, therefore, Islam's challenge. Jesus Christ proclaimed that no man knows the Father save through the Son. He is the brightness of the Father's glory. The impress of His essence. Whoever has seen Jesus has seen the Father. Mohammed by denying Christ's Deity also denied that He came on a unique and transcendent mission from the court of heaven—*to show us the Father*. Instead of arriving at his theology through the mind of Christ, as revealed in the gospels and developed through the Holy Spirit's teaching in the epistles, Mohammed went back to natural theology. He did not use, or would not use, the channel of knowledge opened by the Incarnation. Instead of learning from Him who *descended* from heaven, Mohammed asserted that he himself *ascended* to heaven and there had intercourse with God. (Surah 17:2 and the Commentaries.) Whether this "night journey" of the prophet be considered a dream, a vision, or, as most Moslems hold, a physical reality, is of minor importance. The Koran and orthodox Tradition leave no doubt that Mohammed gave out this idea himself, and often stated that he had conversation with the angels and the prophets, as well as with God Himself in Paradise.[1]

The account of this "night journey," as given in the Tradition and widely believed, is both puerile and blasphemous. Nor does the story add anything to the sum total of theological ideas as given in the Koran. Mohammed's account of heaven is borrowed from the Talmud. We conclude, therefore, that Mohammedan monotheism, granting all that can be said in its favor, lacks four elements which are present

[1]See Muir's *Mahomet*, Vol. II., p. 221. Sprenger calls the story "an unblushing forgery" on the part of Mohammed.

not only in the Christian idea of the Godhead, but in the Old Testament as well: (1) *There is no Father-hood of God.* We have seen how their initial conception of theology is a bar to any possible filial relation on man's part toward Deity. The Moslem's fear of God is not the beginning of wisdom. Allah produces on them a servile, not a filial, fear. No one approaches God except as a slave. Hegel's criticism, at the head of this chapter, shows the opinion of a philosopher on the elementary character of such monotheism. Where there is no Fatherhood toward man there can be no Brotherhood of Man. Islam is an exclusive brotherhood of *believers,* not an inclusive brotherhood of humanity. Assuredly, this characteristic of Islam is responsible for much of its fanatic spirit and its gigantic pride. The denial of God's Fatherhood changes Him into a desolate abstraction. Who can *love* Ghazzali's definition of Allah or feel drawn to such a negative conception? The very contemplation of so barren a Deity "pours an ice-floe over the tide of human trusts and causes us to feel that we are orphaned children in a homeless world."

(2) *The Moslem idea of God is conspicuously lacking in the attribute of love.* We have seen this in our study of Allah's names. But in gathering up the few precious fragments of this idea from the Koran another thing is evident. Whatever Mohammed taught concerning God's mercy, loving kindness

or goodness has reference only and wholly to what
God is *external* to Himself. In the Bible, love is not
a mere attribute of Deity. God *is* love. God's love
not only shines forth from Genesis to the Book of the
Revelation, but it is often declared to have existed
from all eternity. (Jer. 31:3; John 3:16; 17:24;
Eph. 1:4; Rev. 13:8.) Fairbairn remarks: "The
love which the Godhead makes immanent and essential to God gives God an altogether new meaning and
actuality for religion; while thought is not forced to
conceive monotheism as the apotheosis of an
Almighty will or an impersonal idea of the pure
reason."

Moslem mysticism was a revolt against the orthodox doctrine of Allah. The human heart craves a
God who loves; a personal God who has close relations with humanity; a *living* God who can be touched
with the feeling of our infirmities and who hears and
answers prayer. Such a God the Koran does not reveal. A being who is incapable of loving is also incapable of being loved. And the most remarkable
testimony to this lack in the orthodox Moslem conception of Deity is the fact that the passionate devo-
tional poetry of the Sufis is put down as rank heresy.
Allah is too rich and too proud and too independent
to need or desire the tribute of human love. In consequence Islam is a loveless creed. The Bible teaching that "God is love" is to the learned blasphemy
and to the ignorant an enigma. Orthodox Islam is

a religion without song. Where are there any psalms of devotion or hymns of spiritual aspiration in the Koran or the volumes of Tradition ?

There is no precept nor example in Islam enjoining love to one's enemies. It knows nothing of universal benevolence or of a humane tolerance. (Surah 9:29.) That the element of love is lacking in their idea of God is perhaps the reason also why the Koran, in contrast with the Bible, has so little for and about *children.* Of such is not the kingdom of Mohammed.

(3) *Allah is not absolutely, unchangeably and eternally just.* It is possible, as some allege, that the Western Church may have emphasized the forensic aspect of God's holiness and righteousness unduly and to excess. But the Bible and the human conscience in all ages also emphasize this truth. It is found in the Greek theism. The Bible is not alone in stating that the Judge of all the earth *must* do right. Justice and judgment are the habitation of His throne. It is impossible for God to lie. He will in nowise clear the guilty. The soul that sinneth it shall die. The awful spectacle of Calvary can only be explained in the terms of Divine justice and Divine love. It was, in the words of Paul, "to declare His righteousness; that He might be just and the justifier of him which believeth in Jesus."

Now since Islam, as we have seen, denies the doctrine of the atonement and minimizes the heinousness of sin, it is not surprising that the justice of God

is not strongly insisted on and often presented in a
weak or distorted way. As Hauri says: "Neither
in His holiness nor in His love is Allah righteous.
As regards the wicked, His love does not receive its
due; he is quick to punish, to lead astray and to
harden; His wrath is not free from passion. As regards believers, His holiness comes short of its right.
Allah allows His prophets things otherwise forbidden
and wrong. Even ordinary believers are allowed to
do what is really not right because they are believers.
For example, the prophet said: 'It is better not to
have slave-concubines, but Allah is merciful and
clement.' "[1]

In Islam, God's law is not the expression of His
moral nature, but of His arbitrary will. His word
can be abrogated. His commandments are subject to
change and improvement. A testimony to this on the
part of Moslems themselves is found in their eager
attempts to prove that all the prophets were *sinless;*
i.e., that *their* transgressions of the moral law as recorded in the Koran were not really sinful, but that
they were permitted these slight faults or committed
them in forgetfulness. The greatest feats of exegesis
in this line are found in Ar-Razi's Commentary on
the verses that tell of Adam's sin, David's Adultery
and Mohammed's prayers for pardon. (Surahs 7: 10-
17; 38:20-24 and 47:20, 21.) All the laws of logic

[1] *Der Islam*, p. 45. The Koran offers other examples of such
clemency! Cf. Surahs 2 : 225; 5 : 91, etc.

and etymology are broken to avoid the natural inference that these "prophets" were guilty sinners. Those
who desire to know how far even Indian Moslems
can go in defence of this untenable position must read
the pamphlet of James Munro, Esq., on the recent
Zanb Controversy in Bengal and the Punjaub.[1] It is
evident that this desire to justify "the prophets" is
nothing else than a practical lowering of the standard
of ethics. What Adam or David or Mohammed did
may *appear* to be sinful, but it really was not. God
is merciful and clement.

(4) *There is a lack of harmony in Allah's attributes.* Raymund Lull (1315), the first missionary to
Moslems, pointed out this weakness in the monotheism of Islam. He puts forward this proposition:
"Every wise man must acknowledge *that* to be the
true religion which ascribes the greatest perfection
to the Supreme Being, and not only conveys the
worthiest conception of all His attributes, but demon-
strates the harmony and equality existing between
them. Now their religion [*i.e.,* Islam] was defective
in acknowledging only two active principles in the
Deity, His will and His wisdom, while it left His
goodness and greatness inoperative, as though they
were indolent qualities and not called forth into active exercise. But the Christian religion could not
be charged with this defect. In its doctrine of the
Trinity, it conveys the highest conception of the

[1] Baptist Mission Press, Calcutta.

Deity as the Father, the Son and the Holy Spirit in one simple essence. In the Incarnation of the Son it evinces the harmony that exists between God's goodness and His greatness; and in the person of Christ displays the true union of the Creator and the creature; while in His Passion it sets forth the divine harmony of infinite goodness and condescension."[1]

These words are as true to-day as they were when addressed to the Moslems of North Africa in the Middle Ages. In Islam's theology, mercy and truth do not meet together; righteousness and peace have never kissed each other. The only way in which Allah pardons a sinner is by abrogating His law or passing over guilt without a penalty. There is no Substitute, no Mediator, no Atonement. And, therefore, the law-of-the-letter, with all its terror, and the physical hell, ever yawning for its victims, subject Moslems to the bondage of fear unless formalism has petrified their consciences.

"The distinguishing characteristic of Christianity," says Schiller, "by which it is differentiated *from all other monotheistic systems,* lies in the fact that it does away with the law—the Kantian imperative—and in place of it gives a free and spontaneous inclination of the heart."[2] The law is not abolished, but fulfilled in Christ. He blotted out "the handwriting of ordinances that was against us, which was

[1] Raymund Lull's *Liber Contemplationis in Deo,* liv., 25-28.
[2] Quoted in Shedd's *Hist. of Doctrine,* Vol. I., p. 221.

contrary to us, and took it out of the way, nailing it
to His cross." That cross of Christ is the missing
link in the Moslem's creed. Without the doctrine of
the Cross there is no possible unity in the doctrine of
the divine attributes; for the mystery of redemption
is the key to all other mysteries of theology.

We must go a step further. Not only is the Moslem idea of God lacking in these four important
and essential ideas of Christian theology, but its in-
sufficiency is most of all evident from its results.
The influence of such teaching regarding God and
His relation to the world is apparent everywhere in
Moslem lands, but especially in Arabia. The present
intellectual, social and moral condition of Arabia
must be due to the power (or the impotence) of
Islam, for no other intellectual or religious force has
touched the peninsula for centuries. Islam has had
undisputed possession of Arabia almost since its
birth. Here, too, the reformation of Islam under
the Wahabis exercised its full power. In other lands,
such as Syria and Egypt, it remained in contact with
a corrupt form of Christianity, or, as in India and
China, in conflict with cultured paganism; and there
is no doubt that in both cases there were (and are to-
day) mutual concessions and influences. But on its
native Arabian soil the tree planted by the prophet
has grown with wild freedom and brought forth fruit
after its kind.

As regards morality, Arabia is on a low plane.

Slavery and concubinage exist everywhere. Polygamy and divorce are common. The conscience is
petrified; legality is the highest form of worship; virtue is to be like the prophet. The Arabic language
has no every-day word for conscience and the present
book-term does not even occur in the Koran. Intel-
lectually, there has been little progress. The
Bedouins are nearly all illiterate and book-learning
in the towns is compressed into the mould of Koran
philosophy. Arabia has no unity except the unity of
intolerance and suspicion. Fatalism has paralyzed
progress. Injustice is stoically accepted and the bulk
of the people are passive. No man bears another
man's burden and there is no public spirit. Treachery
and murder are the steps to petty thrones in free
Arabia, and in the Turkish provinces justice is sold
to the highest bidder. Cruelty is common. Lying is
a fine art and robbery a science. Islam has made the
hospitable Arab hostile to Christians and wary of
strangers. If Mohammedan monotheism had in it
the elements of salvation and progress for its devotees, surely Arabia would have witnessed the result. For thirteen hundred years the experiment
has been tried—and, by the witness of all travellers,
it has piteously failed.

A stream can rise no higher than its source. Islam
has no lofty conception of ethics and of holiness like
that of the Christian religion. Mohammed's life soon
became the standard of morality for all Moslems. In

the Koran he is human; in tradition he becomes sinless and almost divine. *To be as good as Mohammed is the ideal of the Moslem.* Christ rises higher: "Be ye therefore perfect even as your Father which is in heaven is perfect." Paul's command "to be imitators of God as dear children," is to the orthodox Moslem a double blasphemy. Allah can neither be imitated nor have children. He is unique and nothing can be like Him.

Martensen points out the importance which faith in the *Triune* God has for ethics (*Christian Ethics,* Vol. I., pp. 65-75), and concludes: "If, therefore, Christian dogmatics had not asserted and developed the doctrine of the Trinity, ethics must postulate it in its own interests." All church history shows that a genuine and even a scientific knowledge of God has been better maintained with the doctrine of the Trinity than without it. A knowledge of God as full as we need, as full as He Himself intended we should have, is impossible without the doctrine of the Holy Trinity. So-called pure monotheism has always degenerated into some form of pantheism, whether among Jews, Mohammedans or in Christendom.

Finally, it is evident from our study that the Moslem doctrine of God is sterile. It has neither grown nor been fruitful of new ideas in all the history of Islam. The sheikhs of Al Azhar in Cairo, in the twentieth century, are still content with the definition of Al Ghazzali. On the contrary, the Christian doctrine of the Godhead beginning with the Old Testament revelation of Jehovah, interpreted in the fulness of time by the Incarnation, developed by the Holy Spirit's teaching through the apostles and systematized in the conflict with heresies and philosophies, is even to-day a growing concept and a fruitful idea. "Let any one trace the course of thinking by the theological mind upon the doctrine of the Trinity, and perceive how link follows link by necessary consequence; how the objections of the heretic or the latitudinarian only elicit a more exhaustive, and at the same time more guarded statement, which carries the Church still nearer to the substance of revelation and the heart of the mystery; how, in short, the trinitarian dogma, like the Christian life itself, as described by the apostle, 'being fitly joined together and compacted by that which every joint supplieth, maketh increase unto the edifying of itself' into a grand architectural structure—let this process from beginning to end pass before a thinking and logical mind, and it will be difficult for it to resist the conviction that here is science, here is self-consistent and absolute truth."[1]

Islam is proud to write on its banner, the Unity of God; but it is, after all, a banner to the Unknown God. Christianity enters every land under the standard of the Holy Trinity—the Godhead of Revelation. These two banners represent two armies.

[1] Shedd's *Hist. of Doctrine*, Vol. I., p. 4.

There is no peace between them. No parliament of religions can reconcile such fundamental and deep-rooted differences. We must conquer or be vanquished. In its origin, history, present attitude and by the very first article of its brief creed, Islam is anti-Christian. But that does not mean that the battle is hopeless. Christian monotheism is as superior to Mohammedan monotheism as Christ is superior to Mohammed. *There is no god but the God-head.* Islam itself is beginning to realize the strength of the Christian idea of God, and our chief prayer for the Moslem world should be that they may know the Only True God and Jesus Christ whom He hath sent. When the great Mohammedan world acknowledges the Fatherhood of God they will also understand the brotherhood of men and the mystery of Calvary.

134

THE PROPHET'S MOSQUE AT MEDINA.

In this place, according to Moslem tradition, Jesus Christ will finally be buried.

Frontispiece.]

THE
MOSLEM CHRIST

An Essay on the Life,
Character, and Teachings of
Jesus Christ according to the
Koran and Orthodox Tradition

BY

SAMUEL M. ZWEMER
D.D., F.R.G.S.
AUTHOR OF "THE MOSLEM DOCTRINE OF GOD" "ARABIA
THE CRADLE OF ISLAM" "ISLAM, A CHALLENGE
TO FAITH" ETC.

ANM
publishers

TO

James Cantine

PIONEER MISSIONARY, YOKE-FELLOW AND FRIEND
FOR TWENTY YEARS IN ARABIA

" Who, thinkest thou, might that have been, conceived without an earthly father, and to whom at His birth Satan could find no way of approach?

"Who could that have been, named in the Koran 'The Word of God and a Spirit from Him'; called also in the Sunnat 'The Spirit of God'? For what Being, one would ask, could be greater than the Spirit of God?

" Who could that have been who, we are told, spoke to those around Him while yet in the cradle? Who, that could, as Beidhawi explains, give life to the dead and to the hearts of men (*i.e.* to their bodies and to their spirits); who other than the Almighty and the Holy Ghost?"—From the *Minar ul Haqq* (An Apology for the Christian Faith), p. 159.

INTRODUCTION

ISLAM is the only one of the great non-Christian religions which gives a place to Christ in its book, and yet it is also the only one of the non-Christian religions which denies His deity, His atonement, and His supreme place as Lord of all in its sacred literature. In none of the other sacred books of the East is Christ mentioned; the Koran alone gives Him a place, but does it by displacing Him. With regret it must be admitted that there is hardly an important fact concerning the life, person, and work of our Saviour which is not ignored, perverted, or denied by Islam.

Yet Moslems acknowledge Jesus Christ as a true prophet, and no less than three of the chapters of the Koran, namely, that of *Amran's Family* (Surah III), that of *The Table* (Surah V), and that of *Mary* (Surah XIX), are so named because of references to Jesus Christ and His work. The very fact that Jesus Christ has a

place in the literature of Islam, and is acknowledged by all Moslems as one of their prophets,
in itself challenges comparison between Him and
Mohammed, and affords an opportunity for the
Christian missionary to ask every sincere Moslem,
"What think ye of the Christ?" This is still
the question that decides the destiny of men
and of nations. To help our Moslem brethren
answer this question, however, we must know
what Moslems believe in regard to Christ, and
lead them up to higher truth by admitting
all of the truth which they possess. Not our
ignorance, but our accurate knowledge of the
Moslem Christ, will enable us to show forth the
glory and the beauty of the Christ revealed in
the New Testament to those who ignorantly
honour Him as a mere prophet.

Moreover, at a time when the study of other
religions is so common, it must be of interest to
all Christians to know what two hundred million
Moslems think of their Lord and Saviour, and to
compare His portrait taken from the Koran and
later Moslem literature with that given in the
Gospels.

This volume, as in the case of my earlier essay
on *The Moslem Doctrine of God*, is based entirely

on the Koran, the commentators, and orthodox
tradition. The Koran text quoted is from
Palmer's translation (*Sacred Books of the
East*, vols. vi. and ix. Oxford, 1880), together
with references to the three standard commentaries of Beidhawi, Zamakhshari, and Jellalain.
For Moslem tradition in regard to Jesus Christ,
the references will be found in the Bibliography,
but I have specially used a standard work on the
subject, and, in fact, the only popular work I
know which gives a connected account of the
life of Jesus Christ according to Moslem sources,
namely, *Kitab Kusus al Anbiah* (also called
Al 'Ara'is), by Abu Ishak Ahmad bin Mohammed
bin Ibrahim Eth-Thalabi, a doctor of theology of
the Shafi school, who died 427 A.H. (A.D. 1036).
Eth-Thalabi, the author of the work mentioned, is thus described in Ibn Khallikan's
Dictionary of Biography (vol. i. p. 22): "He
was the first of his age in the science of
interpretation, and wrote the great commentary
which is superior to many others. He also wrote
the book called *Kusus-al-Anbiah* and other
books. It is related that Abu Kasim el Kashiri
said, 'I saw the Lord Most Mighty in a dream,
and He was talking with me, and I was talking

with Him. And the Lord said, "The man of good character has approached"; and I looked and, behold, Eth-Thalabi was approaching.'" His work is found in MS. in several of the libraries of Europe, and was printed at Cairo, 1293, 1306, 1308, 1310, 1325 A.H., and at Bombay, 1306 A.H. I have used the latest Cairo edition.

I have also compared the account of Jesus Christ given in *Bible de l'Islam* by E. Lamairesse, a French translation of Mirkhond's *Rauzat-as-Safa* (Paris, 1894) and the Arabic text found in *Akhbar ad Duwal wa Athar al Awwal* by the historian Abu 'l 'Abbas al Qaramani, who was born in A.D. 1532 and died 1611. Neither adds much to the fuller biography of Eth-Thalabi. Except for C. F. Gerock's *Versuch einer Darstellung der Christologie des Koran* (Gotha, 1839), and a more recent French work, *Jésus-Christ d'après Mahomét* par Edouard Sayous (Paris, 1880), both limited to the Koran and not giving the traditional accounts, I do not know of any treatise on the subject in the languages of the West; nor have I been able to trace anywhere in Moslem literature a monograph on Jesus Christ as the last of the prophets before Mohammed's advent.

The question may well be raised concerning the sources of Mohammed's information. How and from whom did he learn of Jesus Christ? Whatever may have been the condition of Christianity in Arabia, there is no doubt that he came in contact with it all through his life.[1] One of the chief stories he must have heard from his boyhood days was that of the Christian invasion from the south and the defeat of Abraha's troops. Later in life he went to Syria, met the monks, and also passed through the territory of the Christian tribes in north Arabia. After he professed to be a prophet, his favourite concubine was Miriam, a Coptic Christian, the mother of his darling son Ibrahim. In addition to all this, Moslems themselves admit that there were Christians and Jews who assisted Mohammed and instructed him. A recent study by P. L. Cheikho, entitled *Quelques Legendes Islamiques Apocryphes* (Beirut, 1910), enumerates some of the sources to which Mohammed was indebted for his knowledge of Christianity. First in order, he states, were his contemporaries Waraka bin Naufel, Zobeir bin 'Amru, Zaid, and Kaab. The author also

[1] Wright's *Early Christianity in Arabia* (London, 1855).

speaks of a book called *Kitab bin Munabah*, of which a dozen pages were recently found in a collection of papyri. According to Sprenger, the man who his countrymen said assisted Mohammed in writing the Koran, was a foreigner; for Mohammed himself said (Surah 16 : 105), "It is only some mortal who teaches him. The tongue of him they lean towards is barbarous, and this is plain Arabic." Sprenger says [1] that the man referred to was "Addas, a monk of Nineveh, who was settled at Mecca." The commentators inform us further that Mohammed used to listen to Jaber and Yassar, two sword manufacturers at Mecca, when they read the Scriptures; and Ibn Ishak says that he had intercourse with Ar-Rahman, a Christian of Yamama. [2] Koelle goes even further than Sprenger in indicating the sources of Mohammed's information. He says: "Not want of opportunity, but want of sympathy and compatibility kept him aloof from the religion of Christ. His first wife introduced him to her Christian cousin; one of his later wives had embraced Christianity in Abyssinia, and

[1] Sprenger's *Life of Mohammed* (Allahabad, 1851), p. 99.

[2] Cf. W. St. Clair Tisdall, *The Original Sources of the Quran*, (London, 1905), pp. 136–179.

the most favoured of his concubines was a Christian damsel from the Copts of Egypt. He was acquainted with ascetic monks, and had dealings with learned bishops of the Orthodox Church. In those days the reading of the Holy Scriptures in the public services was already authoritatively enjoined and universally practised; if he wished thoroughly to acquaint himself with them, he could easily have done so. But, having no adequate conception of the nature of sin and man's fallen estate, he also lacked the faculty of truly appreciating the remedy for it which was offered in the Gospel." [1]

A recent critical study on Mohammed's sources for his knowledge of Christianity and the Christ, [2] confirms the conclusions reached by Sprenger and others. The author makes Harnack his starting-point, who shows in his *History of Dogma* that there was a close and striking resemblance between the teaching of Jewish-Christian gnosticism and that of Mohammed. He questions, however, whether Mohammed came in direct contact with any one

[1] S. W. Koelle, *Mohammed and Mohammedanism*, p. 471.
[2] V. Neusch, "Muhammeds Quellen für seine Kenntnis des Christentums," in *Zeitschrift für Missionskunde und Religionswissenschaft*, 1910, Heft 4, p. 113.

of these sects. History tells us that Judaism
found an early entrance into Arabia, and we
know that there were various sects of Christianity
represented, but we know of the preponderance
of none.   As we have to do with a non-literary
people, we cannot assume much dogmatic
knowledge.   Neusch believes that none of
Mohammed's teachers were prominent enough
or definite enough in their knowledge of
Christianity to warrant us in declaring that
he was dependent on them alone for his sources.
If Mohammed could read, it was probably late
in life that he learned the art, too late to affect
his views which had already been announced.
His conclusion is that although Harnack's
opinion is in general correct, we must not, as
is so often done, simply declare that Mohammed
was dependent on the Jewish-Christian sects
of his day.   We must remember that much of
the present dogma of Islam is much later than
the days of the prophet.   As regards Moslem
traditions which give us fuller information than
the Koran itself, Goldziher has shown that
these were largely contributed by Christian
renegades.[1]

[1] *Muhammedanische Studien*, vol. ii. p. 268.

There are, of course, many references to Jesus in later Moslem literature, and the present-day philosophical disintegration of Islam not only as regards its dogma, but its ethical teaching, has compelled Moslems anew to consider the fact of the Christ. These reform movements and re-adjustments of Moslem teaching to modern conditions, as voiced by the progressive press and the new Islam on the one hand, or the sects that sprang from Islam, the Babis, the Beha'is, and the followers of the late Mirza Quadian, on the other, have, however, scarcely touched the fringe of public opinion among the masses. This book tells of Jesus Christ as known (if known at all) by the vast majority of Moslems, whether learned or illiterate.

SAMUEL M. ZWEMER.

BAHREIN, ARABIA,
March 1912.

NOTE.—The Cufic inscription on the cover-design is from an old manuscript, and reads : "In the name of God the Merciful and Compassionate." May Moslems soon learn of His mercy as revealed in the Christ.

"Le musulman proclame qu'il y a un livre plus récent que l'Evangile et supérieur à lui, le Coran ; il proclame que six siècles après Jésus-Christ est venu un prophète inférieur à quelques égards, notamment par sa naissance, mais moralement et religieusement supérieur, Mahomet. C'est celui-là *le* Maître, et Jésus, n'est qu'*un* maître. Aussi regardons nous l'Islamisme comme une des trois grandes religions monothéistes, à part des deux autres mais non pas indépendante, car sans elles jamais elle n'aurait existé." — EDOUARD SAYOUS (*Jésus-Christ d'après Mahomét*).

The MOSLEM CHRIST

CONTENTS

LIST OF ILLUSTRATIONS

I

HIS NAMES AND THEIR SIGNIFICANCE

" The Christ of History brings the cardinal problem of religion down from the clouds of speculation to the world of hard and prosaic and determinable facts, and that is a dangerous place for either things or persons to stand who are not what they seem. Criticism must handle and speak of all who stand there, the more strenuously if they make extraordinary claims on the faith and reverence of all men and times ; and the now white, now lurid lights it creates enable those piercing and pitiless eyes that love to see the distant past unbury its dread secrets and make confession of its forgotten crimes, to search the period or person on which they fall. That Jesus Christ has so long stood amid those burning lights and before these curious eyes tells an eloquent tale of the quality of His person and the reality of His character. The love of earth has looked at Him till it has grown Divine, the thought of man has studied Him till it has become reverent. The coldest criticism is touched with reverence when it stands before the supreme Person of history, finding Him to be also the supreme Good of man."—A. M. FAIRBAIRN (*The City of God*).

I

HIS NAMES AND THEIR SIGNIFICANCE

AMONG all Orientals, but especially among the Semites, a deep significance is attached to names. This is evident not only from the Bible, but from the practice among the Arabs of to-day. Names, surnames, nicknames, and appellatives are bestowed upon men and places with the intent of expressing the very character of the person or thing named. In considering, therefore, the teaching of the Koran and Moslem tradition concerning our Lord Jesus Christ, we begin first of all by mentioning the names that are applied to Him in Mohammed's Book, and that are therefore those most commonly used among Moslems. In fact, it would be quite inadmissible for an orthodox Moslem to use any other terms in relation to Jesus Christ than those used in the Koran. We give the names in the order of their importance and the frequency of their usage.

'Isa (Jesus). This name, the most commonly used among Moslems, generally with the prefix *Nebi* (prophet) and often with the addition "Son of

Mary," is used twenty-five times in the Koran, as follows :—

Surah 2 : 81. We gave Moses the Book and we followed him up with other apostles, and we gave *Jesus* the son of Mary manifest signs and aided him with the Holy Spirit.

Surah 2 : 130. Say ye, "We believe in God, and what has been revealed to us, and what has been revealed to Abraham, and Ishmael, and Isaac, and Jacob, and the Tribes, and what was brought to Moses and *Jesus*."

Surah 2 : 254. And we have given *Jesus* the son of Mary manifest signs and strengthened him by the Holy Spirit.

Surah 3 : 40. When the angel said, "O Mary! verily God gives thee the glad tidings of a Word from him; his name shall be Messiah *Jesus* the son of Mary, regarded in this world and the next and of those whose place is nigh to God."

Surah 3 : 45. And when *Jesus* perceived their unbelief, he said, "Who are my helpers for God ?"

Surah 3 : 48. When God said, "O *Jesus*! I will make thee die and take thee up again to me, and will clear thee of those who misbelieve, and will make those who follow thee above those who misbelieve, at the day of judgment, then to me is your return."

Surah 3 : 52. Verily the likeness of *Jesus* with God is as the likeness of Adam.

Surah 3 : 78. Say, " We believe in God, and what has been revealed to thee, and what was revealed to Abraham, and Ishmael, and Isaac, and Jacob, and the tribes, and what was given to Moses and *Jesus* and the prophets from their Lord."

Surah 4 : 156. Their saying, " Verily, we have killed the Messiah, *Jesus* the son of Mary, the apostle of God," . . . but they did not kill him.

Surah 4 : 161. Verily, we have inspired thee as we inspired Abraham, and Ishmael, and Jacob, and the tribes, and *Jesus.*

Surah 4 : 169. The Messiah, *Jesus* the son of Mary, is but the apostle of God and His Word, which He cast into Mary and a spirit from Him.

Surah 5 : 50. And we followed up the footsteps of these (prophets) with *Jesus* the son of Mary, confirming that which was before him and the law.

Surah 5 : 82. Those of the children of Israel who disbelieved were cursed by the tongue of David and *Jesus* the son of Mary.

Surah 5 : 109. When God said, " O *Jesus*, son of Mary ! remember my favours towards thee and towards thy mother."

Surah 5 : 112. When the apostles said, " O *Jesus*, son of Mary ! is thy Lord able to send down to us a table from heaven ? "

Surah 5 : 114. Said *Jesus*, the son of Mary, " O God, our Lord ! send down to us a table from heaven to be to us as a festival. . . ."

Surah 5:116. And when God said, "O *Jesus*, son of Mary! is it thou who didst say to men, take me and my mother for two gods, beside God?"

Surah 6:85. And Zachariah and John and *Jesus* and Elias, all righteous ones.

Surah 19:35. That is, *Jesus* the son of Mary,—by the word of truth whereon ye do dispute.

Surah 33:7. And when we took of the prophets their compact, from thee and from Noah, and Abraham, and Moses, and *Jesus* the son of Mary . . . that He might ask the truth-tellers of their truth.

Surah 42:11. He has enjoined upon you for religion what He prescribed to Noah, and what we inspired thee with, and what we inspired Abraham and Moses and *Jesus*.

Surah 43:63. And when *Jesus* came with manifest signs he said, "I am come to you with wisdom, and I will explain to you something of that whereon ye did dispute, then fear God, obey me. . . ."

Surah 57:27. And we followed them up with *Jesus* the son of Mary; and we gave him the gospel.

Surah 61:6. And when *Jesus* the son of Mary said, "O children of Israel! verily, I am the apostle of God."

Surah 6:14. O ye who believe! be ye the helpers of God! as *Jesus*, son of Mary, said to the apostles, "Who are my helpers for God?"

It is interesting to note that among these twenty-five places in the Koran where *'Isa* is used, in sixteen of

them He is called the *son of Mary*; and in five
passages His name is coupled with Moses (Musa),
the great prophet of the old Dispensation. Isidor
Loewenthal, who was a Semitic scholar and a missionary on the Afghan frontier, thought that the
coupling of the name of Jesus with that of Moses
in the Koran might be the reason for the form of
the name, to correspond with other rhymes of that
character; *e.g.*, Harut and Marut, Habil and Kabil,
etc.[1] Of the etymology and significance of this name,
however, we will speak later.

EL MESSIH.—This name, The Messiah, sometimes
joined to that of Jesus and sometimes used by itself,
occurs in the Koran eight times in the following
passages :—

Surah 3 : 40. See above.

Surah 4 : 156. See above.

Surah 4 : 169. See above.

Surah 4 : 170. The *Messiah* doth surely not disdain
to be a servant of God, nor do the angels who are nigh
to Him; and whosoever disdains His service and is
too proud, He will gather them altogether to Himself.

Surah 5 : 19. They misbelieve who say, " Verily
God is the *Messiah* the son of Mary;" say, " Who has
any hold on God, if he wished to destroy the *Messiah*
the son of Mary, and his mother, and those who are
on the earth altogether ? " [1]

[1] Loewenthal, Isidor. *The Name 'Isa : An Investigation.* Calcutta,
1861. Reprinted in *The Moslem World* (London), vol. i. No. 3.

Surah 5 : 76. They misbelieve who say, " Verily, God
is the *Messiah* the son of Mary;" but the *Messiah*
said, " O children of Israel! worship God, my Lord
and your Lord."

Surah 5 : 79. The *Messiah* the son of Mary is only
a prophet: prophets before him have passed away;
and his mother was a confessor; they both used to
eat food.

Surah 9 : 30. The Jews say Ezra is the son of
God, and the Christians say that the *Messiah* is the
son of God; that is what they say with their mouths,
imitating the sayings of those who misbelieved before.
God fight them! how they lie![1]

In one of the passages above quoted (Surah 4 : 170)
there seems to be a reference to the title of the Messiah
in Isaiah as the servant of Jehovah. Mohammed may
have learned of this name from the Jews, although
Surah 9 : 30 (see above) seems to indicate very clearly
that the title of the Messiah was coupled in the
mouth of Christians with the words the *Son of God*.
It is probable, therefore, that both names were learned

---

[1] Palmer's comment on this curious passage is as follows: "The
Moslem tradition is that Ezra, after being dead a hundred years, was
raised to life, and dictated from memory the whole of the Jewish
Scriptures which had been lost during the captivity, and that the
Jews said he could not have done this unless he had been the
son of God. There is no Jewish tradition whatever in support of
this accusation of Mohammed's, which probably was entirely due
to his own invention or to misinformation. Baidhawi, the well-
known commentator, says that it must have been true, because the
Jews themselves, to whom the passage was read, did not deny it."

from the lips of Christians rather than from those of
the Jews, and we are confirmed in this belief by the
use of the third name in the Koran, namely, the *Word
of God.*

KALIMET ALLAH (The Word of God).—This is used
in the Koran twice in direct reference to Christ. In
other passages it occurs, but not as one of the names
of the Messiah. In the following cases the reference
is clear :—

Surah 3 : 40.   See above.

Surah 4 : 169.   See above.

In these two passages Jesus Christ is clearly
referred to as the *Word of God* and as a *Word from
God*; and modern Arabic usage clearly distinguishes
between the Word of God in the sense of Holy Writ,
which is always referred to as *Kalâm Allah*, and the
Word of God as His Messenger, which is *Kalimet
Allah*.   There are, however, only these two passages
in which this New Testament title is given to our
Saviour.

The title given to Moses is *Kalîm Allah*, and the
common explanation is that Moses was the mouthpiece of God in the sense that God spake to him, and
made him His special confidant; but Jesus is the
Kalimet Allah, or Word of God, because He communicates God's word, God's will to men.

RUH ALLAH (Spirit of God, or more correctly,
Spirit from God).—This title is used in the Koran
once concerning Jesus Christ (Surah 4 : 169, quoted

above), but the commentators are not agreed as to its
real significance, and whether it is a name that can be
applied to Jesus Christ, or whether the passage simply
signifies that Jesus, with all other mortals, was par-
taker of the creative Spirit of God.

In addition to these four names which are specially
applied to Jesus Christ in the Koran, He is also
know by the common titles of *Nabi* (prophet) and
Rasûl (apostle).

Surah 19 : 30 (Where Jesus speaks from the cradle,
using these words), Verily, I am the servant of God,
He has brought me the Book, and He has made me a
prophet, and He has made me blessed wherever I be.

Surah 57 : 27.   See above.

Surah 4 : 169.   See above.

The number of prophets and apostles sent by God,
according to Moslem teaching, amounts to 124,000.
Others say 240,000, and others 100,000.   These statements show that the words, prophet and apostle, in
Moslem usage have not the same dignity, which
we infer from their usage in the Old and New
Testaments.   Three hundred and thirteen are said to
have been apostles who came with a special mission.
A prophet, according to Moslem teaching, is a man
inspired by God, but not sent with a special dispensation or book ; while an apostle is one who comes
either with a special dispensation or to whom a
special book has been revealed.   All apostles are
prophets, but not all prophets are apostles.   Jesus

was both. According to the commentators this is the definition of a prophet: "A prophet must be a male[1] person, free, not a slave, of the sons of Adam; of sound mind and without bodily defect or disease, to whom has been revealed a revelation which he himself accepts; nor must he come with a message before he is of age."[2]

The qualifications of a prophet are four:—

1. *Faithfulness.*—That is, during his work as a prophet he is kept from the commission of any outward sinful act. The sinlessness of all the prophets has become a favourite dogma of Islam, in spite of the Koran testimony regarding the sins of many of the prophets, including Mohammed himself.

2. *Truthfulness.*—They speak the truth in accordance with the real state of the case, or at all events, in accordance with what they believe to be the truth.

3. *Sagacity,* or intelligence, enabling them to silence objectors or opponents. This quality the apostles are said to possess in much higher degree than the prophets.

4. *The Delivery of their Message.*—In other words, they must on no account conceal what God has revealed to them.

Because Jesus Christ was an apostle and a prophet

---

[1] Maryam, Eve, and Sarah are admitted by some Moslems among the list of prophets, but it is contrary to the teaching of the leading commentators. Cf. El Jowhara, "No female ever was a prophet" (Klein, *Religion of Islam*, p. 74).

[2] El Jowhara, quoted in Klein, *The Religion of Islam*, p. 72.

He also had the power of working miracles, as we shall see in a later chapter.

In order to understand the title *prophet* and *apostle* ascribed to Jesus, we must remember that the highest in rank among the prophets and apostles is said to be Mohammed. He is considered not only the greatest prophet and apostle, but the most excellent of all created things. After him come Abraham, Moses, and Jesus. These four are distinguished by the title, '*Ulu-el-'Azîm*, possessors of constancy or endowed with a purpose. This name was taken from Surah 46 : 34. "Then do thou be patient as the apostles endowed with a purpose were patient, and hastened not on their punishment." Six of the company of the prophets are classed apart by Moslems and said to have brought in new dispensations and a new law, and they therefore have each of them a special title.

Adam: *Safi Allah* (Chosen of God); Noah: *Nebi Allah* (prophet of God); Abraham: *Khalil Allah* (the friend of God); Moses: *Kalîm Allah* (the mouthpiece of God); Jesus, *Ruh Allah* (Spirit of God); Mohammed, *Rasul Allah* (the apostle of God). It is clear from the above and at the very outset of our investigation that Jesus Christ does not occupy the supreme place, but at the best ranks only with Abraham, Moses, and Mohammed.

We turn now to consider what significance is attached to the proper names given by Moslems to our Lord, both as regards their form and their etymology.

The question why Mohammed used the word '*Isa* instead of *Yesu'a*, is more easily asked than answered. It is a stumbling-block to every Moslem convert who reads the Arabic Scriptures. Kamil Abd ul Messiah, writing to Dr. Jessup from Aden after his conversion to Christianity, says : "Will you kindly send me a reply to this question : Why is Jesus styled '*Isa* in the Moslem books, and did this name exist among the Arabs before Mohammed's time during the days of Ignorance ? " [1]

Dr. Jessup in his reply called attention to some of the explanations given. The first among them is that there is no particular significance in the form of the word, and that Mohammed invented it as a rhyming couplet to the name of Moses (Musa), in the same way as he changed the name of Goliath to Jalut, and that of Saul to Talut, apparently as a matter of rhythm, in the second chapter of the Koran (verses 248–253); and the names of the sons of Adam to Habil and Kabil in Moslem usage for Cain and Abel ; or as he used the fanciful names, Harut and Marut, for the names of angels who taught men sorcery (Surah 2 : 96). The difficulty with this theory is, as we have seen, that only in five cases is the name '*Isa* joined to that of Musa in the Koran text. In every other case there is no apparent reason for this particular form of the word because of the rhythm.

A second explanation given by some Arabic lexico-

[1] Jessup, Rev. H. H., *Kamil*, p. 122. Philadelphia, 1898.

3

graphers is that the word has been deliberately formed by inverting the order of the letters in the Hebrew word *Yesu'a*. This explanation seems forced; nor can it be satisfactorily explained by the laws of etymology, for in reversing the letters not only are the vowels altered, but one of the weak consonants must be changed in *Yesu'a* to make *'Isa*. Beidhawi in his *Commentary* asserts that *'Isa* is the Arabic form of the Hebrew *Yesu'a*, and goes on to say that it comes from a root *Al-'Ayos*, which signifies white mingled with red.[1]

A fourth explanation is offered by Dr. Otto Pautz.[2] "The Koran expression *'Isa* corresponds with the Hebrew Esau, the name of the brother of Jacob (Israel). Because his descendants all through their history stood hostile over against the Israelites, who were the people of the promise, the later Jews caricatured the name of Jesus by making it Esau. Mohammed took this form of Esau from the Jews at Medina, without being conscious of the sinister import connected with the name in their minds." We would like further proofs of this ingenious theory before accepting it, although it appears most plausible in view

---

[1] Beidhawi, vol. i. p. 96. He also gives a curious, but unchaste, derivation for the name of Jesus' mother, Mary: "*Hooa bil Arabiya min el nisa ka el zir min er rijal, etc.*" On the derivation of *'Isa*, cf. Fairozabadi's *Kamoos*, vol. i. p. 125, and *Katr ul Muhit* (Beirut), vol. ii. p. 1478. And on *Zir*, vol. i. p. 874.

[2] Pautz, Otto. Muhammed's *Lehre von der Offenbarung*, p. 191. Leipzig, 1898.

of all that Mohammed borrowed and adapted from Judaism.[1]

In regard to the name *El Messih*, although this term is evidently taken from the Hebrew and has the Hebrew significance of *the anointed*, the Moslems explain it differently. Bringing everything back to Arabic roots, they connect it with the word *Sah* (to wander, to go on pilgrimage), and say it is the intensive form of that root, and that Jesus was the leader of wanderers, "Imam al sa'yihin." The homelessness of Jesus has always strongly impressed itself on the Mohammedan imagination. C. H. A. Field relates:[2] Once on entering a Pathan village, I was met by a youth who asked, "Is this verse in the Injil: 'The Son of Mary had nowhere to lay His head'?" In the *Kusus-al-anbiya* (Stories of the Prophets) this takes the following grotesque shape:—

One day Jesus saw a fox roaming through the wilderness. He said to him, "O fox! whither art thou going?" The fox answered, "I have come out for exercise; now I am returning to my own home." Jesus said, "Every one has built himself a house; but for Me there is no resting-place." Some people who heard it said, "We are sorry for Thee, and will build Thee a house." He replied, "I have no money." They answered, "We will pay all the expenses." Then He said, "Very well, I will choose the site." He led them down to the edge of the sea and, pointing where the waves were dashing highest, said, "Build Me a house there." The people said, "That is the sea, O

---

[1] Geiger, Abraham, *Judaism and Islam.* Madras, 1898; *Was hat Mohammed aus dem Judenthume aufgenommen?* Bonn, 1833.

[2] *Church Missionary Review,* July 1910.

Prophet ! how can we build there ?" "Yea, and is not the world a sea," He answered, " on which no one can raise a building that abides ? "

A similar echo of Christ's words is found in the famous inscription over a bridge at Fatehpur Sikri: " Jesus (upon whom be peace) said, ' The world is a bridge; pass over it, but do not build upon it.' " [1]

Although this explanation of the word which Moslems have generally adopted is ingenious, it is evidently an attempt to escape from the ordinary significance of the root. Even in his Arabic dictionary Fairozabadi gives the name *Messih* under the Arabic root *Masaha*, to anoint, but states that this name was given to Jesus Christ because He was often on journeys, and did not spend His days in one place. Concerning other derivations he says there are no less than fifty explanations enumerated by him in his book *Masharik Al Anwar.*[2]

The Moslem interpretation of the name of Jesus, *Kalimet Allah*, has already been given. In Surah 19: 35, He is called *Kaul ul Hak*, the Word of Truth. An argument can easily be based on these expressions for the eternal nature of Jesus Christ and His supreme office, but it is doubtful whether most Moslems would admit its force. Dr. W. St. Clair Tisdall rightly says: [3] " The term *Kalimah* (λόγος, word, speech) denotes

[1] *Church Missionary Review*, July 1910.

[2] Fairozabadi, *Kamoos*, vol. i. p. 156 ; cf. Beidhawi on Surah 3 : 40.

[3] Revised *Mizanu'l Haqq*, p. 185. London, 1910.

the expression of what is in the mind of the speaker,
who in this case is God Most High. If Christ were
a Word of God, it would be clear that He was only
one expression of God's will; but since God Himself
calls Him "the Word of God," it is clear that He must
be the one and only perfect expression of God's will,
and the only perfect manifestation of God. It was
through Him that the prophets spoke when He sent
them His Holy Spirit. Since then the title *Kalimatu
'llâh* shows that Christ only can reveal God to men.
It is clear that He Himself must know God and His
Will perfectly."

In closing this account of the names of Jesus Christ
in the Koran and their significance, there are two
more expressions to which we must call attention.

The first of these occurs in Surah 21 : 91, where
Mary is referred to, and the statement is made, "We
made her and her Son a sign unto the worlds." The
use of the singular instead of the plural in this connection brings to mind the name of our Saviour in
Isaiah's prophecy, *Wonderful*. Beidhawi's comment
on this text is an evident attempt to minimise the
significance of the expression. He says: "We made
her and her Son a sign unto the worlds; that is, the
story of their life or their condition, for whosoever
thinks of their condition is convinced of the perfection
of power in God Most High, Who is the Creator."

The other occurs in Surah 3 : 40: When the angel
said, " O Mary ! verily, God gives thee the glad tidings

of a Word from Him; His name shall be The Messiah, Jesus the son of Mary, *Illustrious in this world and the next*, and of those whose place is nigh unto God." If Moslems were willing to admit all that these words imply, it would not be difficult to prove that in this passage of the Koran the person and character of Jesus Christ are superior to those of all other prophets and apostles. The commentator Beidhawi, commenting on this passage, uses these remarkable words: "His illustriousness in this world is the gift of prophecy, and in the world to come, the power of intercession; and 'whose place is nigh to God' signifies His high position in Paradise, or the fact that He was raised up to heaven and enjoys the companionship of the angels." [1]

[1] Beidhawi on Surah 3 : 40.

II

THE KORAN ACCOUNT OF HIS LIFE, DEATH, AND TRANSLATION

"The contents and the arrangement of the Koran speak forcibly for its authenticity. All the fragments that could possibly be obtained have with artless simplicity been joined together. The patchwork bears no marks of a designing genius or a moulding hand. It testifies to the faith and reverence of the compilers, and proves that they dared no more than simply collect the sacred fragments and place them in juxtaposition. Hence the interminable repetitions; the palling reiteration of the same ideas, truths, and doctrines; hence, scriptural stories and Arab legends, told over and over again with little verbal variation; hence the pervading want of connection, and the startling chasms between adjacent passages."—Muir's *Life of Mahomet*, p. 557.

II

THE KORAN ACCOUNT OF HIS LIFE, DEATH, AND TRANSLATION

IN attempting to give an account of the life of Jesus
Christ in the very words of the Koran, there are
three difficulties that meet us at the outset.

The first relates to the general piecemeal character
of the Koran as a book. It has no chronological order
nor logical sequence. Its verses were revealed at
different times and in different places, and throw
together in confusion, laws and legends, facts and
fancies, prayers and imprecations. Very few Bible
characters are mentioned in the earliest group of the
Surahs, and although there are distinctively Christian
features in some of the early revelations, Jesus Himself
is not mentioned.[1]

A more serious difficulty is that the Koran statements about the Lord Jesus Christ are not free from
contradiction, any more than some of its other teaching.
Some passages speak of Him as a mere man and a
prophet; others, as we have seen, give him such titles
as are given to no other human being. Especially in

[1] Cf. Smith, H. P., *The Bible and Islam*, pp. 86–87; Rodwell's
Koran, p. 4.

relation to His death, the statements are contradictory, and cannot be reconciled without violence to the text.

A third difficulty relates to the chronological order of the Surahs. If it were our purpose to show the development of Mohammed's ideas in regard to Jesus Christ, it would be important to begin with the earliest mention of Jesus Christ in the Koran, and follow out this teaching to the final Surahs. But there is no agreement as regards the chronological order of the various chapters in the Koran.[1] Moslems themselves

[1] I had occasion recently to investigate the chronological place of one of the Surahs, and the more authorities consulted the less certainty appeared. In Hughes' *Dictionary of Islam* three distinct lists are given—that of Jalal ed Din, of Rodwell, and of Muir. Nöldeke's *History of the Koran* afforded a fourth list. All of them are authorities on the subject, each professing to have arrived at his results by internal evidence and criticism of the accepted text, with the help of authoritative tradition. After reading of their painstaking efforts, and persuaded by the logical reasons for many of Nöldeke's deductions in his elaborate treatment of the subject, I was curious to know in how far there was agreement between the authorities mentioned. The following was the result :—

By actual count there were sixty-five among a hundred and fourteen possible instances where *two* agreed. There were only five instances where three agreed on the order of certain chapters. There were forty-five instances where all disagreed, *and there was not a single instance where all were agreed* as to the place of a Surah in chronological order. The greatest agreement was between Nöldeke and Rodwell, but even they differed on the chronological place of fifty-two of the hundred and fourteen chapters. Where Muir followed the Arabic commentator, Nöldeke rejected his order altogether, and where the latter approached the traditional order, Rodwell and Muir agreed to disagree with both. There was the widest divergence in nearly every case. The first Surah according to Muir is the 103rd, while Nöldeke makes it the 97th. The Surah of The Pen is considered by Jalal ed Din the second in order, and by the others the seventeenth, fifty-second, and eighteenth respectively.

acknowledge that the present order of the Surahs is not at all chronological, and yet they admit the importance of ascertaining the time when and the place where each Surah was revealed.

As our purpose is not to trace the growth of this idea in the mind of Mohammed, but to collect all the passages on which the common opinion in regard to Jesus Christ, among Moslems, rests, we need not trouble about the chronology of the Surahs, but, grouping them as far as possible in the order of the Gospel history, give herewith a life of Jesus Christ in the words of the Koran only.

HIS ANNUNCIATION [1]

Surah 3 : 37-43. And when the angels said, "O Mary! verily, God has chosen thee and has purified thee, and has chosen thee above the women

Surah 19 : 16-21. And mention, in the Book, Mary ; when she retired from her family into an eastern place ; and she took a veil (to screen herself)

---

[1] The following index of the leading passages in the Koran that relate to Jesus Christ, as they occur in Beidhawi's *Commentary* (Cairo edition, 2 vols.), will prove useful to those who have found difficulty in locating them, as Beidhawi's *Commentary* does not number the verses :—

The Annunciation : Surah 3 : 37-43, vol. i. p. 206, 207 ; Birth : Surah 19 : 22-24, vol. ii. p. 34 ; Surah 23 : 52, vol. ii. pp. 121, 122 ; Miracles : Surah 3 : 43-46, vol. i., pp. 207, 208 ; Surah 5 : 112-115, vol. i. pp. 365-367 ; Mission : Surah 2 : 81, vol. i. p. 96 ; Surah 2 : 254, vol. i. p. 173 ; Surah 3 : 44, vol. i. p. 207 ; Surah 4 : 157, vol. i. p. 316 ; Surah 4 : 50-51, vol. i. p. 340 ; Surah 6 : 85, vol. i. p. 389 ; Surah 17 : 26, 27, vol. i. p. 695 ; Surah 61 : 6, vol. ii. p. 517 ; Crucifixion : Surah 3 : 47-50, vol. i. p. 209 ; Surah 4 : 155, 156, vol. i. p. 315 ; Divinity and Sonship denied : Surah 3 : 51, 52, vol. i. p. 210 ; Surah 3 : 72, 73, vol. i. pp. 215, 216 ; Surah 5 : 19, vol. i.

of the world. O Mary! be
devout unto thy Lord, and
adore and bow down with those
who bow. That is (one) of the
declarations of the unseen
world which we reveal to thee,
though thou wert not by them
when they threw their lots
which of them should take
care of Mary, nor were ye by
them when they did dispute."
When the angel said, "O Mary!
verily, God gives thee the glad
tidings of a Word from Him;
his name shall be the Messiah
Jesus the son of Mary, regarded
in this world and the next and
of those whose place is nigh to
God. And he shall speak to
people in his cradle, and when
grown up, and shall be among
the righteous." She said,
"Lord! how can I have a son
when man hath not yet touched
me?" He said, "Thus God
creates what He pleaseth.
When He decrees a matter He
only says 'BE,' and it is; and
He will teach him the Book, and
wisdom, and the law, and the
gospel, and he shall be a prophet to the children of Israel."

from them; and we sent unto
her our spirit; and he took
for her the semblance of a well-
made man. Said she, "Verily,
I take refuge in the Merciful
One from thee, if thou art
pious." Said he, "I am only a
messenger of thy Lord to bestow
on thee a pure boy." Said she,
"How can I have a boy when
no man has touched me, and
when I am no harlot?" He
said, "Thus says thy Lord, It
is easy for Me! and we will
make him a sign unto man,
and a mercy from us; for it is
a decided matter."[1]

p. 830; Surah 9: 36, vol. i. p. 498; Surah 19: 35, 36, vol. ii. p.
36; Surah 43: 57–65, vol. i. pp. 411, 412; The Trinity: Surah 4:
169, vol. i. pp. 318, 319; Surah 5: 76–79, vol. i. pp. 351–352;
Surah 5: 116, 117, pp. 367, 368.
[1] Jelal-ud-Din comments on these passages as follows: "Inflavi-
mus eam de spiritu nostro, cum inflavit in aperturam tunicae ejus

His Birth

Surah 19 : 22–34. So she conceived him, and she retired with him into a remote place. And the labour pains came upon her at the trunk of a palm tree, and she said, "O that I had died before this, and been forgotten out of mind!" and he called to her from beneath her, "Grieve not, for thy Lord has placed a stream beneath thy feet; and shake towards thee the trunk of the palm tree, and it will drop upon thee fresh dates fit to gather; so eat and drink and cheer thine eye; and if thou shouldst see any mortal say, 'Verily, I have vowed to the Merciful One a fast, and I will not speak to-day with a human being.'"

Then she brought it to her people, carrying it; said they, "O Mary! thou hast done an extraordinary thing! O sister of Aaron! thy father was not a bad man, nor was thy mother a harlot!"

Surah 23 : 52. And we made the son of Mary and his mother a sign; and we lodged them both in a high place, furnished with security and a spring.

(Mariae) ad collum, efficiente Deo, ut flatus ejus perveniret ad vulvam ejus et ex eo conciperet Jesum." Beidhawi (vol. ii. p. 33) agrees with this, and states that Gabriel took the form of a beautiful young man "ut excitaret Mariae cupidinem et ita," etc. It is the opinion of Gerock that Mohammed's idea of the conception of Jesus Christ by the Virgin Mary was wholly sensual, and that Gabriel was his natural father. Cf. *Christologie des Koran*, pp. 36–40. His argument is based on the Koran text itself.

And she pointed to him, and they said, "How are we to speak with one who is in the cradle a child?" He said, "Verily, I am a servant of God; He has brought me the Book, and He has made me a prophet, and He has made me blessed wherever I be; and He has required of me prayer and almsgiving as long as I live, and piety towards my mother, and has not made me a miserable tyrant; and peace upon me the day I was born, and the day I die, and the day I shall be raised up alive."

His Miracles

Surah 3:43-45. And He will teach him the Book, and wisdom, and the law, and the gospel, and he shall be a prophet to the people of Israel (saying) that I have come to you with a sign from God, namely, that I will create for you out of clay as though it were the form of a bird, and I will blow thereon, and it shall become a bird by God's permission; and I will heal the blind from birth, and lepers; and I will bring the dead to life by God's permission; and I will tell you what you eat and what you store up in your houses. Verily, in that is a sign for you if ye be believers. And I will confirm what is before you of the law, and will surely make lawful for you some of that which was prohibited from you. I have come to you with a sign from your Lord, so fear God and follow me, for God is my Lord, and your Lord, so worship Him: this is the right path.

And when Jesus perceived their unbelief, He said, "Who are my helpers for God?" Said the apostles, "We are God's helpers." We believe in God, so bear witness that we are resigned. Lord, we have believed in what Thou hast revealed, and we have followed the apostle, so write us down with those which bear witness." [1]

Surah 5 : 112–115. When the apostles said, "O Jesus, son of Mary ! is thy Lord able to send down to us a table from heaven ?" He said, "Fear God, if ye be believers"; and they said, "We desire to eat therefrom that our hearts may be at rest, and that we may know that what thou hast told us is the truth, and that we may be thereby amongst the witnesses." Said Jesus, the son of Mary, "O God, our Lord ! send down to us a table from heaven to be to us as a festival—to the first of us and to the last, and a sign from Thee,—and grant us provision, for Thou art the best of providers."

God said, "Verily, I am about to send it down to you; but whoso disbelieves amongst you after that, verily I will torment him with the torment which I have not tormented any one with in all the worlds." [2]

HIS MISSION AND MESSAGE

Surah 57 : 26–27. And we sent Noah and Abraham ; and placed in their seed prophecy and the Book ; and some of them are guided, though many of them are workers of abomination !

Then we followed up their footsteps with our apostles ; and we followed them up with Jesus the son of Mary ; and we gave him the gospel ; and we

Surah 2 : 254. These apostles have we preferred one of them above another. Of them is one of whom God spake ; and we have raised some of them degrees ; and we have given Jesus the son of Mary manifest signs, and strengthened him by the Holy Spirit. And, did God please, those who come after them would not have fought after there came to

---

[1] These verses are the only reference in the Koran to the miracles of Jesus Christ. How meagre compared with any of the Gospels ! And yet later tradition has built up on these verses or added to them a whole mass of legendary wonders, many of them puerile in the extreme.

[2] The reference is undoubtedly to the institution of the Lord's Supper. The later explanations, as we shall see, are wide of the mark. Cf. 1 Cor. xi. 27 and 29–34.

placed in the hearts of those that followed him kindness and compassion. But monkery, they invented it; we only prescribed to them the craving after the goodwill of God, and they observed it not with due observance. But we gave to those who believe amongst them their hire; though many amongst them were workers of abomination !

them manifest signs. But they did disagree, and of them are some who believe, and of them some who misbelieve, but, did God please, they would not have fought, for God does what He will.

Surah 5 : 50–51. And we followed up the footsteps of these (prophets) with Jesus the son of Mary, confirming that which was before him and the law, and we brought him the gospel, wherein is: guidance and light, verifying what was before it of the law, and a guidance and an admonition unto those who fear.

Then let the people of the gospel judge by that which is revealed therein, for whoso will not judge by what God has revealed, these be the evil-doers.

Surah 2 : 81. We gave Moses the Book and we followed him up with other apostles, and we gave Jesus the son of Mary manifest signs and aided him with the Holy Spirit. Do ye then, every time an apostle comes to you with what your souls love not, proudly scorn him, and charge a part with lying and slay a part?

Surah 6 : 85. And Zachariah and John and Jesus and Elias, all righteous ones.

Surah 61 : 6. And when Jesus the son of Mary said, " O children of Israel ! verily, I am the apostle of God to you, verifying the law that was before me, and giving you glad tidings of an apostle who shall

Surah 4 : 157. And there shall not be one of the people of the Book but shall believe in him before his death; and on the day of judgment he shall be a witness against them.

come after me, whose name shall be Ahmed."

Surah 3 : 44. "I have come to you with a sign from your Lord, so fear God and follow me, for God is my Lord, and your Lord, so worship Him—this is the right path."

HIS DEATH

[The assertion of His death and the denial of His crucifixion are here placed in parallel columns to show a discrepancy in statement which has been the despair even of Moslem commentators.]

Surah 3 : 47–50. But they (the Jews) were crafty, and God was crafty, for God is the best of crafty ones !

When God said, "O Jesus ! I will make thee die and take thee up again to me, and will clear thee of those who misbelieve, and will make those who follow thee above those who misbelieve, at the day of judgment, then to me is your return. I will decide between you concerning that wherein ye disagree. And as for those who misbelieve, I will punish them with grievous punishment in this world and the next, and they shall have none to help them." But as for those who believe and do what is right, He will pay them

Surah 4 : 155–156. And for their misbelief, and for their saying about Mary a mighty calumny, and for their saying, "Verily, we have killed the Messiah, Jesus the son of Mary, the apostle of God." . . . But they did not kill him, and they did not crucify him, but a similitude was made for them. And verily, those who differ about him are in doubt concerning him ; they have no knowledge concerning him, but only follow an opinion. They did not kill him, for sure ! nay, God raised him up unto Himself.

4

their reward, for God loves not
the unjust.[1]

Surah 19:34. "And peace
upon me the day I was born,
and the day I die, and the day
I shall be raised up alive."[2]

HIS CHARACTER AS AN APOSTLE AND PROPHET
(Denial of His Deity)

Surah 4:169. O ye people
of the Book! do not exceed in
your religion, nor say against
God aught save the truth.
The Messiah, Jesus the son of
Mary, is but the apostle of God
and His Word, which He cast
into Mary, and a spirit from
Him; believe then in God and
His apostles, and say not
"Three." Have done! it were
better for you. God is only
one God, celebrated be His
praise that He should beget a
Son! His is what is in the
heavens and what is in the
earth; and God sufficeth for a
guardian.

Surah 5:116–117. And when
God said, "O Jesus, son of

Surah 5:76–79. They mis-
believe who say, "Verily, God
is the Messiah the son of
Mary;" but the Messiah said,
"O children of Israel! worship
God, my Lord and your Lord;"
verily, he who associates aught
with God, God hath forbidden
him Paradise, and his resort is
the Fire, and the unjust shall
have none to help him.

They misbelieve who say,
"Verily, God is the third of
three;" for there is no God
but one, and if they do not
desist from what they say,
there shall touch those who
misbelieve   amongst   them
grievous woe.

Will they not turn again
towards God and ask pardon

[1] Beidhawi says on this passage (vol. i. p. 209), after various
attempts to escape the ordinary meaning of the words: "It is said
God caused him to die for seven hours and then raised him to heaven."

[2] Beidhawi makes no comment on this clear declaration of the *death*
of Christ. Moslems say it refers to his death after his second coming.

Mary! is it thou who didst say to men, take me and my mother for two gods, beside God?" He said, "I celebrate Thy praise! what ails me that I should say what I have no right to? If I had said it, Thou wouldst have known it; Thou knowest what is in my soul, but I do not know what is in Thy soul; verily, Thou are one who knoweth the unseen. I never told them save what Thou didst bid me, —'Worship God, my Lord and your Lord,' and I was a witness against them as long as I was amongst them; but when Thou didst take me away to Thyself Thou wert the watcher over them, for Thou art witness over all."

of Him? for God is forgiving and merciful.

The Messiah the son of Mary is only a prophet: prophets before him have passed away; and his mother was a confessor; they both used to eat food.— See how we explain to them the signs, yet see how they turn aside!

HIS CHARACTER AS AN APOSTLE AND PROPHET [1]

Surah 19 : 35–36. That is, Jesus the son of Mary,—by the word of truth whereon ye do dispute!

God could not take to Himself any son! celebrated be His praise! when He decrees a matter He only says to it, "BE," and it is; and verily, God is my Lord and your Lord, so worship Him; this is the right way. And the

Surah 3 : 51–52. That is what we recite to thee of the signs and of the wise reminder. Verily, the likeness of Jesus with God is as the likeness of Adam. He created him from earth, then He said to him, "BE," and he was.

---

[1] For a summary of the teaching of these passages see Chapter V.

parties have disagreed amongst
themselves.

Surah 9 : 30. The Jews say
Ezra is the son of God ; and
the Christians say that the
Messiah is the son of God;
that is what they say with
their mouths, imitating the
sayings of those who mis-
believed before.—God fight
them ! how they lie !

Surah 5 : 19. They mis-
believe who say, " Verily, God
is the Messiah the son of
Mary ; " say, " Who has any
hold on God, if he wished to
destroy the Messiah the son of
Mary, and his mother, and
those who are on earth
altogether ? "

Surah 47 : 57–64. And when the son of Mary was set forth as
a parable, behold thy people turned away from him and said,
" Are our gods better, or is he ? " They did not set it forth to
thee save for wrangling. Nay, but they are a contentious
people.

He is but a servant whom we have been gracious to, and we
have made him an example for the children of Israel. And if
we please we can make of you angels in the earth to succeed you.
And, verily, he is a sign of the Hour. Doubt not then concerning it, but follow this right way ; and let not the devil turn you
away ; verily, he is to you an open foe !

And when Jesus came with manifest signs, he said, " I am come
to you with wisdom, and I will explain to you something of that
whereon ye did dispute, then fear God, obey me ; verily, God,
He is my Lord and your Lord, serve Him then ; this is the
right way."

Surah 3 : 72–73. And, verily, amongst them is a sect who
twist their tongues concerning the Book, that ye may reckon it
to be from the Book, but it is not from the Book. They say,
" It is from God," but it is not from God, and they tell a lie
against God, the while they know.

It is not right for a man that God should give him a Book and
judgment and prophecy, and that then he should say to men,

" Be ye servants of mine rather than of God ; "-but be ye rather masters of teaching the Book and of what ye learn.

The texts above given are the total contents of the Koran as far as they relate to the life of Jesus Christ, and have formed the basis for the traditional account of His life, among Moslems. A study of the Koran commentaries on the texts given will show how later tradition has taken the outlines of Mohammed's revelation and made the picture more real, more full, but also more fantastic. Whatever was unintelligible or contradictory in the words of Mohammed's revelation could only be interpreted and made clear by means of tradition, and this applied not only to the legislative portions of the Koran, but also in its historical material. Tradition in Islam, we must remember, occupies a totally different position to what we understand by tradition in the Christian Church.[1] Orthodox tradition consists of the record of what Mohammed did or enjoined, or that which he allowed, *as well as the authoritative sayings and doings of the companions of the prophet.* There is not a single Moslem sect that looks to the Koran as the only rule of faith and practice, or as the only reliable source of historical information on the earlier prophets. Therefore we must necessarily go to tradition for the fuller portrait of Jesus Christ. According to Goldziher, tradition is the normative principle in Islam. " Before the end of the first

[1] Hughes, *Dictionary of Islam*, art. " Tradition."

century," he says, "they had already laid down the canon : The *Sunna* (tradition) is the judge over the Koran, and not the Koran the judge of the *Sunna*," [1] and he goes on to show that the authority of tradition increased century after century.

There is no doubt that much of the traditional account of the life of Jesus Christ came from the lips of Mohammed but was not recorded in the Koran. Other portions of it were accredited to him, although they were the invention or contribution of Christian renegades who became Moslems. [2] Students of Islam are in disagreement regarding the reliability of tradition in general and the authenticity of many traditions in particular. While Dozy expresses astonishment that so much of Moslem tradition is authentic and reliable, [3] Goldziher, on the other hand, thinks the greater part was manufactured by those who came after Mohammed, for private ends in Church and State. [4] Moulavi Cheragh Ali says, "The name of Mohammed was abused to support all manner of lies and absurdities, or to satisfy the passion, caprice, or arbitrary will of the despots, leaving out of consideration the creation of any standards of test. I am seldom inclined to quote traditions, having little or no belief in their genuineness, as they

---

[1] Goldziher, *Mohammedanische Studien*, vol. ii. p. 19.

[2] *Ibid.*, vol. ii. pp. 382-399.

[3] *Essai sur l'Histoire de l'Islamisme*, p. 12.

[4] Vol. ii. p. 5, Goldziher.

generally are unauthenticated, unsupported, and one-sided." [1]

When one reads the standard commentaries on the above passages of the Koran, or the net result of their investigations based on tradition, as given in our following two chapters, it seems impossible to determine in how far we have a portrait of Christ as given by Mohammed himself, or a portrait of Christ by those who followed him. Muir's conclusion is unbiassed, and may well lead us from this chapter into the next.

"That the Collectors of Tradition rendered an important service to Islam, and even to history, cannot be doubted. The vast flood of tradition, poured forth from every quarter of the Moslem empire, and daily gathering volume from innumerable tributaries, was composed of the most heterogeneous elements ; without the labours of the traditionists it must soon have formed a chaotic sea, in which truth and error, fact and fable, would have mingled together in undistinguishable confusion. It is a legitimate inference from the foregoing sketch, that Tradition, in the second century, embraced a large element of truth. That even respectably derived traditions often contained much that was exaggerated and fabulous, is an equally fair conclusion.

---

[1] Quoted from *Political and Social Reform in the Ottoman Empire,* etc. (Bombay, 1883), pp. 19 and 147, in Hughes' *Dictionary of Islam.* The most voluminous authority quoted in Moslem Tradition is Abu Huraira, known by this surname, "the Father of the little Cat," on account of his fondness for cats. He joined the followers of Mohammed in A.H. 629, and lived with him. More traditions are attributed to him than to any other source. He was renowned for his infallible memory, and yet Moslems themselves raise suspicion in regard to his trustworthiness. Sprenger calls him "the extreme of pious humbug," but we must take into account the fact that most of the sayings which tradition attributes to him were foisted on him probably at a much later date.—*Encyclopedia of Islam,* p. 94, art. "Abu Huraira."

It is proved by the testimony of the Collectors themselves that thousands and tens of thousands were current in their times, which possessed not even a shadow of authority.   The mass may be likened to the image in Nebuchadnezzar's dream, formed by the unnatural union of gold, or silver, of the baser metals, and of clay ; and here the more valuable parts were fast commingling hopelessly with the bad." [1]

---

[1] Muir, *The Life of Mahomet*, vol. i. p. xlii.

III

JESUS CHRIST ACCORDING TO TRADITION

Low lies the Syrian town behind the mountain
  Where Mary, meek and spotless, knelt that morn,
And saw the splendid Angel by the fountain,
  And heard his voice, "Lord Isa shall be born!"
                                ARNOLD'S *Pearls of the Faith.*

The Christ of post-Koranic tradition is far more life-like than the Christ of the Koran. The latter is a mere lay-figure, bedecked with honorific titles indeed, such as the "Spirit of God and a word proceeding from Him," and working miracles, but displaying no character. In the post-Koranic writers, on the other hand, we have His sinlessness, His return to judgment, His humility, His unworldliness, His sufferings, His doctrine of the New Birth, topics upon which the Koran is entirely silent.—C. H. A. FIELD in the *C. M. S. Review.*

III

JESUS CHRIST ACCORDING TO TRADITION

FROM HIS BIRTH TO HIS PUBLIC MINISTRY

THE account of the life of Jesus Christ given in this and the next chapter is a connected summary of all that is given by leading commentators and orthodox tradition on the Koran passages of Chapter II. as collected by Imam Abu Ishak Ahmed bin Mohammed bin Ibrahim Eth-Thalabi.[1] My reasons for using the account of Eth-Thalabi have already been given in the Introduction. There are other accounts, but they are largely parallel, and Eth-Thalabi, who was himself a commentator on the Koran of some reputation, based his work on traditions which are universally acknowledged as authoritative by most Moslems. The translation given is as far as possible literal, although some few passages are omitted because characterised by the crude indecency which so often occurs in Moslem

[1] The work of Thalabi was made the thesis for his doctoral degree by Lidzbarski. He investigated the sources of all the legends found in it, and gives special references. His work is entitled *De Propheticis . . . legendis Arabicis.* Leipzig, Drugulin, 1893.

literature. I have also omitted the long preliminary account found in *Kusus-al-Anbiah* on Zechariah and the family of Amran, as not strictly germane to our topic.

Although no footnotes are given, the authority for every statement and story can easily be found in Beidhawi, Zamakhshari, etc., under the appropriate Koran passages.

On the Birth of Jesus (upon whom be peace) and on Mary's Conception of Jesus (on both of them be peace).[1]

Said God Most High, and it is recorded in the Book " that Mary when she separated from her people, went to an eastward place." In explanation of this the learned say that when three days had passed since Mary conceived Jesus,—and she was at that time a girl of fifteen years old, and some say thirteen years old,—she dwelt in a mosque; and there was with her in the mosque her cousin, named Joseph the carpenter, and he was a sweet-tempered man, who earned his living by his trade. And Joseph and Mary were also servants of the mosque as water-carriers, and when Mary had emptied her water-jar and Joseph his, each of them took the jar and went to a cave where the water-spring was, to draw water. And then they returned to the Mosque.

And when the day came on which Gabriel (upon whom be peace) encountered her, it was the longest

[1] A translation of the life of Jesus Christ from *Kusus-al-Anbiah*, by Imam Abu Ishak Ahmed bin Mohammed bin Ibrahim Eth-Thalabi. The account of the birth and life of Jesus Christ is found in this work on pp. 241-255, Cairo edition, 1325 A.H.

day of the year and the hottest. She, when her
water-jar was emptied, said, "Will you not go with
me, O Joseph, and we will draw water?" He said,
"I still have abundance of water sufficient until
to-morrow;" but she said, "But as for me, by God, I
have no water." So she took her jar and went away
alone until she entered the cave. And she found there
with her Gabriel (upon whom be peace), and God had
made him resemble a beautiful young man. And he
said to her, "O Mary, truly God hath sent me to you
that I may give you a pious child." Said she, "I take
refuge with the merciful One from you if you are an
honest person," that is, a true believer, obedient to God.

'Ali bin Abi Talib [1] says (may God be gracious to his
countenance) she knew that the pious person was
merciful and modest, and she considered him a man of
the sons of Adam.[2]

Akrima says that Gabriel appeared to her in the
form of a beautiful young man of fine countenance, with
curly hair and an erect form. And the learned say
that God sent Gabriel in the form of a human being
that Mary might have confidence in him and be able
to hear his words, for if he had come down in his angel

---

[1] The reference to those who are authority for the various and
sometimes contradictory traditions are introduced in Moslem
literature by these words: "Ali bin Abi Talib said, Abu Huraira said,
Katada said, etc." We have not thought it worth while to give a
biographical note in every case. Those interested can consult *Ibn
Khallikan.*

[2] Cf. footnote on page 44.

form, she would have been terrified and have fled from him and not been able to hear his message.

And when Mary said, "I take refuge from you," he said unto her, "Verily I am the apostle of thy Lord to give you a pious child." Said she, " Shall there be to me a child, and no one has touched me, and I have committed no folly ?" Said he, "That is true, but thy Lord finds a miracle easy;" and when he said that, she submitted to the decree of God. And he breathed in the opening of her chemise; and she had taken it off; and when he departed from her, Mary put it on, and so she conceived Jesus, on whom be peace. Then she filled her water-jar and went back to the mosque.

Here follows an indecent explanation at considerable length. Its character may be indicated in a footnote from another source.[1]

Then she went to an eastward place, because it was in the winter, the shortest day of the year. Hasan says in relation to this tradition that therefore the

---

[1] As-Suhaili states that in "She guarded her *farj*," God intended by *farj* the opening of her shirt ; that is to say, there was no suspicion attached to her dress, she being clean in her clothes. The openings (*faruj*) of a shirt are four, namely, the two sleeves and the upper and under parts. Do not let your thoughts take you to any other than this meaning, this being an excellent metaphor, for the Kur'an is too pure in meaning, too laconic in words, too delicate in suggestions, and too beautiful in expressions, to intend that to which the imagination of the ignorant may lead, especially as the breathing (into her) of the spirit of sanctity was by the order of the Holy One, so that sanctity joined with the Holy One, and the sanctified one (Mary) thus became free from any false thought and suspicion (about her).—AD-DAMIRI's *Hayat Al-Hayawan*, p. 521.

Christians worship toward the east, because Mary
went to an Eastward place when she met Gabriel.
And there was with her at the time, they say, a
relative of her's, called Joseph the carpenter, and they
were employed in the mosque which was near Mount
Zion; and this mosque at that time was one of the
largest of their places of worship, and Mary and Joseph
did service there which was of great reward, namely,
keeping it in order and purifying it. And there were
not known at that time people who were more diligent
or more worshipful than these two.

And the first one who doubted her because she had
conceived a son was her relative and friend, Joseph
the carpenter. And when he marvelled and was surprised, and did not know what to do in regard to her, he
spoke to her concerning the matter.[1] Said El Kelbi:

[1] We condense here again and quote from the French translation of
Mirkhond's *Rauzat-us-Safa*, by Lamairesse :—

"Le charpentier Yusuf (Joseph), son cousin du côté maternel,
s'aperçut le premier de la grossesse de Mariam. Il venait habituelle-
ment adorer dans le Ville Sainte et à l'occasion causait avec Marie.
Fort affligé, il lui dit un jour : 'J'ai sur ta piété et sur ta dévotion
un soupçon dont je désire te faire part.' 'Soit,' répondit Marie.
Yusuf reprit : 'A-t-on jamais obtenu récolte sans semence ? A-t-on
jamais eu une semence qui ne provînt pas d'une moisson ?' Mariam
réplique : 'Si tu admets que Dieu a créé une moisson, elle est venue
sans semence ; si tu crois qu'il a créé une semence, celle-ci n'est pas
parvenue d'une moisson ; si tu admets que Dieu a créé en même temps
la moisson et la semence, aucune des deux ne provient de l'autre.'
Yusuf demanda ensuite : 'A-t-il jamais existé un enfant sans père ?'
'Oui,' répondit Marie, 'et même sans une mère. Adam et Ève
n'eurent ni père ni mère.' Yusuf ne contesta pas, mais il ajouta :
'Mes questions étaient purement philosophiques, maintenant,
pardonne ma hardiesse et apprends-moi comment tu es devenue

Joseph the carpenter afterwards took Mary and Jesus
to a cave, and caused them to enter, and she lived there
for forty days. Then after she had brought forth her
child, she left the cave and walked on the road; and
Jesus spake to her and said, "O my mother, all hail to
thee! because I am the servant of God and His
Messiah." And when she came to her people, and the
young child was with her, they wept and were sorrowful, because they were pious folk, saying, "O Mary!
you have done great wickedness and abomination, O
sister of Aaron." Katada said that Aaron was a pious
man, of the upright of the children of Israel, and this
was not Aaron the brother of Moses. And it is related
that he followed the funeral on a certain day when
40,000 of the children of Israel died, all of whom were
named Aaron! But Wahab said that Aaron was one of
the most corrupt of the children of Israel and taught
them corrupt practices, and that is why they compared
Mary to Aaron, saying, "Your father Amran was not
wicked, and your mother was not a transgressor nor
impure; whence, then, is there come to you this
child?"

Then Mary told them to talk to Jesus, and they grew
angry and said, "How can we speak to him who is
in the cradle, a little child?" Wahab says that then
Zachariah came to her, when she showed herself to

grosse.' Marie répondit: 'Allah m'a fait savoir qu'il enverrait au
monde son Verbe, procédant de lui-même, le Messie Isa, fils de
Miriam.'"—pp. 290-291.

the Jews, and said to Jesus, "Speak up, and give us your argument if you are so commanded." And at that instant Jesus (upon Him be peace), and He was only forty days old, said, "Verily, I am the servant of God to whom He has given a wonderful Book." And by saying this He confessed that He worshipped God and proved that Christians are liars, and established His argument against them. Amru bin Maimun said that when Mary came to her people with Jesus, they took up stones and tried to stone her, but when Jesus spake, they left her alone. It is also said that after this Jesus did not speak again until He was of the ordinary age of children who begin to talk. And God knows best.

On the Departure of Mary to Egypt.—Said God Most High in the Koran: We have made the son of Mary and His mother a sign, and given them refuge for a time and a resting-place appointed. They say that the birth of Jesus took place forty-two years after the beginning of the reign of Augustus, and fifty-one years had passed of the Kingdom of the Ashkanin, the kings of the tribes. And the kingdom at that time was in the hands of the kings of these tribes, and the sovereignty of Syria and its provinces was to Cæsar, the king of Rome. And the ruler of the provinces on behalf of Cæsar was Herod. And when Herod the king heard the news of Christ, he desired to kill Him, and it was because they had looked at a star, and they knew by their reckonings to what this referred, from a book which they had.

5

Then God sent an angel to Joseph the carpenter, and
told him what Herod desired to do, and commanded
him to flee with the young child and His mother into
Egypt; and God revealed also to Mary that she should
go to Egypt: "For if Herod gets hold of your son, he
will kill him, but when Herod dies, return then to
your country." Then Joseph put Mary and his son
upon a donkey which he had, until they came to
Egypt, and this was the place which God spoke of
in His Book. 'Abdullah bin Salaam said that the
place where they took refuge was Damascus; Abu
Huraira says it was Ramleh; and Kitada says it
was Jerusalem. Kaab says it was that part of the
world which is nearest heaven, and Abu Zaid says
it was Egypt; Dhahak said it was the plain of
Damascus, etc. etc.

Mary remained in Egypt twelve years, spinning
cotton and gleaning after the reapers. And she was
gleaning after the reapers, and when she gleaned,
she carried Jesus on one of her shoulders and her
gleaning basket on the other till He was twelve years
old. And it is related that Mohammed the son of
Ali el Bakir said : When Jesus was born and He was a
day old, it was as though He was a month old; and
when He was nine months old, His mother took Him
by the hand and led Him to the school and placed
Him between the hands of the teacher; and the
teacher said to Him, "Say, *Bismillah er-rahman er
rahim*." Then Jesus said it. The teacher said, "Say

Abjad."[1]   Then Jesus (upon whom be peace) lifted up
His head and said to him, "Do you know what *Abjad*
means?"   Then the teacher lifted up his rod to strike
Him, and Jesus said, "O teacher! do not strike me if
you know; if you do not know, ask me, so that I can
explain it to you." When the teacher said, "Explain
it to me." And Jesus said, "*Alif* means that there is
no God but God; the *ba* stands for the glory of God;
the *jím* for the majesty of God; and the *dal* for the
religion of God. *Hawwaz*: *Ha* stands for hell, and the
waw stands for woe to the people of the fire, and the
za stands for their groanings in hell. *Hatta* signifies
that their sins can never be forgiven. *Kalman* signifies
the Word of God Uncreated and Unchangeable.
Safas signifies measure for measure and part for part.
Karshat signifies that God will collect them at the
time of the resurrection." Then the teacher said to
His mother, "O Woman, take thy child, for He knows
everything and does not need a teacher."

According to another tradition it is related that
the prophet of God said: Verily, Jesus, when His
mother sent Him to be taught, and the teacher said to
Him, "Say Bismillah," replied, "What is Bismillah?"
and the teacher said, "I do not know." Jesus said,
"The *ba* is the Glory of God, and the *sín* is the sub-

[1] Abjad, the first word in a mnemonic series containing the Arabic
alphabet, following the ancient or numerical order, and used as
numerals by the Arabs until superseded by later notation. Each
word in the series is here interpreted fancifully with a play on the
Arabic root.

limity of God, and the *mîm* is the kingdom of God Most High and Exalted," etc. etc.

On the Form and Figure of Jesus. (upon Him be peace).—Said Kaab: Jesus, the son of Mary, was a ruddy man, inclining towards white. His hair was not lank, and He never oiled it. He went bare-footed; and He never owned a place, or a change of garments, or property or vesture or provisions, except His daily bread. And whenever the sun began to set, He would kneel and pray until the morning. He was in the habit of healing the sick and the lepers, and raising the dead by the will of God. He could tell those about Him what they ate in their houses, and what they laid up against the morrow. He walked on the face of the water on the sea. He had dishevelled hair, and His face was small. He was an ascetic in this world and greatly desirous of the world to come; diligent in serving God. And He was a wanderer in the earth till the Jews sought Him and desired to kill Him. Then God lifted Him up to heaven, and God knows best.

Concerning the signs and wonders which were manifested by the hand of Jesus in His youth until He became a prophet.—Wahab said that the first miracle of Jesus which people saw was as follows: His mother was living in the house of the ruler in Egypt where Joseph the carpenter left her, and this was the house where the poor congregated. Money was stolen from the treasury of the ruler, and the poor did not care.

And Mary was grieved by this occurrence. Now when Jesus saw the sorrow of His mother at what had happened to their host, He said, "O my mother! do you wish that I should show him where his property is?" And she said, "Yes, my son." He said to her, "Say to him that he gather together all the poor in his courtyard." So Mary told the ruler to gather the poor together; and when they were collected Jesus pointed out two men. One of them was blind and the other was lame. He put the lame man upon the back of the blind man and said to him, "Get up!" and the blind man said, "I am too weak to do it." Then Jesus said to him, "How were you able to do it yesterday?" And when they heard that, they struck the blind man till he got up. And when he got up, the lame man showed him the way to the treasure house. And Jesus said to the ruler, "Thus they played the trick upon the owner of the property yesterday; because the blind man helped with his strength and the lame man with his eyes." Then the blind man and the lame man said, "He speaks the truth; by God"; and they returned his property to the ruler, and he received it and put it in the treasury; and said, "O Mary! take half of it." And she said, "I am not poor enough for that." Then said the ruler, "Give it to your son"; and she said, "He is greater in dignity than I am."

Not long after the ruler desired to have the marriage of his son take place, so he made a feast and collected all the people of Egypt and fed them for two months.

And when it was finished, certain people from Syria came to see him, and he did not know of their coming until they came down upon him. And on that day he had no drink for them. And when Jesus saw his anxiety on this account, He entered some of the chambers of the ruler in which there were rows of jars; and He passed by them one by one, touching them with His hand; and every time He touched one it was filled with drink until He came to the last one. And He was at that time twelve years old.

Es Sadi said concerning another miracle of Jesus (upon Him be peace): When He was in school with His playmates, He told them what their fathers were eating. He would say, for example, to one of the boys, "Go home, for your people are doing thus and thus; and they are eating so and so; or, they have prepared for you this and this." Then the boy would run home to his people and cry until they gave him what they had been eating. Then they said to him, "Who told you of it?" and he said, "Jesus." So they kept their boys away from Him, and said, "Do not play with this sorcerer." And when they were gathered together in a house, Jesus came seeking them. And they said, "They are not here;" and He said, "What is there in this house?" They said, "Swine;" said He, "Let it be so." And when they opened the door the boys had turned into swine. And when this was noised abroad the children of Israel understood that He was a prophet. And when His mother was afraid for His life, she put Him upon a donkey and carried Him up to Egypt.

Another miracle: said Es Sadi, When Jesus and His mother went out on their wanderings throughout the earth, they came to the land of Israel and alighted in a village at the house of a man who entertained them as his guests and was kind to them. The king at that time was a mighty man and an oppressor. So one day their host came in greatly worried and sorrowful, and he entered his house, and Mary was then sitting with his wife. So she said to her, " What is the matter with your husband, for I see him sad of countenance ? " and she said, " Do not ask me." And Mary said, " Tell me, for perhaps by my hand his sorrow will be lightened." And she said, " We have a king who puts a burden upon every man of us in his turn, because he compels us to feed and to give wine to him and his soldiers on a certain day ; and if he does not do it, he punishes him. To-day it is our turn, and we have no sufficiency." Said Mary, " Say to him, ' Do not be anxious at all, for he has been kind to us, and I will command my son that He make supplication for him, and it will suffice him.' " Then Mary told Jesus. And Jesus said, " If I do it, evil will befall." Mary said, " We do not care, because he was kind to us and honoured us." Said Jesus, " Then say to him that he bring together and fill up all his vessels and pots with water, and then come and tell me." So he did so, and called Jesus. Then the water in the vessels was changed into meat and gravy, and the water in the pots was changed into wine such as men had never tasted before. So when the king came, he ate and drank and asked, "Whence is this wine?" And they said to him, "From such and such a country." Said the king, "My wine comes from the same country, but it is not as good as this." Then they mentioned another country, and when this again was a mistake and the king became suspicious, he said, "Tell me the truth"; and he said, "I will tell you. There is with me a young man who never asks God for anything but He gives it to Him. He asked God Most High, and He made the water, wine."

Now this king had a son whom he desired to be his successor; and he had died some days previous, and the king loved him more than anyone else. So he said, "If there is a man who can ask God to make water into wine, let him make intercession so that my son may live again." So they called Jesus and spoke to Him concerning this. And Jesus said to him, "Do not do it, because if he lives again, evil will befall you." The king said, "I do not care, if only I can see him." And Jesus said to him, "If I make him live for you, will you allow me and my mother to go where we please?" And he said, "Yes." So Jesus called upon God, and the young man came to life. And when the people of the kingdom saw that his son was alive, they got together their weapons and said, "This one has devoured us, and now when his death is near, he desires to have his son rule over us, who will also devour us as his father did." So they killed them, but Jesus and his mother went away.

Said Wahab: While Jesus was playing with his playmates, one of them jumped upon another and kicked him with his feet till he died. So they threw him between the arms of Jesus, and He was covered with blood; and when the people came upon them, they took notice of it and carried Him to the Kadi of Egypt, and said to him, "This boy has killed the other." So the Kadi asked Him, and Jesus said, "I do not know who killed him, and I am not his companion." They desired to fall upon Jesus (upon Him be peace), and He said to them, "Bring me the boy who was killed"; and they said, "What do you wish to do with him?" He said, "I wish to ask him who killed him." Said they, "How can he speak to you when he is dead?" They took Jesus and brought Him to the place where the boy was killed; and when Jesus offered a prayer, God raised him from the dead, and Jesus said to him, "Who killed you?" The boy said, "So and so." Then the children of Israel said, "Who is this?" and he said, "This is Jesus, the son of Mary." And they said, "Who is that with Him?" and he said, "The judge of the children of Israel." Immediately he died again. Then Jesus went back with His mother, and a great multitude followed Him. And His mother said, "Shall I defend you from them? And he said, "God will keep us, and He is the Most Merciful."

Another miracle. Said 'Atta: When Mary took Jesus, after He left school, to various workmen to learn His trade, the last to whom she gave Him were dyers. And she put Him with the chief dyer to learn the trade. So he brought together different coloured garments. Then he said to Jesus, "Now you have learned this part of your trade, and I am going out on a journey. I will not return for ten days. These garments are a different colour, and you have learned how each is to be dyed. When I come back, I hope the work will be finished." So Jesus (upon whom be peace) prepared one kind of dye, and put all the garments in it, and said to them, "By the permission of God Most High, be ye as I order. And when the dyer came back and found all the garments in one vessel, he said to Jesus, "What have you done?" He said, "I have finished the work." The dyer replied, "Where?" He said, "In this vessel." Said the dyer, "All of them?" Jesus said, "Yes." "How is it possible for them all to be in one vessel? You have spoiled the garments." Said Jesus, "Rise and see." So he arose; and Jesus pulled out a yellow garment, a green garment, a red garment, etc., according to the desire of the dyer. And he was astonished, and knew it was from God most great and glorious; and he said to the people, "Come and see what Jesus has done." So he and his friends believed in Him, and these his friends became the apostles. And God knows best.[1]

Concerning the return of Mary and Jesus (upon them be peace) to their own country after the death of Herod.— Wahab said that when Herod the king died twelve years after the birth of Jesus (upon Him be peace), God Most High revealed to Mary the news of the death of Herod and commanded her to return with her cousin Joseph the carpenter to Syria. So Jesus and His mother (upon them be peace) returned and dwelt in the mountains of Galilee, in the village of Nazareth. From this the *Nasara* (Christians) get their name. And Jesus used to learn in one hour the knowledge of a day, and in a day the knowledge of a ' month, and in a month the knowledge of a year. And when He had completed his thirtieth year, God revealed to Him that He must manifest Himself before men and call them to God; and speak parables to them, and heal their sick and palsied and their blind; and should tame and subdue

---

[1] Another miracle of the boyhood days of Jesus is given as follows : "While Jesus, the son of Mary, and John, the son of Zacharias, were once going together, they saw a wild she-goat (or ewe) in labour, upon which Jesus said to John, ' Say these words, "Hanna (Hannah) gave birth to John, and Mary gave birth to Jesus ; the earth calls thee, O young one, come forth, O young one ! " ' Hammad b. Zaid states that if these words are uttered near any woman in labour in a tribe, she will not be long in delivering by the order of God. John (Yahya) was the first one to believe in Jesus ; they were the sons of (each other's) maternal aunts, and the former was older than the latter by six months ; John was killed before the translation of Jesus to heaven."—AD-DAMIRI's *Hayat-Al-Hayawan*, p. 111.

those possessed of devils, and they died for fear of
Him. So He did what was commanded Him; and
men loved Him, and turned to Him and were pleased
with Him; and the number of those that followed
Him increased, and His reputation became great, and
perchance there collected around Him of the sick
and palsied in one hour, fifty thousand. And every
one who could get to Him, went to Him, and whosoever was not able, Jesus went to them. And He
healed them by prayer on condition of faith. And
the prayer by which He healed the sick and raised
the dead is as follows: O God! Thou art the God who
art in heaven and the God who art on earth. There
is no God in them save Thee; and Thou art the
Strong One in the heavens and the Strong One upon
earth, and there is no Strong One save Thee. And
Thou art the King of all who are in heaven and
the King of those who are on earth, and there is
no king in them save Thee. Thou art the Ruler in
heaven and the Ruler upon earth, and there is no
Ruler in them save Thee. Thy power on earth is as
Thy power in heaven, and Thy authority in heaven
is as Thy authority on earth. I ask Thee by Thy
names most gracious, for Thou art all-powerful.[1]

[1] All of the above is translated from the Arabic text of Eth-Thalabi.

IV

JESUS CHRIST ACCORDING TO TRADITION

"Traditions can never be considered as at all reliable unless they are traceable to some common origin, have descended to us by independent witnesses, and correspond with the statements of the Koran itself—always of course deducting such texts as (which is not infrequently the case) have themselves given rise to the tradition. It soon becomes obvious to the reader of Muslim traditions and commentators that both miracles and historical events have been invented for the sake of expounding a dark and perplexing text; and that even the earlier traditions are largely tinged with the mythical element."— J. M. RODWELL, *Introduction to Koran Translation,* p. 7.

"The Cross of Christ is the missing link in the Muslim's creed; for we have in Islam the great anomaly of a religion which rejects the doctrine of a sacrifice for sin, whilst its great central feast is a *Feast of Sacrifice.*"— T. H. HUGHES, *Dictionary of Islam,* p. 233.

IV

JESUS CHRIST ACCORDING TO TRADITION

HIS PUBLIC MINISTRY TO HIS SECOND COMING

BEFORE we pass on to the continuation of Eth-Tha-labi's account, it is important to remember that the death of Jesus Christ is both affirmed and denied in the Koran. In order to unify its teaching, the only escape possible was to affirm that although He died for a few hours or days, *He was not crucified.* In addition to this, Moslems add that when He comes the second time He will die again, emphasizing, as it were, the frailty of His human nature, which, even after His return from glory, is subject to death; and so contradicting all the teaching of the New Testament that "He died for sin once," and "death hath no more dominion over Him." We take up Thalabi once more:

The Story of Jesus' Disciples.—Said God Most High (in the Koran), When Jesus called them back from infidelity, He said, "Who are my helpers for God?" Then the disciples said, "We are your helpers for God.

We have believed in God, and we bear witness that we
are Moslems." And said God Most Glorious and
Praiseworthy, When it was revealed to the disciples,
that is, they were inspired to know, that they should
believe in Him and in His apostle, they said, "We
have believed and we witness that we are Moslems.
Know that the disciples were the chosen of Jesus, the
son of Mary, and His favourites; those in whom He
was pleased, and His helpers and viziers.   They were
twelve in number, and their names were: Simon, the
yellow one (pale), who was called Peter, and Andrew
his brother; James, the son of Zebedee, and Yahya his
brother; Philip and Bartholomew and Thomas and
Matthew, the toll-gatherer; James the son of Halfa,
and Liya (Levi) who was called Thaddeus, and Simon
the Canaanite, and Jude Iscariot (upon them be peace)."
And the learned men are disagreed as to why they had
these names.[1]   Said Ibn 'Abbas: They were fishermen
who plied their trade, and Jesus passed by them and
said to them, "What are you doing?" and they said,
"We are catching fish."   And He said, "Will you not
walk with me, so that we may catch men?"   And
they said to Him, "How is that?"   And He said,
"We will call the people to God."   They said, "Who

[1] The apostles are not called *rusul* as Mohammed is called *rasûl*
(apostle), but *Hawari* (Surah 3 : 4, 5 ; 4 : 111, 112 ; 61 : 14). The word
is derived from the Æthiopic *hora*=to go, *hawarya*, an apostle.
According to Beidhawi it comes from *hawira*, to be white, and was
given to the disciples of Jesus because of their purity of life and sincer-
ity. Others say because they wore white garments or dyed them white.

art Thou?" And He said, "I am Jesus, the son of Mary, and servant of God, and His apostle." And they said, "Will any of the prophets be above Thee?" And He said, "Yes, the Arabian prophet." So they followed Him, and believed in Him, and departed with Him.

Said Sa'di: They were sailors. Ibn Artat said: They were dyers, and they were called by their name, *Hawari*, because they dyed garments and made them white.

It hath been told us by Ibn Fatuh in his tradition received from Mass'ab, that the disciples were twelve men who followed Jesus; and when they were hungry they said, "O Spirit of God! we are hungry." Then He would strike with His hand upon the ground, whether it was a plain or a mountain, and there would come forth to every man of them two loaves, and they would eat them. And when they were thirsty they would say, "O Spirit of God! we are thirsty." And He would strike the earth, whether it was a plain or a mountain, and water would gush forth, and they would drink. Then they said, "O Spirit of God! who is happier than we: when we wish, Thou dost feed us, and when we are desirous, Thou dost give us drink, and we believe in Thee and have followed Thee." Said Jesus, "The best of you is he who works with his hands and eats what he has earned." So it is related that they began to make clothes for their living.

Said Ibn 'Aun: One of the kings of the earth made a feast and invited the people, and Jesus was one of the
6

guests. And the repast did not grow less. Then the king
said to Him, "Who art Thou?" and He said, "I am
Jesus, the son of Mary." Said the king, "I will leave
my kingdom and follow Thee." So he departed with
those that followed Him, and they were the disciples.
And some say this was the dyer and his friends, whose
story we have already related. Said Dhahak: They
were called *Hawariyûn* (disciples) because of the purity
of their hearts. And said 'Abdullah ibn Mubarak:
They were so called because they were luminous with
light. On them was the sign of worship, its brightness
and its purity. And the old meaning of *Hûr* among
the Arabs is intensity of whiteness. And Hassan said:
The disciples were the helpers; and Katada said: They
are the ones who became the caliphs after Christ.
[Here the author quotes Mohammed as saying that
every apostle had his disciples, and then goes into a
discussion as to who were the disciples (*Hawariyûn*)
of Mohammed.]

*An account of the special characteristics of Jesus (upon
Him be peace), and the miracles which came from His
hand after His call until He was lifted up (God's blessing
be upon Him).*—Among His special characteristics was
this, that God strengthened Him by the Holy Spirit.
Said the Book of God: And We strengthened Him by
the Holy Spirit. A similar expression is used in the
Surah of the Table when God said, O Jesus, son of
Mary, remember My mercy upon Thee and upon Thy
mother when We strengthened thee with the Holy

Spirit. And the learned are disagreed in regard to the significance of these words. Rabi'a said: It is the Spirit which was breathed upon Him, which is related to God Himself in the same sense as we use the words *House of God* and *Camel of God* in the Koran. And the Holy One He is God Most High, as is indicated by the expression "Spirit from Him" and the expression "We breathed in Him of our Spirit." Others say that the significance of Holy is purity, the Pure Spirit. And Jesus (upon Him be peace) was called a Spirit because He had no male parent. He was not born after the manner of other men [the expressions here used are unfit for translation], but He was created by the command of God. Kaab and Sadi, however, say that the Holy Spirit is Gabriel, and that Jesus was strengthened by Gabriel's presence because he was His companion and His helper, going with Him wherever He went until He took Him up to heaven. And Seyyid, the son of Jabir, and Obeid, the son of Amir, state, The Holy Spirit is the name of God Most High, and by it Jesus raised the dead and showed men these wonders.

And among his characteristics was that God taught Him the Gospel and the Torah, and He read them from memory, as God said in His book, "When we taught you the book," namely, by memory. It is said that memory consists of ten parts, and that Jesus possessed nine of them, as well as wisdom and a knowledge of the Torah and the Gospel.

And among His characteristics was that He created

birds from clay, as God Most High said, Truly I have come to you with a sign from your Lord. I will create for you from clay the appearance of birds; I will breathe upon them and they will fly, by permission of God. And in accordance with this word of the Koran Jesus fashioned clay into the form of birds, and then He breathed upon them and they were birds, by permission of God. And He only created bats. And He selected this variety because the bat is the most perfect of birds in its powers, because it suckles its young, and gives birth to them, and has teeth, and is a mammal, and flies. Wahab said the birds would fly while men looked at them, and when they disappeared from sight they fell down, to distinguish the work of a mere man from the work of God Most High; and that it might be known that the only one who is perfect is God Most High.

And among His characteristics was that He cured the blind from birth and lepers, as God said in His book, And Thou shalt heal the blind and lepers, by My permission. And these two special diseases were selected because physicians could not cure them; and as medicine was the most celebrated science in the days of Jesus, He showed them a miracle after this sort. And it is related that Jesus (upon Him be peace) passed by a village in which there were blind people, and He said, Who are these? They told Him, These are people who sought for justice, and they put out their eyes with their own hands. And

Jesus said to them, "What made you do it?" and they said, "We feared the punishment of the judge, so we did it ourselves, as you see." And He said to them, " Ye are the learned, and the judges, and the advocates and the noble are the ignorant. Now wipe your eyes with your hands and say 'Bismillah'"; and they did so, and immediately all of them had their sight.

And among His characteristics was raising of the dead by the permission of God. As God said, And when Thou dost come, the dead come forth by My permission. And among the dead whom He raised was Lazarus, His friend. His sister sent to Jesus, saying, Your brother Lazarus is dying; so He came to him. And He was three days' journey away from him, and when He and His friends came, they found that he had already died three days ago. And He said to his sister, Depart with us to his grave; and it was in a rock built up like a tomb. Then Jesus said, O God! Lord of the seven heavens and the three earths, verily, Thou hast sent me to the children of Israel to call them to Thy religion, and Thou hast told them that I can raise the dead by Thy permission, so raise up Lazarus. Then Lazarus arose and came out from his grave, and remained alive and had children.

And among those whom He raised from the dead was the son of an old woman, and this is the story. Jesus passed in His wanderings with the disciples by a city, and He said, " Verily in this city there is treasure. Who will go and get it out for us?" And they said, "O Spirit of God, no stranger can enter this city, for they will kill him." And said Jesus, "Stay where you are until I return." And He went till He came to the city and stood at the gate and said, "Peace be to you, O people of this place; I am a stranger: give me to eat." And an old woman said to him, "Don't you wish me to go with you to the governor so that you may say to him, 'Give me to eat'?" And while Jesus was standing at the door, behold, a young man, the son of the old woman, approached. Jesus said to him, "Make me thy guest this night;" and the young man replied as did his mother, the old woman. And Jesus said to him, "I tell you that if you will do it, I will marry you to the daughter of the king. The young man said to Him, "Either you are crazy, or you are Jesus the son of Mary." And He said, "I am Jesus." So he gave Him lodging, and He spent the night with him; and when He arose in the morning, He said to him, "Take your breakfast and go to the king, and say to him, 'I have come to be engaged to your daughter.' Then he will command them to strike you and cast you out. So the young man went to the king, and said to him, "I have come that I may be engaged to your daughter." So he commanded him to be beaten, and they did so, and cast him out. Then the young man came back to Jesus and told Him the news. And Jesus said, "On the morrow

go to him again with the same request, and he
will give you the same punishment, but less." So
the young man did as he was told, and they struck
him with fewer blows than the first time, and he
came back to Jesus and told Him. Then Jesus
said, "Go to him to-morrow, and he will say to you,
'I will marry you to my daughter upon one condition,
and my condition is a castle of gold and silver, and
all that is in it of gold and silver and precious
stones.' Then say to him, 'I will do it.' And if he
sends some one with you, go outside with him, for
you will find it, and nothing will happen to you."
Then he went in to the king and became engaged
to his daughter; and the king said, "Will you give
her the dowry according to my desire?" And he said,
"What is your desire?" And he commanded in accordance with what Jesus had told him. So he said,
"Yes, I am willing. Send with me some one who
will give it to you." So he sent a man with him,
and he gave him what the king wished, and the
people all marvelled at that. And so the king gave
him his daughter. And the young man marvelled
and said, "O Spirit of God, you are able to do things
like this, and still you are poor?" And Jesus said
to him, "I have preferred that which remains to that
which fades away." Said the young man, "I also prefer
it, and I will be your companion." So he forsook
the world and followed Jesus. Then Jesus took him
by the hand and brought him to his companions,

and said to them, "This is the treasure concerning whom I told you." And the son of the old woman remained with Him till he died. And when they passed by with him on the bier, Jesus cried to God; and the young man sat up and took up the bier from the necks of the men that carried it, dressed himself, and carried it on his back and went back to his people, and remained alive; and to him also children were born.

And among the miracles of raising the dead was the daughter of the toll - gatherer. They said to Jesus, "Will you raise her, for she died yesterday?" And He called upon God Most High, and she lived.

Among those He raised was Shem, the son of Noah. Said the disciples unto Him, when He was describing Noah's ark, "If you had sent us some one who had seen the ark and could describe it to us, we would believe." So He arose and came to a little hill, and struck it with His hand and took a handful of the earth and said, "This is the grave of Shem, the son of Noah. If you wish, I will raise him for you." They said, "Yes;" and He called upon God by His greatest name, and struck the hill with His staff and said, "Come to life by permission of God." Then Shem, the son of Noah, came forth from his grave, white haired. And he said, "Is this the resurrection day?" Said Jesus, "No, but I have called you out in the name of God Most High." Shem had lived five hundred years and he was still young. So he told them the news of the ark. Then Jesus said to him, " Die ; " and he said, " Only on one condition, that God protects me from the agonies of death." Jesus granted his request by permission of God ; and all this is mentioned in the story of Noah the prophet (upon whom be peace).

And among those whom He raised from the dead was Ezra (upon whom be peace). They said to Jesus, Raise him from the dead, or we will burn you with fire. So they collected a great lot of wood of the vine ; and in those days it was the custom to bury people in coffins made of stone. When they found the grave of Ezra with his name written on the outside, they tried their best to open it and were not able, so they could not get him out from the grave. They went back to Jesus and told Him, and He handed them a vessel with some water and said, Sprinkle this upon his grave ; and they did so. Then the coffin was easily opened, and they came with him to Jesus. And behold, he was wrapped in a shroud, and the earth does not consume the bodies of the prophets. Therefore when they took off his garment, He began to sprinkle the water upon his body and his head. Then He said, " Come to life, O Ezra, by permission of God Most High ; " and behold, he sat up in the sight of their eyes. And they said to Ezra, " Will you not witness to this man, namely, Jesus ? " And he said, " I witness that He is the servant of God and His apostle. And they said to Jesus, "Ask your Lord to allow him to stay with us, that he may be alive among us." And Jesus said, "Take him back to his grave;" and he died. And some believed in Jesus, the son of Mary, and some were rebellious.[1]

[1] To complete this series of miracles we add one more story popular in Arabia : Historians and authors of stories of the deeds (of the ancients), relate that a man among the Beni-Israil in the time of Jesus, whose name was Ishak, had a wife (cousin) who was one of the handsomest women of her time. He was devotedly attached to her, and she happened to die. He therefore stayed near her grave, and for a long time never flagged in visiting it. One day Jesus happened to pass by him while he was by her grave crying. So Jesus asked him, "What makes you cry, O Ishak ?" He replied, "O Spirit of God, I had a cousin who was also my wife, and I used to love her very much ; she is now dead, and this is her grave. I have no patience, and her separation has killed me." Jesus asked him, "Do you wish me to revive her for you, by the permission of God ?" And he replied, "Yes, O Spirit of God." Jesus then stood over the grave and said, "Rise up, O dweller in this grave, by the permission of God," whereupon the grave clave open, and there stepped forth out of it a black slave with fire coming forth from his nostrils, his eyes, and other openings in his face, and saying, "There is no deity but God, and Jesus is His Spirit, His Word, His Servant, and His Apostle." Ishak said, "O Spirit and Word of God, this is not the grave in which my wife is, but it is this one," pointing to another grave. Jesus then said to the black slave, "Return to the state in which you were," upon which he fell down dead, and he buried him in his grave. He then stood over the other grave and said, "Rise up, O dweller in this grave, by the permission of God," and thereupon the woman rose up, scattering off the dust from her face. Jesus asked him, "Is this your wife ?" and he replied, "Yes, O Spirit of God." Jesus then said, "Take her then by the hand and go away." He therefore took her and went away, but having been overcome by sleep he said to her, "The want of sleep over your grave has killed me ; I wish therefore to rest." She replied, "Do so." So he placed his head on her lap and slept. While he was asleep, the king's son happened to pass by her ; he was beautiful and handsome, had a large frame (of body) and was mounted

Among His characteristics is knowledge of secret things, for He used to tell them what they ate, and what they treasured up in their houses. Said El Kalbi: When Jesus healed the blind and the lepers and raised the dead, they said, "This is a sorcerer, but let Him tell us what we eat and what we drink in secret, and we will believe." So He told them what

on a beautiful courser. When she saw him, love for him entered her mind, and she stood up hurriedly for him ; and when he saw her, love for her also entered his mind; so she came to him and said to him, "Take me." He therefore caused her to mount behind him on his courser and went away. When her husband woke up from his sleep, he looked about for her, but not finding her, he went in search of her, following the footsteps of the courser. He at last overtook them and said to the [king's son, "Give me my wife and cousin." But she denied it, saying, " I am the slave-woman of the king's son ;" and he said, "No, you are my wife and my cousin." She then said, "I do not know you, I am only the king's son's slave-woman." The king's son then said to him, " Do you want to spoil my slave-woman ?" upon which Ishak said, "Verily, by God, she is my wife, and Jesus the son of Mary has revived her for me by the permission of God, after she had died." While they were thus quarrelling, Jesus happened to pass that way, so Ishak said to him, "O Spirit of God, is not this my wife whom you have revived for me by the permission of God ?" and he replied, "Yes ;" but she said, "O Spirit of God, he lies ; I am the slave-woman of the king's son." The king's son also said, "This is my slave-woman." Jesus therefore asked her, "Are you not the one whom I have revived by the permission of God ?" and she replied, " No, by God, O Spirit of God," upon which he said to her, "Return to us what we have given you," and she fell down dead. Jesus then said, "Whoever wants to see a man whom God caused to die an unbeliever, then revived him and caused him to die a second time, a Muslim, let him look at the black slave, and whoever wants to see a woman whom God caused to die a believer, then revived her and caused her to die a second time an unbeliever, let him look at this one." Ishak the Jew then swore to God that he would never marry again, and went away crying into the deserts.—AD-DAMIRI's *Hayat-Al-Hayawan*, pp. 497–498.

they would eat the following day, or what they had eaten in the past.

Another characteristic was His walking upon the water. It is related that He went out once on His wanderings, and there was with Him a man of short stature; and he was a close companion of Jesus. And when they approached the sea, He said, " In the name of God, good health and certainty." So He walked upon the face of the waters. Then the man of short stature said, "In the name of God, in health and certainty;" and he walked upon the face of the waters. Then astonishment seized him, and he said, " This is Jesus, the Spirit of God, walking on the water, and I am walking on the water." No sooner had he said so than he began to sink, and he cried aloud to Jesus to pull him out. And He said, " What was it that you said, O man of short stature?" So he told Him; and Jesus said to him, "You have put yourself in the wrong place and God is angry at what you said; so repent to God." And the man repented, and regained his position with Jesus. [Here the author draws a comparison between Mohammed and Christ, and quotes Mohammed as saying that if Jesus had possessed more faith and trust, He would have walked not only on the water, but on the air.]

Other Traditions concerning Jesus Christ.—Wahab said: Jesus (on whom be peace) went out one day on His wanderings, and a Jew accompanied Him, who had two loaves of bread, and Jesus had only one loaf.

Said Jesus unto him, "Share me your food; and the Jew said, "Yes;" but when he saw that Jesus had only one loaf, he was sorry. And when Jesus went up to pray, His companion went aside and ate one of his loaves. When Jesus had finished His prayer, He asked him, "Where is the other loaf?" and he replied, "I had only one." So they both ate one loaf, and then they departed. [The story goes on to relate how Jesus performed miracle after miracle (mostly of an inane character), which convinced the Jew of His divine mission; and how the Jew continued to deny having eaten the loaf, until finally the Jew was punished for his greed, and Christ went on His way.]

Concerning the sending down of the Table.—Said God Most High, in the Koran, When the disciples said, " O Jesus, son of Mary, is thy Lord able to cause a table to come down from heaven?" He said, "Trust in God if you are believers." The learned are at disagreement concerning how the table came down, and its character, and what was upon it. Katada says in a tradition which he got from Jaber, who got it from Omar, who got it from Yasar, who received it from the Apostle of God (upon him be prayers and peace): The table came down, and upon it was bread and meat, and this was because they asked Jesus for food to eat, which would not prove insufficient. He said, "I will do it, and it will abide with you as long as you do not hide it or conceal it; but if you do that, it will punish you." And the first day had not passed by when they began to deceive and hide of it; and some of the traditions relate that they stole of it, for they said, It will not come down always. So the table was taken up, and those who deceived were turned into apes and swine. And Ibn 'Abbas said that Jesus said, " O Children of Israel, fast ye for thirty days, and then ask God whatsoever you wish, and He will give it to you." So they fasted thirty days, and when they were ended they said, " O Jesus, whenever we work for anybody and we finish his job, he feeds us. Behold we fasted to God, and we are hungry; now ask God that He make a table come down to us from heaven." Then Jesus put on sackcloth and sprinkled Himself with ashes and called upon God Most High, and said, " O God, our Lord, cause to come down to us a table from heaven." Then the angels brought the table, upon which were seven loaves and seven fishes, and they placed it between their hands and they ate of it from the first to the last. 'Atta the son of Ibn Saib relates that when the table came down to the children of Israel it contained all manner of food except meat. 'Attiah al 'Ufi said that a big fish came down from heaven in which was the taste of all kinds of food. Katada said that when the table came down from heaven it had on it the fruits of paradise, and it came down every morning and every night wherever they happened to be, like the manna and the quails to the children of Israel in the wilderness. Wahab said: God made a barley loaf to come down and two fishes, and this was sufficient for all of them. Some would come and eat and depart satisfied, and others would follow them and eat, until they had all eaten and there was food remaining. Kaab said: Verily the table came down from heaven, upside down, and the angels flew with it between heaven and earth, and all kinds of meat and food were on it. Makátal and Kalbi said that God heard Jesus (upon Him be peace), and said, "Verily, I will make a table come down to you as you have desired, and whosoever eats of this food and does not believe in Me, I will make him an example and a curse to those that follow after." They said, "We are agreed." So He called Simon, and he was the best of the apostles, and He said to him, "Have you any food?" Simon said, "I have two small fishes and six loaves." And He said, "Give them to me." So Jesus cut them up into tiny pieces, and said, "Sit down upon the grass;" and they sat down in companies of ten. Then Jesus arose and called upon God Most High, and He answered Him and sent the blessing upon it, and the bread became loaves, and the fish became whole fish. Then Jesus got up and walked about, and threw before each company handfuls. Then He said, "Eat, in the name of God." And the food increased until they all had a great sufficiency; and there was food remaining, and the number of people was five thousand and over. Then the people said, "We have borne witness that Thou art the servant of God and His apostle."

Then at another time they asked Him, and God sent

down five loaves and two fishes, and He did with them as He did at the first. And when the people went back to their villages and spread this report, some of those who had not observed it laughed and said, " Woe be unto you; verily, He hath bewitched your eyes." So those to whom God wished good, retained their sight; and those to whom He wished punishment, returned unto their unbelief and were changed into monkeys and swine.

'Atta bin Abi Rabah relates that no one followed Jesus who was His equal; and He never scolded an orphan; and He never laughed immoderately; and He never even drove a fly from off His face; and He never broke a promise once given;[1] and He never was frivolous. And when the disciples asked that He should make a table come down, He said, "O God, send down upon us a table from heaven, and furnish us with food upon it that we may eat, for Thou art the best of providers." Then a large, red, covered dish came down between two clouds, a cloud above it and a cloud below it; and they were looking at it. And it came down slowly until it came in their presence. Then Jesus wept and said, " O God, make me of the thankful ones; and make it a mercy to us, and do not make it an example and a punishment." And when they looked upon it, they saw a sight which no one had seen before, and they never smelled a meal better than

---

[1] The text here is very obscure; this is the best rendering I could find.

this meal. Then Jesus said to them, " Let the best of you in good works uncover the dish and say grace and eat from it." Then said Simon, the pale one, the chief of the apostles, " You are the one to do it rather than we." Then Jesus got up and performed the ablution, and prayed a long prayer and wept very much. Then He took off the cloth cover and said, " In the Name of God, the best of Providers." And behold, it was a fish, broiled, without scales and without bones; overflowing with oil; and at its head was a pot of salt, and at its tail some vinegar, and around it all sorts of vegetables except leeks. And there were also five loaves of bread: upon one of them there were olives, and upon another was honey; upon another, butter; upon the fourth, cheese; and upon the fifth, salted meat. And Simon said, " O Spirit of God, is this food from this world or from the other world?" Jesus said, " What ye see is not the food of this world nor of the other world, but God has created it by His mighty power; eat, in accordance with your request, as much as ye like, and there will be enough for you." Then they said, " O Spirit of God, show us another miracle beside this." And Jesus said, " O fish, live, by permission of God." Then the fish shook itself, and its scales returned upon it, and its bones, and they were terrified. Said Jesus, " Why ask a thing which, when I give, you do not like? But I do not wish to frighten you; O fish, go back as you were, by permission of God." And the fish returned to its broiled state as it was. Then they said, " O Spirit of

7

God, you be the first to eat from it, and then we will eat." Jesus said, "God forbid that I should eat, but those who have asked for it shall eat it." And they were afraid to eat from it, so Jesus invited the poor, and the sick, and the lepers, and the maimed, and the halt, and said to them, "Eat that which God has provided for you, and may you have good health and the others punishment." And those that ate of it were thirteen hundred men and women, of the poor and needy, and the sick and the lepers, and all of them were filled. And Jesus looked upon the fish, and behold, it was as it was before when it came down from heaven. Then the table flew back while they were looking, until it disappeared from them. And none of those that were sick on that day ate from it but they got well, and the weak became strong; and no poor man but became rich, and remained so until his death. So the disciples and those who did not eat repented. And it came to pass that when it came down, the rich and the poor, the small and the great, men and women, crowded together round it; and it came down for forty mornings; but when the shadows lengthened, it went up again while they beheld, and disappeared from their sight. And it came down irregularly: one day it would come and another day not, like the camel of Thamud. And God revealed to Jesus, "Surely I have prepared my table and my food for the poor, not for the rich." And this did not please the rich, so that they doubted and made men to doubt, and they said, "Do you really think a table came down from heaven?" Then Jesus said to them, "Ye have perished, and deserve the punishment of God." And God Most High revealed to Jesus, "Truly I have laid two conditions upon those that belie my miracle, if they continue to disbelieve after it comes down to them, and I will punish them with a severe punishment. Then Jesus said, "If you punish them, they are your servants; and if you forgive them, you are the mighty and wise." So God changed three hundred and thirty of them in one night; men who were with their families in bed; and when they arose in the morning they were swine, wandering about in the streets and among the sewers and eating filth. And when the people saw this, they were terrified at Jesus, the son of Mary, and they wept, and the friends of those who were changed into swine also wept. And when the swine saw Jesus, they wept, and they went round about Him; and Jesus called them by their names, one after the other, and they wept and wagged their heads and were not able to speak. And they lived three days and then died.

And among His characteristics was His being taken up into heaven. When God said, "O Jesus, verily, I will cause you to die, and will raise you to myself and will purify you above those who disbelieve" (the Koran). And their saying, "Verily we have killed the Messiah, Jesus the son of Mary, the apostle of God; but they did not kill Him, and they did not

crucify Him, but," etc., until the Koran verse says,
"But God raised Him to Himself, and God is Most
Mighty and Wise." Concerning these Koran verses,
Kalbi says that Jesus (upon whom be peace) met a
mob of Jews; and when they saw Him, they said,
"There comes the sorcerer, the son of the sorceress;"
and they thrust out Him and His mother. And when
Jesus saw that, He called to God and said, "O God,
Thou art my Lord, and I am of Thy Spirit, and by
Thy word am I created; and I did not come to them
on my own account. O God, curse them that curse
me and curse my mother." And God answered His
prayer, and changed those who cursed Him and His
mother into swine. And when the chief of the Jews
saw that, he was terrified and affrighted, and the
Jews agreed that Jesus should be killed. So they
collected together on a certain day, and began to
ask Him questions, but He said to them, "O company
of Jews, verily God hates you." Then they hated
Him because of that saying, with a strong hatred,
and gathered together to murder Him. Then God
Most High sent Gabriel (upon whom be peace), who
caused Him to enter into a hovel and concealed Him
on the roof. Then God Most High lifted Him from
its parapet. Then the chief of the Jews commanded
one of his men who was called Phelatanus, that he
should enter the hovel and kill Him. And when
Phelatanus entered he did not see Him, and he
remained behind a long time, so they thought that

he was killing Him. Then God made him appear like Jesus, and when he came out they thought he was Jesus and they killed him and crucified him.

Wahab relates that Jesus, when God Most High made Him know that He was about to leave the world, was terrified at death and in great doubts, so He called together the disciples and made them a meal; and He said to them, Stay with me this night, for I have need of you. And when they came to Him that night, He gave them a supper and stood up to serve them; and when they had finished the meal, He washed their hands, and gave them commandments and wiped their hands with His garment. And this seemed strange to them, and they despised Him. Then He said to them, "Unless you return the thing which I have done, I have no part in you and you have no part in me." And He repeated this, and when He had finished He said to them, "What I have done to you this night by serving you with food and washing your hands with my hand, has not been except that ye might be equals on my account; for ye see that I am best among you. Do not therefore be proud the one above the other, but let every one humble himself for the other, and give up his own will for the others, as I have given up my will for you. But in regard to the need which I said I felt for you, my request is that you call upon God for me and persevere in your prayer that He may put off my time of death." And when they arranged themselves for prayer and desired

to persevere, God sent upon them sleep, so that they
were not able to pray. Then Jesus began to awaken
them and to say, "God be praised! can you not be
patient for a single night and help me in it?" And
they said, " By God, we do not know what is the matter
with us. We were anxious to keep awake the night,
but we were unable to keep awake; and whenever we
wished to pray, some one prevented it." Then Jesus
said, " The shepherd is going away and the sheep will
stay behind." And He continued to speak words of
this sort concerning Himself. Then He said, " Verily,
one of you will disbelieve in me before the cock
crows three times; and one of you will sell me for
a few dirhems, and then he will devour his hire."
Then they went out and scattered, and the Jews
were seeking Him; and they took Simon, one of the
disciples, and said, " This is one of His companions."
Then he became anxious and said, " I am not of His
companions," and they left him. Then another took
hold of him in the same way; then he heard the
voice of the cock and wept, for it made him sorrowful.
When it was morning one of the disciples came to
those Jews and said to them, " What will you give me
if I indicate to you where He is?" And they agreed
with him for thirty dirhems; and he took them and
showed them where Jesus was. So they took Him
and bound Him with ropes and led Him out; and
while they were leading Him, they kept saying, " Thou
art He that didst raise the dead, and cure the blind

and the lepers, now why cannot you loosen yourself
from these ropes?" And they spat upon Him and
put thorns upon Him; and they erected the wood to
crucify Him upon it. And when they came to crucify
Him upon the tree, the earth was darkened, and God
sent angels, and they descended between them and
between Jesus; and God cast the likeness of Jesus
upon him who had betrayed Him, and his name was
Judas. And they crucified him in His stead, and they
thought that they crucified Jesus. Then God made
Jesus to die for three hours, and then raised Him up
to heaven; and this is the meaning of the Koran verse,
" Verily, I will cause Thee to die, and raise Thee unto
me, and purify Thee above those who disbelieve."

And when he who resembled Jesus was crucified,
Mary his mother came, and another woman whom
Jesus had cured of possession; and they wept at the
feet of the one who was crucified. Then Jesus came
to them and said, " For whom are ye weeping?" And
they said, " For Thee." Then He said, " Truly God
Most High hath lifted me up and no evil has befallen
me. Verily, this person only resembled me to them."

And Makátal said: Verily, the Jews appointed a
man to keep guard over Jesus, and to go wherever
He went; and when Jesus went up a mountain, an
angel came and lifted Him up to heaven. Then
God made the man who watched Him resemble Jesus,
and the Jews thought that it was Jesus; so they took
him. And he kept on saying, " I am not Jesus; I am

So and So, the son of So and So ; " but they would not
believe him, and they killed and crucified him.   Katada
said : It has been related that the Prophet of God, Jesus,
said to His companions, "Which of you is willing to
take my form, and he will be killed."   Then a man
of the crowd said, "I, O Prophet of God."   So he was
killed, and God prevented them from killing Jesus
and lifted Him up to Himself.   And it is said that
the man who resembled Jesus and was crucified in
His place was an Israelite called Ashua (this is the
common form of Joshua, or Jesus), the son of Kandir.
And God knows best.

*An account of the Descent of Jesus from Heaven seven
days after His Ascension.*—Said Wahab and others of
those who are learned in books : When God lifted up
Jesus, He tarried in heaven seven days.   Then God said
to Him, " Your enemies, the Jews, are trying to prevent
your covenant with your companions, so go down to
them and give them commandment ; and go to Mary
Magdalene, for no one is weeping for you as much as
she is, and no one is sorrowful for you as much as she
is.   So go down to her, and tell her that she will be
the first to meet you ; and instruct her to gather
together your disciples, so that you may send them
throughout the earth, calling men to the worship of
God."

Now the story of Mary Magdalene is that she
belonged to the children of Israel from a little village
of Antioch, called Magdala ; and she was a pious

woman, but she had a flow of blood and was not purified from it. So the learned of Israel tried to cure her, but she was not cured; she only concealed her sickness from them. And when she heard of the coming of Jesus (upon Him be peace), and how God cured people at His hand, she approached Him, hoping for a cure. When she saw Jesus and the dignity with which God had clothed Him, she was ashamed, and came up from behind and touched His back. Then Jesus said, "Some one hath touched me for a cure; and God hath granted her her desire and purified her with my purity."

So when God commanded Jesus to come down to her seven days after His ascension, He came down upon her, and a mountain burned with light when He came down. So the disciples gathered together, and He sent them out into the world to call men to God. Then God took Him up, and clothed Him with feathers and covered Him with light; and deprived Him of all desire for food and drink. And He flies with the angels around the throne. So He is human and angelic, and earthly and heavenly.

And the disciples scattered as He had commanded them, [and that night on which He came down is a night of glory with the Christians. Now they say that Peter turned his face to Rome; and Andrew and Matthew to the country of the cannibals; and Thomas and Levi to the land of the East; and Philip and Jude to Kairwan and Africa'; and John to Ephesus, a

village of the companions of the cave; and James and
his brother to Jerusalem, which is the Holy Land;
and Bartholomew to Arabia, that is Hejaz; and Simon
to the land of Barbar.   And every one of the disciples
when he came to the people to whom he was sent,
spoke in their language.

Here ends the account of Eth-Thalabi.   It needs no
comment.   Other accounts of the death, resurrection,
and return of Jesus Christ, however, add new legends
about Jesus and put new touches to the Moslem
caricature of the Christ.   Karmani relates that Jesus
commended His mother at the time of His death to
the care of two men, namely, Simon and John; and
He said to them, "Take care of her, and do not leave
her at all."   Then God lifted Him up and clothed Him
with feathers, etc.   Mary lived after Jesus was taken
up into heaven six years, and her age was fifty-three
years.   Then she died and was buried in the Church
of the Incarnation in Jerusalem.   But it is also related
by Abu-'l-Leeth, the Samarkandi, that Mary died
before Jesus was taken up into heaven, and that Jesus
attended her funeral Himself.

Abu Huraira says that the apostle of God (upon
Him be peace) said: All the prophets are brethren.
Although their mothers are different, their religion is
one, and I am the nearest of all men to Jesus, because
there was no prophet between Him and me.   And the
days will come when He will come down upon you and

judge with a righteous judgment, for He will come down to my people ; and when you see Him you will know Him, for He is a man neither tall nor short, between red and white, with dishevelled hair as if it rained from His head. And He will break the Cross, and kill the swine, and take away the poll-tax ; property will be plentiful, and He will grant peace, and fight for the religion of Islam until God shall destroy in His day the people of every other faith except Islam, and worship shall be God's alone. And in His day God will destroy the anti-Christ, who will be slain by His hand and those of His servants ; and there will be safety in the land, so that the lion will herd with camels and the leopard with kine, and the wolves with the sheep ; and little children shall play with serpents, and they will not harm them. Then Jesus will tarry in the earth forty years, will marry a wife from the daughters of Ghassan and will have children. Then He will die in Medina, and be buried next to the grave of Omar bin Khitab (may God be pleased with him), and blessed be Abu Bakr and Omar, who will be raised in the resurrection between two prophets.

In Burton's *Pilgrimage to El Medina and Mecca*, he refers to this tradition in these words, and gives a sketch of the *Hujrah*.

" It is popularly asserted that in the Hujrah there is now spare place for only a single grave, reserved for Isa bin Maryam after his second coming. The historians of Al-Islam are full of tales proving that though many of their earlier saints, as Osman the

Caliph and Hasan the Imam, were desirous of being buried there ; and that although Ayishah, to whom the room belonged, willingly acceded to their wishes, son of man has not yet been able to occupy it."

"The *Hujrah*, or tomb in which Mohammed died and was buried, was originally the apartment of 'Ayesha, the Prophet's favourite wife. At present it consists of an irregular square of fifty-five feet, separated from the mosque of the Prophet by a passage about twenty-six feet wide. Inside the *Hujrah* there are three tombs, supposedly those of Mohammed, Abu Bakr, and Omar, surrounded by a stone wall, or some say by strong planking. Whatever the material may be, it is covered by a curtain, and the outer railing is separated by a darker passage from the inner, and is of iron work painted green and gold. Above the *Hujrah* is a green dome surmounted by a large gilt crescent. There is much confusion among Moslems in regard to the whole arrangement of this grave chamber. Fatimah, the Prophet's daughter, is supposed to be buried in a separate part of the building. Mohammed is said to be stretched full length on his right side, with the right palm supporting the right cheek and his face toward Mecca. Close behind him Abu Bakr is placed, whose face fronts Mohammed's shoulder ; then Omar, who occupies the same position with respect to his predecessor. The space left for the grave of Jesus when He returns to earth, occupies the same relation described above, to the grave of Omar, as can be seen on Burton's sketch.

"There are reasons for doubting whether the prophet is really buried in the mosque raised to his honour. No less than twelve arguments can be given against the supposition.[1] The garden annexed to the tomb is called *ar Raudha*. The *Hujrah* has four gates, all kept locked except the fourth one, which admits only the officers in charge of the treasure, the eunuchs who sweep the floor, light the lamps, and carry away the presents thrown into the enclosure by Moslem devotees. It is commonly asserted that many early Moslem saints and warriors desired to be

---

[1] See Zwemer, *Arabia the Cradle of Islam*, pp. 47, 48.

THE PROPHET'S MOSQUE AT AL-MADINAH.

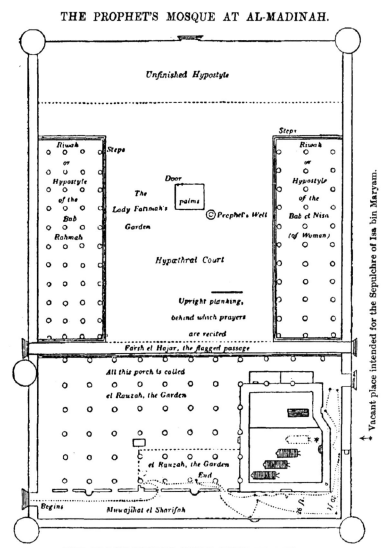

THE PLACE WHERE JESUS WILL BE BURIED.

(From Burton's " Pilgrimage to Madinah and Mecca.")

buried in the remaining space next to the grave of Omar, but that by Mohammed's own wish it was reserved for 'Isa on his second coming and death. When Medina was taken by the Wahabis in 1804, their chief stripped the tombs of all valuables and proclaimed that all the prayers and exclamations addressed to it were idolatrous. At present, however, many superstitious practices are indulged in, and Medina is almost as much a centre of pilgrimage as Mecca.

"All Moslem pilgrims, therefore, know of the place where Jesus the Messiah is to be buried."[1]

We are indebted to C. H. A. Field for the following account of the trial of our Lord before the Sanhedrin and Pilate. It occurs in the Dabistan of Mohsin Fani (A.D. 1647), and resembles the Gospel narrative more than the earlier traditions.

"When Jesus appeared, the high priest said, 'We charge Thee upon Thy oath by the living God, say art Thou the Son of God?' The blessed and Holy Lord Jesus replied to him, 'I am what thou hast said. Verily, We say unto you, you shall see the Son of Man seated at the right hand of God, and He shall descend in the clouds of Heaven.' They said, 'Thou utterest a blasphemy, because, according to the creed of the Jews, God never descends in the clouds of Heaven.'

"Isaiah the prophet has announced the birth of Jesus in words the translation of which is as follows: 'A branch from the root of I'shai shall spring up, and from this branch shall come forth a flower in which the Spirit of God shall dwell; verily, a virgin shall be pregnant and shall bring forth a Son.' I'shai is the name of the father of David.

"When they had apprehended Jesus, they spat upon His blessed face and smote Him. Isaiah had predicted it. 'I shall

---

[1] This tradition is given as reliable by Ibn Khaldoon (*Mukadimet Ibn Khaldoon*, Beirut edition, pp. 226, 227). This author gives the other traditions regarding Christ's return in the same form as above.

give up My body to the smiters, and My cheek to the diggers of wounds. I shall not turn My face from those who will use bad words and throw spittle upon Me.' When Pilatus, a judge of the Jews, scourged the Lord Jesus in such a manner that His body from head to foot became but one wound, so was it as Isaiah had predicted. 'He was wounded for our transgressions ; I struck Him for his people.' When Pilatus saw that the Jews insisted upon the death and crucifixion of Jesus, he said, 'I take no part in the blood of this Man ; I wash my hands clean of His blood.' The Jews answered, 'His blood be on us and on our children.' On that account the Jews are oppressed and curbed down in retribution of their iniquities. When they had placed the cross upon the shoulder of Jesus and led Him to die, a woman wiped with the border of her garment the face, full of blood, of the Lord Jesus. Verily, she obtained three images of it and carried them home ; the one of these images exists still in Spain, the other is in the town of Milan in Italy, and the third in the city of Rome."

Later accounts like these, however, are evidently largely based on the Gospel story or Christian traditions, and are neither generally known nor accessible to the masses. It is not correct to quote them as belonging to the common stock of ideas on Jesus Christ. The masses are wholly dependent on what the Mullahs teach, and these do not read historians nor poets, but orthodox tradition and the Koran.

V

THE PERSON AND CHARACTER OF
JESUS CHRIST

"Jesus Christ is a name that represents the most wonderful story and the profoundest problem on the field of history—the one because the other. There is no romance so marvellous as the most prosaic version of His history. The Son of a despised and hated people, meanly born, humbly bred, without letters, without opportunity, unbefriended, never save for one brief and fatal moment the idol of the crowd, resisted by the religious and the learned, persecuted unto death by the priests, destined to a life as short as it was obscure, issuing from His obscurity only to meet a death of unpitied infamy, He yet, by means of His very sufferings and His cross, enters upon a throne such as no monarch ever filled and a dominion such as no Cæsar ever exercised. He leads captive the civilised peoples; they accept His words as law, though they confess it a law higher than human nature likes to obey; they build Him churches, they worship Him, they praise Him in songs, interpret Him in philosophies and theologies; they deeply love, they madly hate, for His sake."—A. M. FAIRBAIRN, *Christ in Modern Theology.*

V

THE PERSON AND CHARACTER OF JESUS CHRIST

THE chapters that preceded have clearly shown that Christ has a place in Islam as one of the greater Prophets, and that the Koran gives precious glimpses of the Messiah's greatness, but yet falls short of unveiling his glorious perfection and Divine majesty. Mohammed leads his followers to the portal, but he fails to open the door. A perusal of the Koran and of the traditions on the part of any sincere Moslem who tries to interpret Jesus Christ, may indeed kindle the flame of curiosity, but will ever leave his heart-longing unsatisfied. Yet no Moslem who reads his book can escape forming some opinion of Jesus Christ, the son of Mary, and therefore of giving a verdict on His person and character.

This chapter is intended to show what the conclusion is in the mind of the average Moslem from the accounts already given in regard to the person and character of Jesus Christ. It sums up all the data found in Chapters I–IV, in the completed idea of the man

8

Jesus Christ as He stands before the Moslem mind and heart. The chapters that precede are largely historical: in this we attempt dogmatic treatment. And yet it is impossible to approach the subject and use Christian terminology, because Islam eliminates all the Christian ideas back of this terminology, by its denials and contradictions.

The doctrine of the person of Jesus Christ is central, determinative, and supreme in Christian theology.[1]   In dealing with the person of Jesus Christ the Church throughout the centuries has taught that He was very God and very Man, and to His person there have always been ascribed, according to the teaching of the Bible, the threefold office of Prophet, Priest, and King. His eternal existence as the Son of God, His wonderful humiliation as the Son of man, and His exaltation in glory, are the commonplaces of theology and the comfort of all believers.

Yet no Moslem can study the person and character of Jesus Christ according to these categories.   For him they do not exist.   In considering the person of Jesus Christ from a Moslem standpoint, we must first, therefore, take up the subject *negatively*.

I. The Moslem idea of Christ, as of God, consists not only in what is asserted of Him, but also, and more emphatically, in what is denied. As James Freeman Clarke remarks: "The error in every theory

[1] Fairbairn, A. M., *The Place of Christ in Modern Theology*. London, 1894, *passim*.

is usually found in its denials, that is, its limitations.
What it sees is substantial and real; what it does not
see is a mark only of its limited vision."[1] The Koran
denies the Deity and the eternal Sonship of Jesus
Christ. He is a creature like Adam. "Verily, Jesus
is as Adam in the sight of God. He created him of
dust; He then said to him, BE, and he was" (Surah
3 : 52). Those who assert that Jesus Christ is more
than human are infidels. "The Christians say that
the Messiah is the Son of God. God fight them! how
they lie!" (Surah 9 : 30). Not only is Jesus Christ
a mere creature, but He is not essential to God nor to
God's plans in the world. "Who can obtain anything
from God if He chose to destroy the Messiah, the son
of Mary, and His mother and all who are on the earth
together?" (Surah 5: 19). To Moslems a consideration of the person of Jesus Christ begins by the
assertion that He was only a man among men.[2]
"Jesus is no more than a servant whom we favoured,
and proposed as an instance of divine power to the
children of Israel, and, if we pleased, we could from
yourself bring forth angels to succeed you on earth"
(Surah 43: 59).

Nothing so arouses the hostility of the Moslem mind
as the statement that Jesus Christ is the Son of God.
The Mohammedan ideas and misconceptions of the

[1] Quoted in *The Moslem Doctrine of God*, p. 77.
[2] Cf. the refutation, in most bitter terms, of the doctrine of the
Trinity in Carletti's translation of *Idhar-ul-Hak*, vol. i. pp. 388–
417.

Trinity are more fully treated elsewhere,[1] but two passages from the Koran will make clear how important this denial of the Trinity is as regards their doctrine of the person of Jesus. "They say the Merciful has taken to Himself a son—ye have brought a monstrous thing! The heavens well-nigh burst asunder thereat, and the earth is riven and the mountains fall down broken, that they attribute to the Merciful a son! But it becomes not the Merciful to take to Himself a son" (Surah 19: 91–93). "Praise belongs to God, who has not taken to Himself a son and has not had a partner in His kingdom, nor had a patron against such abasement" (Surah 17: 112).

Whatever the Koran and tradition may state, as we have already seen and shall see afterwards, concerning Jesus Christ, His dignity, His sinlessness, or His power to work miracles, Moslems do not distinguish His person in any way as to His *nature* from the other prophets who came before Him. The pre-existence of Christ is everywhere denied, while Moslem tradition is full of stories about the Light of Mohammed, created before all things and existing before all worlds.[2] It seems incredible that Islam, while imputing to Mohammed that which he never asserted of

---

[1] *The Moslem Doctrine of God*, chapter vi.

[2] See *Insan al Ayoon*, by Burhan ud Din al Halibi, and the evidence collected by Kœlle, *Mohammed and Mohammedanism*, pp. 246–252.

FACSIMILE OF LETTER FROM A MULLAH IN CHEFOO, CHINA (1911),

in which he objects to the doctrine of Christ's deity, urges that Mohammed is superior to Christ in every respect, and that the fact of the Virgin birth does not necessarily prove the superiority of Jesus, because "Adam had neither father nor mother, and was in this respect superior to Jesus, while it is well known that even scorpions propagate miraculously."

himself, namely, pre-existence, should deny this in connection with Jesus Christ.[1]

The bitter attacks of Islam on Christianity in the Moslem press of Egypt and of India nearly always find their centre in the Deity and the atoning work of Jesus Christ. To Christians Jesus Christ is God and man; He is Prophet, Priest, and King. To Moslems He is only human, and while they admit that He is a Prophet, His kingship and His priesthood are neither understood nor admitted. Islam is a religion without a priesthood, without a clear idea of the Atonement, and therefore this central thought in the work of Jesus Christ is absent from the Moslem mind.

Dr. Sayous calls attention to the absence of this idea from Mohammed's own mind in this striking way:—

"En un mot, Mahomet n'a pas vu le péché, et il n'a pas besoin de rédemption. Il a même rendu ses disciples de tous les siècles presque incurablement rebelles à cette idée. C'est pour cela que le monde de l'Islam est sans comparaison celui dans lequel la foi chrétienne a recruté le moins de prosélytes. La doctrine du péché et de la grâce est comme un mur, à la rencontre duquel le musulman curieux de christianisme se détourne en levant les épaules et revient sur ses pas."[2]

---

[1] Carletti's *Idhar-ul-Hak*, "Refutation de la Trinité par les paroles de Jesus Christ, vol. i. pp. 396–417.

[2] Sayous, Edouard, *Jésus Christ d'après Mahomet*, p. 64.

We are not surprised, therefore, that the Cross is still a stumbling-block to most of Mohammed's followers, as it was to Mohammed himself.

Recent Moslem literature of every sect and every school of thought is as positive in its rejection of these distinctively Christian doctrines as is the Koran and orthodox tradition. A missionary in Egypt writes that the bitter antagonism of learned Moslems to the Deity and the Cross of Christ is again coming to the front. As a rule, Moslems refrain from reviling the Christ. He is reverenced among them as a Prophet, " but," says Mr. J. Gordon Logan, " a recent writer, who signed himself ' A Moslem,' set aside the teaching of the Koran, and proceeded to prove from what he called ' *history* ' the true character of Christ and His mother, using the most blasphemous language and casting the vilest accusations on the Son of God." [1] Another Moslem distributed broadcast throughout Cairo a poem of which the following is a free translation.[2] It was headed, " A Wonderful Question for the People of the Cross."

" You who worship Jesus, I have a question for you, and can you answer it ?
If Jesus was Almighty God, with power to strike terror into all men,

---

[1] J. Gordon Logan, Leaflet, *Islam defies your King!* Egypt General Mission.

[2] " El Khalasat el Burhanieh fi Sahet Dianet el Islamieh," by Mahmood bin Seyyid 'Ali (Cairo, 1319), contains it in full, with comments.

Why do you believe that the Jews could make him endure the
    agony of the Cross ?

And why do you believe that God died, and was buried in the dust,

And sought from his creatures a draught of water, that he
    might quench his fiery thirst ?

And that they gave him instead myrrh and vinegar, a nauseous
    mixture,

So that he threw it on the ground because he could not take it ?

And that he died a miserable death in an agony of thirst ?

And that they put on his head a crown of thorns,

So frightful that it could turn raven locks to whiteness ?

And that the blood flowed down his cheeks, and stained his
    face like henna ?

And that he rode on a donkey's colt to save himself from the
    toil of the journey ?

You say too that Perez, son of Tamar, was his ancestor ;

One who was born of incest, and the Lord will not receive a
    bastard into His assembly.

And after that will you count him God, and not be in grievous
    error ?

Nay, he is only one of the creatures of God, as he said of himself
    plainly in the Book.

And if he was God as you suppose, why did he pray to be
    delivered from the torment ?

And who restored his Spirit when it left his body ?

And who kept the world in its state until he came back from
    the dead ?

Was there a second Lord watching its affairs ?

Or did he suffer it to go to destruction ?

And was he crucified for some evil he had done ?

Or why did he merit the punishment ?

And did the Jews do well when they crucified him, in order
    that you might be saved ?

Or did they do evil that you might be delivered ?

An extraordinary thing !

And if you say that they did well, I ask you, why

Do you count them enemies ?

And if you say they did wrong, as they crucified God,

And this is fearful sin,

I say, why was it wrong, if without it you could not be saved from the judgment?

And was he himself pleased with the crucifixion, or angry? Tell me truly.

And if you say he was pleased with it in order that he might atone for the fault of the repentant,

I say that Adam sinned and repented by the grace of God, and God forgave him (*i.e.* without atonement).

You therefore lie about your Lord : for the matter is plain as the Book put it ;

For he fled from his cross, and wept much for himself,

And prayed to the God of heaven :

And said, 'I beseech thee, save me from this trial,'

And cried, 'Eli, Eli, why do you leave me this day to the torment?'

'And if it is possible, O my Creator, to save me,

Save me, O best of Fathers.'

And this is a proof that he was only a servant of the Lord without doubt.

And this is a proof that you lie about him,

And say what is false.

And if you say that the cross was forced on him in spite of himself :

Then this Almighty God is not Almighty, for he hung on the Cross, cursed on every side as it is written.

Do not blame me for thus putting the matter.

Answer my questions.

And do not fail, because silence in this is a disgrace to you.

I have given you advice, and desire only that it may profit you.

For myself, I will die a firm believer in the religion of Mohammed, the noblest of men,

As I do not wish to see the horrors of the day of Judgment."[1]

---

[1] Quoted in *Islam defies your King !*

Not on a par with this sort of popular antagonism to the doctrine of the person of Jesus Christ as held by Christians, and yet equally decisive are the statements of Seyyid Ameer Ali of Calcutta, the latest and most able apologist for Islam: " So far as the divinity of Christ is concerned, one can almost see the legend growing. But assuming that Jesus made use of the expressions attributed to him, do they prove that he claimed to be 'the only-begotten of the Father?' With all his dreams and aspirations, his mind was absolutely exempt from those pretensions which have been fixed on him by his over-zealous followers. · That Jesus ever maintained he was the Son of God, in the sense in which it has been construed by Christian divines and apologists, we totally deny."[1]

Here we should notice a boastful assertion common among Mohammedans when arguing with Christians, that they honour the Lord Jesus Christ more than Christians do. After their deliberate and systematic lowering of His dignity and depreciation of all His claims and work as given in the Gospel, such statements seem strange, but most workers among Mohammedans have been surprised and shocked to see how great is the misconception and ignorance implied in such an assertion. In the *Life of Bishop French* we read: " Another was only come to dispute and entangle us in our talk, a learned Mullah, full of captious quibbles and subtle disputations. He said he was

[1] Ameer Ali, *The Spirit of Islam*, pp. 121–122.

sure he loved Christ more than I did, for he did not believe such bad things as I did, that He was crucified, dead and buried, for he believed, and all Mohammedans believed, He never died at all." [1]

II. So far we have considered the Moslem idea of the person and character of our Saviour negatively. We pass on to consider what Moslems admit and believe as regards the dignity of person and the purity of character found in Jesus Christ. One cannot help feeling that the Moslem who has carefully studied the Koran will come to the conclusion, independently of all the commentators, that Christ is superior to Mohammed; and it is a joy to all missionaries to know that occasionally one finds persons who come to this conclusion, and in consequence turn to the Gospels, led to them by the Koran. The Rev. T. Bomford of Peshawar tells of such an instance: a man from Mecca writing to the Bible Society Depôt in Lahore, and asking for a New Testament to learn more of the Christ mentioned in the Koran; Dr. Pennell of Bannu mentioned other cases of a similar nature. There is no better way of preaching Christ to Moslems than by beginning with the testimony of the Koran to Jesus.[2]

First of all, Moslems admit the dignity of Christ as prophet and apostle, *with names given to Him which*

---

[1] *Life of Bishop French*, vol. ii. p. 119.

[2] Cf. *Christ in Islam: The Testimony of the Quran to Christ*, by Rev. Wm. Goldsack. Christian Literature Society, Madras.

are applied to no other prophet and to no other apostle,
as we have seen in Chapter I.   Every sincere Moslem
admits the force of this argument for the unique
character and personality of Jesus Christ, although
a man among men.

Nevertheless, the average Moslem does not see the
force of this argument until his attention is called to it
specially, because, even although these titles are applied
to Jesus Christ, he himself is ranked with the other
apostles and prophets in such a way as to give Him
no special dignity of position.   Moslems are fond of
quoting the text, "We make no distinction between
them" (*i.e.* between the prophets)—Surah 2: 130, 2:
285, and 3: 78: "Say, We believe in God and what
He has sent down to us, and what has come down to
Abraham and Ishmael and Isaac and Jacob; and what
came down to Moses and to Jesus and the prophets
from their Lord.   We make no distinction between
any of them."   And it is remarkable that the name of
Jesus is mixed up with the other prophets in the only
complete list given in the Koran (Surah 6: 84):
"Isaac, Jacob, David, Solomon, Job, Joseph, Moses,
Aaron, Zechariah, John, Jesus, Elias, Ishmael, Elisha,
Jonah, Lot."   To the average Moslem the Koran and
tradition yield no chronological conception of the
order of prophetic history, and one would not infer
from the Koran necessarily that Jesus was the last
of the prophets before Mohammed or the greatest.

In the second place, Mohammedans teach the sinlessness of Jesus Christ. And although this sinlessness, according to present teaching, does not put Jesus Christ in a class by Himself, as all the prophets are sinless in the Moslem sense of that word, yet the Koran, while mentioning the sins of Adam, David, Solomon, and other prophets, leaves no doubt as regards the purity of the character of Jesus. Mohammed himself, of course, is also considered by all Moslems as the paragon of excellence and purity, and as one who has never sinned. In regard to Jesus Christ, however, the statements of orthodox tradition are very remarkable. The prophet said, we are told, "There is no one of the sons of Adam except Mary and her son but is touched by the devil at the time of his birth, and the child makes a loud noise from the touch."[1] Here we have the doctrine of the Immaculate Conception not only of the Virgin Mary but of Jesus.

We are also told, "When Mary was standing under the palm tree, the angels defended her, and when Satan tried to get at her from above, they flocked above her. Then he tried to get at her from beneath, and behold, the feet of the angels protected her. And when he tried to get in between them, they prevented him. So Satan went back and said, There is nothing ever born which was defended against me so successfully as this birth."[2]

One of the commentators, Er-Razi, says that Jesus was given the title Messiah "because He was kept

[1] *Mishkat*, Bk. I. chap. iii.   [2] *Qarmani*, vol. i. p. 70.

clear from the taint of sin." There is a remarkable
tradition related by Anas, which seems by implication
to prove that while Mohammed admitted his own
sinfulness, he could not charge Jesus with sin. It
reads as follows :—

"In the Day of Resurrection Muslims will not be able to
move, and they will be greatly distressed, and will say, 'Would
to God that we had asked Him to create some one to intercede
for us, that we might be taken from this place, and be delivered
from tribulation and sorrow.' Then these men will go to Adam
and will say, 'Thou art the father of all men, God created
thee with His hand, and made thee a dweller in Paradise, and
ordered His angels to prostrate themselves before thee, and
taught thee the names of all things. Ask grace for us, we
pray thee !' And Adam will say, 'I am not of that degree
of eminence you suppose, for I committed a sin in eating of
the grain which was forbidden. Go to Noah, the Prophet,
he was the first who was sent by God to the unbelievers on
the face of the earth.' Then they will go to Noah and ask
for intercession, and he will say, 'I am not of that degree
which ye suppose.' And he will remember the sin which
he committed in asking for the deliverance of his son (Hud),
not knowing whether it was a right request or not; and he
will say, 'Go to Abraham, who is the Friend of God.' Then
they will go to Abraham, and he will say, 'I am not of that
degree which ye suppose.' And he will remember the three
occasions on which he told lies in the world ; and he will say,
'Go to Moses, who is the servant to whom God gave His law,
and whom He allowed to converse with Him.' And they will
go to Moses, and Moses will say, 'I am not of that degree
which ye suppose.' And he will remember the sin which he
committed in slaying a man, and he will say, 'Go to Jesus,
He is the servant of God, the Apostle of God, the Spirit of God,
and the Word of God.' Then they will go to Jesus, and He
will say, 'Go to Muhammad who is a servant, whose sins

God has forgiven both first and last.' Then the Muslims will come to me, and I will then ask permission to go into God's presence and intercede for them." [1]

There is also this curious version of the temptation of Jesus which may indicate His victory over the devil, but is not very conclusive: Ta'us of Yemen, one of the early followers of Mohammed, used to say, "There is nothing which a man says but is counted against him, even his moaning in illness." He said, "Jesus having met Iblis, the latter said to him, 'Do you not know that nothing will betide you but what is destined for you?' Jesus replied, 'Yes.' Iblis then said, 'Ascend to the summit of this mountain and throw yourself down: see whether you will live or not.' Jesus replied, 'Do you not know that God has said, "My servant cannot test me, for I do what I please?" Verily, a servant does not try his Lord, but God tries His servant.'" Ta'us said, "Iblis therefore became his enemy." [2]

In the third place, Jesus Christ is the great Miracle-Worker, especially as the healer of the sick. It is the common opinion among Moslems that the science of medicine had reached a high degree of perfection in the days of Jesus Christ, and that God glorified His apostle by making it possible for Him to heal the sick through miraculous power. We have seen in the story of the miracles of Jesus how this con-

[1] *Mishkat*, Book XXIII. Chapter 12.
[2] Ad-Damiri's *Hayat Al-Hayawan*, p. 227.

ception is elaborated. Jesus Christ as the Great Physician is a familiar picture to Moslems.

The following beautiful account of Jesus healing the sick occurs in the Masnavi,[1] and may well compare with our evening hymn,

> "At evening, ere the sun was set,
> The sick, O Lord, around Thee lay " :—

"The house of 'Isa was the banquet of men of heart,
Ho ! afflicted one, quit not this door !
From all sides the people ever thronged,
Many blind and lame, and halt and afflicted,
To the door of the house of 'Isa at dawn,
That with his breath he might heal their ailments.
As soon as he had finished his orisons,
That holy one would come forth at the third hour ;
He viewed those impotent folk, troop by troop,
Sitting at his door in hope and expectation ;
He spoke to them, saying, ' O stricken ones !
The desires of all of you have been granted by God ;
Arise, walk without pain or affliction,
Acknowledge the mercy and beneficence of God ! '
Then all, as camels whose feet are shackled,
When you loose their feet in the road,
Straightway rush in joy and delight to the halting-place,
So did they run upon their feet at his command."

Lastly, Christ is alive and in heaven, where He is able to intercede for His people. Zamakhshari in his *Commentary* on the Koran text, "illustrious in this world and the next " (Surah 3 : 46) says, "This signifies the office of prophet and supremacy over

[1] *Masnavi-i-Manavi of Jalal-ud-Din*, Whinfield's translation, p. 116.

men in this world, and in the next world the office of Intercessor and loftiness of rank in Paradise." Moslems disagree as to where Jesus Christ now is. The Sunni divines agree that He saw no corruption, but they differ as to the exact state of celestial bliss in which He now resides in His human body. Some say He is in the second heaven; some say He is in the third; some say the fourth.[1] A learned doctor of the Shiah Sect assured me that the Shiah belief is that He is in the highest, or the seventh heaven.

Gathering up these ideas of the character of Jesus and His person, and yet remembering what they deny in regard to our Saviour, it is evident that to Moslems the Founder of the Christian religion, although miraculously born, with power to work miracles, and the last and greatest of all the prophets until Mohammed, who also had the special honour of being taken up into heaven, is nevertheless a mere man, sent of God, and one of the objects of His mission (and this is always the climax of Moslem teaching) was that Jesus came to announce the coming of Mohammed. This idea has taken a permanent and prominent place in all later Moslem teaching concerning the person of Jesus, and is often the first argument on Moslem lips. Every Moslem, even boys who are well read in their religion, can glibly quote Surah 61:6: "And remember when Jesus the son of Mary said, 'O children of Israel! of a truth I am

[1] Hughes, *Dictionary of Islam*, p. 235.

God's Apostle to you to confirm the law which was
given before me, and to announce an apostle that
shall come after me, whose name shall be *Ahmed.*' "
By this token from the lips of Mohammed himself,
and alleged to be a revelation from God, the prophet
of Arabia not only succeeds but supplants the Prophet
of Nazareth.

Moslems have always been eager to find further
proof of the coming of Mohammed in the Old and
New Testament Scriptures in addition to their mis-
interpretation of John 16: 7: *The Paraclete.*[1] They
therefore not only quote the words of the Koran, but
refer to Deuteronomy 33: 2, Isaiah 21: 6; the parable
in Matthew 20, John 4:21, and 1 John 4: 1–3.

The passage in Deuteronomy states that Jehovah
came from Sinai, and rose from Seir unto them; He
shined forth from Mount Paran. Sinai is a Jewish
mountain; Seir, they say, is a mountain in Galilee
where Christ died, but Paran is a mountain near
Mecca, and signifies the Mohammedan religion.

As for Isaiah's prophecy, in which he sees a troop
coming of horsemen and of men riding asses, and of
those who ride camels, to which the prophet should
hearken diligently, their interpretation is that the
horses refer to Moses' dispensation, the asses to that
on which Christ rode, and the camels to Mohammed.

The parable in the twentieth chapter of Matthew's
Gospel of the labourers in the vineyard is cleverly

[1] See following chapter.

9

applied to the threefold dispensation: the morning, Judaism; the noonday labourers, the apostles of Christ; and those to whom he came in the evening, the Moslems. This interpretation is based on a most interesting statement attributed to Mohammed in the traditions.

"Your likeness, O Moslems, in comparison to the Jews and Christians, is like that of a man who hired labourers. He said, 'Who will work for me a whole day for a shekel?' These are the Jews, for they have laboured a long time for a small wage. Then said the man, 'Who will work from noon until night for a shekel?' These are the Christians. Then he said, 'Who will work from afternoon prayer time until sunset?' Such labourers are ye, and remember that for you there is a double wage, because ye have acknowledged the prophet of Truth, and in him all the other prophets." The tradition goes on to show how the Jews and Christians complained, in the terms of the parable, and how God said, "I will give those whom I love what I will."[1]

According to John 4:21, the true worshippers of God are those that "neither on this mountain nor in Jerusalem" worship Him; namely, the Mohammedans.

The most daring use of Scripture, however, as a prophecy of the coming of Mohammed, is the Moslem interpretation of the last passage mentioned. ":Hereby know ye the Spirit of God. Every spirit that

[1] *Mishkat*, vol. ii. p. 814. Captain Mathew's translation.

confesseth that Jesus Christ is come in the flesh is of God." Mohammed is the true Spirit of God because he taught that Jesus Christ was come in the flesh; namely, He came as man and man only, not as God.[1]

After this fashion the Koran and its interpreters unite to obscure the glory of the person and character of Jesus Christ, by obtruding ever and anon Mohammed as the last of the prophets and the one to whom even Jesus Christ bears witness. And what Moslems have done as regards the person of Jesus Christ, they have not hesitated to do in regard to His teaching, as we shall see in the next chapter.

[1] For other passages of Scripture used by Moslems to establish the fact that Jesus and His apostles foretold the coming of Mohammed, see Carletti's translation of *Idhar-ul-Hak*, vol. ii. pp. 190–250. He quotes the following passages with comment:—

Deut. 18 : 17–22.	Isa. 42 : 9–17.
,, 32 : 21.	,, 65 : 1–6.
,, 33 : 2.	Matt. 13 : 31, 32.
Gen. 17 : 20.	,, 20 : 1–16.
,, 49 : 10.	,, 22 : 33–45.
Dan. 2 : 31–45.	Jude 14 : 15.
Ps. 45 : 1–18.	Rev. 2 : 26–29.
,, 149 : 1–9.	

Cf. Tisdall's *Mohammedan Objections to Christianity*, Rice's *Crusaders of the Twentieth Century*, and Gerock's *Christologie des Koran*, pp. 110–112.

VI

HIS TEACHING

"There seems to be no satisfactory proof that an Arabic version of the New Testament existed in Mohammed's time. Even in the "Orthodox" Church, the Gospel was neglected in favour of legends of saints which appealed more to the popular taste for the marvellous. . . . We shall see that the agreement in detail between what the Koran relates on these subjects and what may be found in apocryphal and heretical literature is very remarkable. Here again Mohammed seems to have had a wonderful talent for rejecting the true and accepting the false, just as in the case of the Jewish traditions."—W. St. Clair Tisdall, *The Sources of the Quran*, pp. 140–143.

" On pourrait faire un volume avec ce que les auteurs musulmans rapportent des paroles ou des actions de Jesus Christ. Les examples que nous venons de donner suffisent pour démontrer que le 'injil' musulman est encore a chercher. Ne serait-ce point l'evangile dont Ibn Salam a fait la traduction, comme il l'assure dans le Fihrist.

"Mais cet évangile n'existe plus ; peut-etre quelque chercheur pourra-t-il un jour le retrouver!"—P. L. Cheikho, *Quelques Legendes Islamiques Apocryphes.*

VI

HIS TEACHING

THE New Testament, and especially the Gospels, give as full an account of the teaching of Jesus as of His life and ministry. This is not the case in the Koran and in Moslem tradition. Both are decidedly meagre on the subject, and Moslems in general are unable to give details regarding the message of Him "who spake as never man spake."

Although, as we have seen, there are many references to Jesus Christ in the Koran, it is remarkable that there is not a single direct quotation from the New Testament in the whole book, and only one from the Old Testament (Surah 21:105).[1] There are passages in the Koran, however, which indicate that Mohammed either directly or indirectly borrowed Scripture thought if not language. Among them are the following:—

In Surah 29:60 we read, "How many a beast cannot carry its own provision. God provides for it and for you. He both hears and knows." We may com-

[1] "The earth my righteous servants shall inherit."—Cf. Ps. 37:29.

pare this with the teaching of Jesus Christ on God's care for the birds (Matthew 6 : 26).

In Surah 18 : 24 the reference is clearer: "Never say of anything, 'Verily, I am going to do that to-morrow,' except (ye say) 'if God please.'" Compare Jas. 4 : 13–15: "Ye ought to say, 'If the Lord will, we shall both live and do this or that.'"

In Surah 42 : 19 there is a reference to the law of sowing and reaping like that in Gal. 6 : 7. "He who wishes for the tilth of the next world, we will increase for him the tilth; and he who desires the tilth of this world, we will give him thereof, but in the next world he shall have no portion."

The passage that approaches nearest to a quotation, however, is found in Surah 7 : 39: "Verily, those who say our signs are lies and are too big with pride for them, for these the doors of heaven shall not be opened, and they shall not enter into paradise until a camel shall pass into a needle's eye" (Matt. 19 : 24).

Passing by these references to the New Testament, for which no credit is given in the Koran, and which are not, therefore, considered by Moslems as a part of the teaching of Jesus, we consider first Mohammed's conception of the message that Christ came to bring to the Jews. It is not evident from the Koran that the mission of Jesus Christ was universal. On the contrary, He is sent to the Jews only, and is not an apostle to the whole world, although His disciples

afterward carry His message into other lands. Jesus
Christ was God's messenger to the Jews who had fallen
into error and unbelief. The miracles were intended
to persuade them of the truth of His message, and to
lead them to accept His revelation received from God,
namely, the Injil or Gospel. The Koran does not
indicate into what particular errors the Jews had
fallen and in what respect they had left the true
religion of Abraham (Islam), that is, the belief in one
God. In one passage it is asserted that the Jews gave
divine honours to Ezra (Surah 9 : 30), but whether this
took place after the mission of Jesus Christ or before,
is left uncertain.

Al Qaramani, in his *History of Ancient Times and
Peoples*, relates that " When Jesus was eight years old,
He was circumcised and named Yasu'a. When He
was thirty years old revelation came to Him, and He
entered the Holy House where the children of Israel
were buying and selling; then He began to strike
them and to say, Ye sons of the children of vipers and
snakes ! have you taken the house of God for a bazaar ?
Then God made the Gospel to come down to Him and
Gabriel ten times " (vol. i. p. 70).

As the Injil, or Gospel, is considered not only by the
Koran, but by all Moslems, as the special message of
Jesus, it is important to know what the Koran teaches
in regard to its character and authority. The word
injil is undoubtedly a corruption of the Greek
εναγγελιον (evangel). It occurs twelve times in the

Koran,[1] and there doubtless refers to the revelations
made by God to Jesus, that is, to His verbal messages,
afterwards put into writing. In later Mohammedan
usage it is applied to the whole New Testament. All
of the passages that mention the Injil occur in the
later Surahs.[2]

Concerning the original divine character and authority of this book, or message or teaching of Jesus, the
Koran expresses no doubt. It confirms all God's
teaching that preceded it; it is a guidance to men; it
is the basis of firm belief and of salvation. Surah
5 : 72 : "Ye rest on naught until ye stand fast by the
law and the gospel." It is "a word of truth." Its
effect is to produce the spirit of adoration (Surah
48 : 29), and to prompt to deeds of kindness and compassion (Surah 57 : 27).

But since Mohammed makes an appeal to the Gospel
for the support of his own mission in what he con-
siders a genuine saying of Christ's, well known to the
Christians of his day, he gave the reason for the later
charge of Moslems against Christians, that they have
either lost or changed the original gospel. This appeal
of Mohammed to Jesus Christ's words occurs in Surah
61 : 6 : "And when Jesus the son of Mary said, ' O

---

[1] Surah 7 : 156 ; Surah 3 : 2 ; Surah 3 : 43 ; Surah 3 : 58 ; Surah
57 : 27 ; Surah 48 : 29 ; Surah 9 : 112 ; Surah 5 : 50, 51 ; Surah 5 : 70 ;
Surah 5 : 72 ; Surah 5 : 110, and perhaps Surah 19 : 31. In this last
passage, the infant Jesus says, " Verily, I am the servant of God.
He hath given me *The* Book, and He hath made me a prophet."

[2] Cf. Rodwell and Nöldeke.

children of Israel! verily, I am the apostle of God to you, verifying the law that was before me, and giving you glad tidings of an apostle who shall come after me, whose name shall be Ahmed.' "[1]

Jesus, they say, foretold the coming of Mohammed; He pointed to him that was to come. The commentators and later tradition assert, therefore, that the teaching of Jesus, originally · pure monotheism, was corrupted by the apostles that followed Him. In commenting on the words of the Koran, " The Christians say that the Messiah is the son of God; that is what they say with their mouths, imitating the sayings of those who misbelieved before—God fight them! how they lie!" El-Kalbi states: " The Christians followed the religion of Islam for eighty-one years after the translation of Jesus, praying with their faces directed to the *Kiblah* and fasting during the month of *Ramadan,* until a war occurred between them and the Jews. There was a brave and bold man among the Jews called Paul, who killed a large number of the followers of Jesus. He said one day to the Jews, 'If the truth is with Jesus, we have misbelieved Him and we shall go to Hell-fire, and we shall be over-reached, if they enter Paradise and we enter Hell-fire; but I

---

[1] Ahmed is the equivalent of Mohammed, and Moslem commentators have ingeniously found an allusion to this promise in the words of Jesus concerning the Paraclete (John 14 : 16, 15 : 26, and John 17 : 7). They assert that the word παράκλητος has been substituted in the Greek for περικλυτός, which would mean the same as Ahmed. The whole context makes clear the futility of this contention.

shall scheme a dodge and mislead them, so that they would enter Hell-fire.' Now, he had a horse called the Eagle, on the back of which he used to fight; he hocked it, showed repentance, and threw dust on his head, upon which the Christians asked him, 'Who are you?' He replied, 'Paul, your enemy. A voice from heaven declared to me, "Your repentance will not be accepted until you become a Christian," and here, I have now repented.'—[This doubtless refers to the history of Paul's conversion, Acts ix.].—They therefore took him into the church, and he entered a room in it and remained in it for a year, not going out either by day or by night until he learnt the New Testament. He then came out and said, 'A voice from heaven has declared to me, "God has accepted your repentance."' They therefore believed him and loved him. He then went to Jerusalem and appointed over them as his successor Nestorius, whom he taught that Jesus, Mary, and God were three. He then went to Greece (ar-Rum) and taught them there the doctrine of the divinity and the humanity. He told them that Jesus was neither a human being nor a jinn, but that he was the son of God, and he taught a man named Jacob this doctrine. He then called a man named Malkan, and told him that God always was and always will be Jesus. When he had got a proper hold over them, he called them three, one by one, and said to each of them, 'You are exclusively mine, and I have seen Jesus in a dream, and he was pleased with me.' He also said to each one of them, 'I shall to-morrow kill myself; then invite people to follow your persuasion.' He then entered the arena and killed himself, saying, 'I am doing this to please Jesus.' When the third day came, each one of them invited the people to accept his creed, and a party followed each of them; so that the Christians became separated into three distinct bodies,—the Nestorians, the Jacobites, and the Malakites. They differed from, and fought with, one another. Hence God said, 'And the Christians say that the Messiah is the son of God; that is what they say with their mouths, imitating the sayings of those who mis-believed before.—God fight them! how they lie!'"[1]

Another account of how the apostles corrupted the original message of Jesus is given in the Biographical Dictionary of Hajji Khalifah, entitled Kashf-uz-Zunun. The statements made are such a curious mixture of fact and fiction that we quote them at length:—

"In the book entitled the *Tuhfatu'l-Adib fi Raddi 'ala Ahli's-Salib*, or 'A Refutation of the Servants of the Cross' (written by 'Abdu'llah, a pervert from Christianity to Islam, A.H. 823), it is said that these four companions are they who corrupted the religion of Jesus, and have added to it. And that they were not of the *Hawariyun*, or apostles mentioned in the Koran. Matta did not see Jesus until the year he was taken up to heaven; and after the ascension of Jesus he wrote in the city of Alexandria, with his own hand, his Injil, in which he gives an account of the birth and life of Jesus, mentioning several circumstances which are not mentioned by the others. Luka

---

[1] Ad-Damiri, *Hayat-Al-Hayawan*, vol. ii. pp. 537–538.

also did not see Jesus, but he was converted to Christianity by
one *Bulis* (Paul), who was an Israelite, who himself had not seen
Jesus, but was converted by Ananiya (Ananias). Marqus also
did not see Jesus at all, but was converted to Christianity, after
the Ascension of Jesus, by the apostle *Bitrus*, and received the
Injil from that apostle in the city of Rome. And his gospel in
many respects contradicts the statements of the other three.
Yuhanna was the son of the sister of Maryam, the mother of
Jesus, and the Christians assert that Jesus was present at the
marriage of Yuhanna, when Jesus changed the water into wine.
It was the first miracle performed by Jesus."

"When Yuhanna saw the miracle, he was converted to
Christianity, and left his wife and followed Jesus. He was the
writer of the fourth Injil. It was written in Greek, in the
city of Ephesus. These are the four persons who altered and
changed the true Injil, for there was only one Injil revealed to
Jesus, in which there was no contradiction or discrepancy.
These people have invented lies concerning God and His
prophet Jesus, upon whom be peace, as is a well-known fact,
although the Christians (*Nasara*) deny it." [1]

It is evident from these traditions which find an
echo in the common belief of Moslems everywhere,
that the gospel story now in the hands of Christians
is not for them a true account of the teachings of Jesus.
Although the Koran in general terms commends both
the Old and the New Testament,[2] in a whole series of
passages which assert that the Torah, the Zaboor, and
the Injil are the very word of God, yet neither the
Koran nor tradition give any adequate indication of

[1] Quoted in Hughes' *Dictionary of Islam*, p. 212.
[2] All the references of the Koran to the sacred scriptures of the
Jews and Christians have been collected by Sir William Muir in his
book, *The Coran*. S.P.C.K. London, 1878.

the contents and message of these books of God as
they relate to sin and salvation.

The curious story of Habib the carpenter, which is
given in Surah 36:12-30 of the Koran, tells of the
preaching of the apostles at Antioch and the conversion of the carpenter, but leaves out any reference
to the character of the message which the apostles
carried to that city where the disciples were first
called Christians.   El Beidhawi, the commentator,[1]
says that the people of Antioch were idolaters, and
that Jesus sent two of His disciples, John and Jude,
to preach to them.   When they arrived, they met
Habib the carpenter, who said, " What signs can you
show that you are sent from God?" They replied,
" We can heal the sick, and give sight to the blind,
and cure leprosy." When Habib brought his sick son
to them, they laid hands upon him, and he was healed.
Habib then believed on Jesus, and published the
Gospel to the people of the city.   When the news
reached the governor, he sent for the disciples, and
asked them, " Is your God different from our God?"
and they said, " Yes, He it is who made both thee and
thy gods." Then the governor put them in prison.
While they were in prison Jesus sent Simon Peter,
who made friends with the servant of the governor
secretly, gained access to his presence, performed a
miracle by raising his child who had been dead seven
days.   This child, when raised from the dead, said he

[1] El Beidhawi on Surah 36 : 12-30 ; cf. also Zamakhshari.

had seen Jesus Christ in heaven, who was interceding for the three disciples in prison. Then the governor believed and many others, but the unbelievers raised a disturbance; and when Habib the carpenter preached to them, he was stoned, and having died, entered Paradise. Habib's tomb is still to be seen at Antioch, and is visited as a shrine by Moslems.

When we turn to later traditions and to later Moslem literature, it is refreshing to find something more real on the teaching of Jesus, although it is not always attributed to Him. In Bokhari we read, "The prophet said, ' At the resurrection God shall say, " O ye sons of men! I was sick and ye visited Me not." They shall say, "Thou art the Lord of the worlds; how should we visit Thee?" He will say, "A certain servant of mine was sick, and if ye had visited him, ye would have found Me with him." ' " This is remarkable teaching, for it brings out a sense of nearness between God and man which is generally ignored by Moslems.

In regard to the teaching attributed to Jesus Christ and alleged to be found in the original Gospel, or Injil, P. L. Cheikho gives the following extracts, taken, he says, from many sources: "Jesus Christ said in the Gospel, ' Hope if ye are afraid, and be afraid if ye hope.' ' Your life consists of a certain number of breaths, and some one is watching over it. Do not forget death, therefore, because death will not forget you.' ' Good health is a secret king.' ' Anxiety is part of the weakness of old age.' 'The son of Adam craves for that which is forbidden.' 'A bribe blinds the eyes of the learned, and what think ye then of the ignorant?' 'Weep with those that weep, and laugh with those that laugh.'"

Another story told in the book of the Israelites, attributed to Wahab bin Munabah, is that Jesus one day passed a skull lying by the wayside and commanded it to speak. It obeyed, and recounted a fantastic story to those who were present, saying, "I am Bilwam, the son of So and So, King of Yemen. I lived a thousand years, and married so many women, and slaughtered so many enemies, and conquered so many cities. Let those who see me remember, and may the world not deceive them as it has deceived me, for all the time that has passed is like the dream of one who sleepeth." Then Jesus wept.[1]

There is one striking instance of a quotation from the epistles,—a favourite with many thoughtful Moslems, which is, however, attributed to Mohammed on the authority of Abu Huraira: "The Most High said, 'I have prepared for my righteous servants what eye hath not seen nor ear heard, nor hath it occurred to the heart of a human being.'" These words are evidently quoted from 1 Cor. 2:4. Yet it is doubtful whether Mohammed ever used them, as much of the later traditions are pure invention.[2]

[1] *Quelques Legendes Islamiques Apocryphes*, pp. 43, 44.
[2] *Mishkat-ul-Masabih*, p. 487.

10

Other instances are given by a recent writer on the subject:

"In the '*Awarifu-l-Mawarif* of Shahab-ud-Din Suhrawardi the doctrine of the New Birth is definitely attributed to Christ. 'The death of nature and of will, which they call "the second birth," even as Jesus has written.'

"Ghazzali in the *Ihya-ul-ulum* thus refers to St. Matthew 11 : 17 : 'Some one said, "I saw written in the Gospel, We have sung to you, but ye have not been moved with emotion; we have piped unto you, but ye have not danced."' He also quotes St. Matthew 6 : 25, 'Jesus said, Consider the fowls, etc.'

"The historian Tabari mentions the institution of the Last Supper, Christ's washing His disciples' hands, requesting them to watch with Him, predicting Peter's denial, and quotes the text, 'The shepherd shall be smitten, and the sheep shall be scattered.'"[1]

Centuries after Mohammed, the poets of Syria and Persia interpreted the teaching of Jesus as they gathered it either from Moslem tradition or from Christian neighbours. In the Bostan of Sa'di the parable of the Publican and the Pharisee takes the following curious shape:—

In Jesus' time there lived a youth so black and dissolute,
That Satan from him shrank appalled in every attribute;

---

[1] "Christ in Mohammedan Tradition," C. H. A. Field, *C.M.S. Intelligencer*, January 1911.

He in a sea of pleasures foul uninterrupted swam
And gluttonised on dainty vices, sipping many a dram.
Whoever met him on the highway turned as from a pest,
Or, pointing lifted finger at him, cracked some horrid jest.
I have been told that Jesus once was passing by the cave
Where dwelt a monk who asked Him in,—
When suddenly that slave of sin appeared across the way,
Far off he paused, fell down and sobbingly began to pray ;
And like a storm of rain the tears pour gushing from his eyes.
" Alas, and woe is me for thirty squandered years," he cries ;
The pride-puffed monk self-righteous lifts his eyebrows with
    a sneer
And haughtily exclaims, " Vile wretch ! in vain hast thou
    come here.
Art thou not plunged in sin, and tossed in lust's devouring sea ?
What will thy filthy rags avail with Jesus and with me ?
O God ! the granting of a single wish is all I pray,
Grant me to stand far distant from this man at Judgment
    Day."
From Heaven's throne a revelation instantaneous broke,
And God's own thunder-words through the mouth of Jesus
    spoke :
" The two whom praying there I see, shall equally be heard ;
They pray diverse,—I give to each according to his word.
That poor one thirty years has rolled in sin's most slimy
    deeps,
But now with stricken heart and streaming eyes for pardon
    weeps.
Upon the threshold of My grace he throws him in despair,
And faintly hoping pity pours his supplications there.
Therefore forgiven and freed from all the guilt in which he
    lies
My mercy chooses him a citizen of paradise ;
This monk desires that he may not that sinner stand beside,
Therefore he goes to hell and so his wish is gratified." [1]

---

[1] Quoted by C. H. A. Field.

And the poet Nizami gives this curious illustration of the compassion and gentleness of Jesus :—

One evening Jesus lingered in the market-place
Teaching the people parables of truth and grace,
When in the square remote a crowd was seen to rise
And stop with loathing gestures and abhorring cries.
The Master and His meek disciples went to see
What cause for this commotion and disgust could be,
And found a poor dead dog beside the gutter laid :
Revolting sight ! at which each face its hate betrayed.
One held his nose, one shut his eyes, one turned away,
And all among themselves began aloud to say,
" Detested creature ! he pollutes the earth and air ! "
" His eyes are blear ! "   " His ears are foul ! "   " His ribs
    are bare ! "
" In his torn hide there's not a decent shoe-string left ! "
" No doubt the execrable cur was hung for theft ! "
Then Jesus spake and dropped on him this saving wreath:
" Even pearls are dark before the whiteness of his teeth ! "[1]

It is easy to understand how close contact with Christians and Christian teaching gave rise to this kind of poetry, but it is not so easy to understand or to explain how after Mohammed's death distinctively Christian teaching, nay, the very words of Christ, His parables and His deepest lessons, are by tradition-mongers put into the mouth of Mohammed, as if he were the originator of them !

When we remember, however, that the biographies of Mohammed by Moslem authors, beginning with the earliest, but especially the later biographies, attribute

[1] Quoted by C. H. A. Field.

to their prophet an equality with, or even a superiority to the Prophet of Nazareth, so that Mohammed
himself becomes a parody of Jesus Christ, it is not
strange that they imputed Christ's teaching also to
him. Koelle devotes the second portion of his critical
treatise, *Mohammed and Mohammedanism*, to a
comparison between Mohammed and Jesus Christ, in
which he shows by literal translation from Moslem
biographical works how almost every detail of the life
of Christ was duplicated by the glowing imagination
and devout admiration of Moslems, who did not scruple
to invent stories as long as they glorified the prophet.[1]

In a special study on the *Hadith* (traditions) and the
New Testament, Ignaz Goldziher points out several
instances where the very words of Christ are attributed
to Mohammed.[2] Among those, said Mohammed, whom
God will cover with His shadow in the day when there
is no shadow, is " the man who does alms and keeps it
secret, so that his left hand does not know what his
right hand doeth."[3] Abdullah bin Mas'ud said: "I saw the
Prophet of God, when the people struck him and abused
him, that he brushed the blood off his face and said, ' O
God! forgive my people, for they know not what they
do.'" The commentators ignorantly add that Mohammed here quoted a saying of Noah the prophet! The
companions of the Prophet are quoted as saying,

---

[1] Koelle, *Mohammed and Mohammedanism*, pp. 242-446.
[2] Goldziher,*Muhammedanische Studien*, vol. 11, pp. 381-404.
[3] *Al Muwatta*, vol. iv. p. 171.

"Be harmless as doves"; and the greater number of
the inhabitants of paradise, Mohammed is reported to
have said, are "the poor in spirit."

The most remarkable example which Goldziher
gives, is the use of the Lord's Prayer, which in the
Hadith is also attributed to Mohammed. Abu al
Darda'[1] is reported to have said that the prophet
said, "When any one is in suffering, or his brother
suffers, then let him pray this prayer: 'Our Lord
God who art in heaven, hallowed be Thy name. Thy
kingdom is in heaven and on earth, and even as Thy
mercy is in heaven, so may Thy mercy also be upon
earth. Forgive us our debts and our sins, for Thou
art the Lord of the good. Send down mercy from
Thy mercy and healing from Thy healing for those
suffering, that they may begin to heal.'"[2]

Goldziher gives other instances, and shows conclus-
ively that even as in the case of Mohammed's life, so
in the case of Mohammed's teaching, any fragments
of the life and teaching of Christ which could add to
the glory of the prophet, were without scruple incor-
porated in later tradition. It is no wonder that if *such*
a Mohammed, transformed at least in measure into the
character if not into the image of Christ, is enthroned
in the hearts of Mohammedans, they should be hard to

[1] One of the younger contemporaries of Mohammed, who was a late
convert to Islam, but afterwards became one of the greatest Koran
scholars. Under Othman he was the public prayer-reader in Damascus,
where he died A.H. 652.—HOUTSMA, *Encyclopedia of Islam*, p. 82.

[2] *Abu Daood,* vol. i. p. 101.

win.[1] As Koelle remarks, "What a mass of rubbish has to be swept away from the path of the pious Moslem before his vision can become unimpeded and free enough to perceive the all-surpassing spiritual majesty of Him who could say, He who hath seen Me hath seen the Father."[2]

Except for the opinion that Jesus Christ is a true prophet and one of the greatest of the prophets before the time of Mohammed, the masses of the people in the Moslem world have no conception of the message which Jesus Christ came to bring, nor of the character of His teaching as distinguished from that of Moses and the Old Testament prophets. And we must add to this that if the death and the resurrection of Jesus Christ are the cardinal truths of the Gospel, these truths are not only obscured, but contradicted by the Koran and tradition, so that in the teaching of Jesus Christ, as understood by Mohammedans, we must leave out everything that relates to the Incarnation, the Atonement, and salvation from sin by faith in His name. Nowhere in the Koran or in tradition is there any trace of the great Christian doctrine of justification by faith. As in regard to the person of Christ, so in regard to His teaching, Islam is anti-Christian.

[1] The great truths of Christianity centre in the person of its Founder. In a different way Islam is bound up with the personality, even in the minutest details, of its prophet; "in all matters small and great he is their perfect example," says Rev. W. A. Rice. No Moslem is apt, therefore, to have a higher opinion of our Saviour than Mohammed himself had.

[2] Koelle, *Mohammed and Mohammedanism*, preface, p. vii.

VII

JESUS CHRIST SUPPLANTED BY MOHAMMED

"As there is only one God, so there can be only one gospel. If God has really done something in Christ on which the salvation of the world depends, and if He has made it known, then it is a Christian duty to be intolerant of everything which ignores, denies, or explains it away. The man who perverts it is the worst enemy of God and men; and it is not bad temper or narrow-mindedness in St. Paul which explains this vehement language (Galatians 1 : 9) ; it is the jealousy of God which has kindled in a soul redeemed by the death of Christ a corresponding jealousy for the Saviour."—JAMES DENNEY in *The Death of Christ*, p. 110.

VII

JESUS CHRIST SUPPLANTED BY MOHAMMED

AS in a total eclipse of the sun the glory and the beauty of the heavenly orb are hidden, and only the corona appears on the edge, so in the life and thought of Mohammedans their own prophet has almost eclipsed Jesus Christ. The general idea of His life, as we have gathered it from many Moslem sources, is, after all, vague, shadowy, and not at all clearly outlined in the mind of Moslems. An Arab from Hassa expressed this truth a few days ago when he said to me: "Until my wife became a Christian I knew nothing of Jesus whatever, only His name, and that He was a Prophet!" Whatever place Jesus Christ may occupy in the Koran—and the portrait there given is a sad caricature; whatever favourable critics may say about Christ's honourable place among the Moslem prophets, it is nevertheless true that the large bulk of Mohammedans know extremely little, and think still less, of Jesus Christ. He has no place in their hearts nor in their lives. All the prophets have not only been succeeded, but supplanted by Mohammed; he is at once the sealer and concealer of all former revelations. Mohammed is always in the foreground, and Jesus Christ, in spite of His lofty titles and the honour given Him in the Koran, is in the background. There is not a single biography of Jesus Christ standing by Himself, alone and unique, as a great prophet of God, to be found in the literature of Islam. Christ is grouped with the other prophets; with Lot, Alexander the Great, Ishmael, Moses, Abraham, Adam.

We cannot forget this fact when we try to form a conception of the Moslem Christ. It is because of this that Islam presents difficulties offered by no other religion in the work of missions. " It cannot be treated like any other religion," says Rev. W. H. T. Gairdner; "it baffles more than any other, for it is more difficult to concede to it what is gladly conceded to other religions that appeared before Christ, that they in some part prepared and prepare the way for Him. How can that which denies the whole essential and particular content of the message be said to prepare for Him, or to be a half-way house to His kingdom? For that is what Islam does. Other religions know nothing of Christianity; one and all they came before it, and speak of it neither good nor evil. But the whole theory of Islam is that it, the latest sent of all religions, does not so much *abrogate* Christianity with its Book;

FACSIMILE PAGE FROM THE BOOK ENTITLED
"DALA'IL EL KHEIRAT,"

in which Mohammed is considered the sole intercessor and the channel
of communication between the believer and God.

TRANSLATION OF PAGE FROM THE BOOK ENTITLED
"DALA'IL EL KHEIRAT."

"O God! pray for the Moon of Perfection. O God! pray for the Light that shines in the darkness. O God! pray for the Key to the door of peace. O God! pray for the Intercessor of all humanity! O Thou Mercy of God! (Mohammed) I am afraid and terrified. O Thou Grace of God! I am bankrupt; help Thou me. I have no good work in which I can put my trust, save Thy great love and my faith in Thee. Be Thou my safety from the evil of this life, and in the hour of death, and deliver my body from the fire."

as specifically and categorically deny both as wilful corruption and lies." [1]

The sin and the guilt of the Mohammedan world is that they give Christ's glory to another, *and that for all practical purposes Mohammed himself is the Moslem Christ.* The life and character of Mohammed as portrayed for us by his earliest biographers, who were all his faithful followers and admirers, leaves no doubt that he was thoroughly human and liable to error. Later tradition has changed all this, and made him sinless and almost divine. The two hundred and one titles of honour given to Mohammed proclaim his apotheosis. These names and titles are current in all popular books of devotion among Moslems, from Morocco to China; are separately printed and learned by heart in Moslem schools. The list which follows contains at least two score of names that Christians would apply only to Christ, and many of them are by Mohammedans themselves applied to God as well as to their prophet, namely—

Mohammed, Ahmed, Hamid, Mahmood, the Unique, The Only, *The Forgiver*, the Raiser of the Dead, The Avenger, "Ta Ha," "Ya Seen," [2] The Pure, The Purified, The Good, The Lord, The Apostle, The Prophet, [3] The Apostle of Mercy, The Manager, The Gatherer, The Follower, The Leader, The Apostle of War, The Apostle

[1] W. H. T. Gairdner, *The Reproach of Islam*, p. 141.

[2] Titles of two chapters in the Koran.

[3] On Mohammed as the foreteller of future events, see Carletti, *Idhar-ul-Hak*, vol. ii. pp. 145–154.

of Rest, *The Perfect*, The Crown, The Wrapped One, The Covered One, Servant of God, Beloved of God, Chosen of God, Companion of God, Mouthpiece of God, Seal of Prophets, Seal of Apostles, *The Quickener*, The Deliverer, The Reminder, The Victorious, The Victor, Prophet of Mercy, Prophet of Repentance, *The Watcher*, The Well-known, The Famous, The Witness, The Martyr, The Witnessed, Bringer of Good Tidings, The Preacher, The One under Vows, The Warner, *The Light*, The Lamp, The Candle, The Guidance, *The Guide*, The Mahdi, The Enlightener, The Summoner, The Called One, *The Answerer of Prayer*, *The Interceder*, The Hidden, *The Pardoner*, The Saint, *The Truth*, *The Strong*, *The Faithful*, The Entrusted One, *The Gracious*, The Honoured, The Valiant, The Mighty, The Evident, *The Mediator*, The Bestower, The Able, The Honourable, The Exalted, The Possessor of Might, The Possessor of Grace, The Obedient, The Subjector, The Benevolent, *The Merciful*, The Good Tidings, The Assister, The Provider, *The Benefactor*, The Mercy of God, The Gift of God, The Strong Refuge, The Way of God, The Straight Way, The Memorial of God, The Sword of God, The Portion of God, The Shining Star, The Exalted, The Corrector of Evil, The Bearer of Faults, The Illiterate, The Chosen One, The Rewarded, The Mighty One, Abu Kasim, Abu Tahir, Abu Tayyib, Abu Ibrahim, The Intercessor, The Interceder, The Pious, The Peace Maker, The Guarder, The Truthful, The Upright, *Verity*, Lord of Apostles, Leader of the Pious, Leader of Pure

Women, Friend of the Merciful, *Righteousness*, *The Justifier*, The Illustrious, The Adviser, The Man of Counsel, The Undertaker, The Entrusted, The Surety, *The Compassionate*, The Founder of the Law, *The Holy One*, *Holy Spirit*, *The Spirit of Truth*, The Spirit of Rectitude, The All-Sufficient, The Sufficer, The Perfect One, The One who Attained, The Healer, The Giver, The Gift, The Fore-runner, The Rear Guard, The Rightly Guided, The Right Guidance, *The Beginner*, The Precious, The Honoured, The Honour-laden, *The Opener*, The Key, The Key of Mercy, The Key of Paradise, The Source of Faith, *The Source of Truth*, The Guide to Plenty, The Selected One, The Purifier of Good Works, *The Pardoner of Sins*, The Lord of Intercession, The Highly Exalted, The Most Noble, The Essence of Power, The Essence of Glory, The Essence of Honour, The One who Helps, The One who has a Sword, The One who has Praise, The One who has a Covering, The Argument, The Sultan, The Possessor of the Cloak, The Possessor of High Degree, The Possessor of the Crown, The Possessor of the Helmet, The Possessor of the Banner, One who ascended to Heaven, The Possessor of the Sceptre, The Possessor of the Seal, The Possessor of Boraak,[1] The Possessor of the Sign, The Possessor of the Proof, The Possessor of the Argument, The Eloquent, The Pure of Heart, *The Gracious One*, *The Pitiful*, The Ear of Goodness, The Perfection of Islam, *Lord of Two Worlds*, The Eye

[1] The famous animal on which Mohammed made his night journey to heaven.

of Kindness, The Eye of Brilliancy, The Helper of God, The Helper of Men, The Pleader for the Nations, The Knowledge of Truth, The Discloser of Secrets, The Elevator of the Lowly, The Glory of the Arabs, The One who has Victory.

Some of these titles, as we have indicated by printing them *in italics*, are similar to those given to God Himself. Mohammed is also called the Light of God, the Peace of the World, the Glory of the Ages, the First of all Creatures, and other names of yet greater import. One tradition goes so far as to say, " No man in whatsoever condition he is can resemble God so much as thou dost. But if there could be an image to represent God as He is, it could be no other than thyself." [1]

No Moslem prays to Mohammed, but every Moslem prays for him in endless repetition daily. In spite of statements in the Koran to the contrary, most Moslems believe that he will be the only intercessor on the day of judgment. The books of devotion used everywhere are proof of this statement. God favoured him above all creatures; he dwells in the highest heaven, and is several degrees above Jesus in honour and station. Mohammed holds the keys of heaven and hell: no Moslem, however bad his character, will perish finally ; no unbeliever, however good his life, can be saved except through Mohammed. Islam denies the need of Christ as Mediator, only to substitute Mohammed as a mediator, without an incarnation, without an atonement,

[1] Quoted in W. A. Rice, *Crusaders of the Twentieth Century*, p. 15.

I N order that those who know Arabic may see for themselves how Mohammed has practically usurped the place of Jesus Christ as the supernatural channel of communication with God, and how he has been practically deified by Moslems, we here print the list of names applied to Mohammed in common books of devotion, such as *Dala'il al Kheirat* Cairo, 1324, pp. 28–33). The list is in two sections : first, a comparative list of those names which have the same grammatical root, and are applied both to Mohammed and to God, and second, those names which although of different etymological origin, have practically the same significance.

NAMES APPLIED TO GOD.	حسب الاشتقاق حرفيًا (اولًا)	NAMES APPLIED TO MOHAMMED.
الرَّحيم		رحيم
القُدُّوس		روح القدس
المُهَيمِن		مُهَيمِن
الجبَّار		جبَّار
الفتَّاح		فاتِح . مفتاح . مفتاح الرحمة . مفتاح الجنَّة
الرافع		رافع الرتَب
المعِزّ		مخصوص بالعزّة
الكريم		كريم
المجيب		مجيب
المجيد . الماجد		مخصوص بالمجد
الشهيد		تشهيد
الحقّ		حقّ
العزيز		عزيز
الوكيل		وكيل
القويّ		قويّ . ذو قُوَّة
المَتين		متين
الوليّ		ولِيّ
المحيي		محيي
البَرّ		بَرّ . مَبَرّ
العفوّ		عفوّ
الرؤوف		رؤوف
المقسط		روح القسط
النُّور		نور . مُنير . مصباح . سراج
الهادي		هادٍ . مُهديّة . هدًى . علم الهُدَى

حسب احتمال المعنى (ثانياً)

سيّد الكونين	الله
صاحب التاج	الملك
صفوح عن الزّلات . مُقيل العثرات	الغفّار
وُصول	الوهّاب
مُبلّغ	الرزّاق
مانح	الغفور
كافٍ	المُقيت
حاشر	الباعث
صاحب الدرجة الرفيعة	المُتعال
شفيع . صاحب الشفاعة . وجيهٌ . صاحب الوَسيلة	التوّاب
عاقب	المنتقم
صاحب السلطان	مالك الملك
غَوْث . غَيِّث . غياث	الغنيّ . المُغني
وَاصل	المُعطي
شافٍ	النافع

The Moslem Christ—page 160.

and without demand for a change of character. One has only to question the Moslem masses, or to read tradition in proof of these statements.[1]

Every detail of the life of Jesus Christ has been imitated and parodied by Mohammed's later biographers and admirers. "En se développant, la théologie musulmane," says René Basset, "plus au courant du christianisme, tendit à en rapprocher de plus en plus le fondateur de l'islam et à attribuer à celui-ci les miracles qui devaient le rendre au moins l'égal de Jesus. Cette déviation de l'idée réelle qu'on avait du Prophète, commença de bonne heure et ne fit que s'accroître avec le temps. De là, les prodiges calqués sur ceux que rapportaient les Evangiles et qui sont en opposition complète avec les sentiments réels de Mohammed."[2] In the commentary on the poem in praise of Mohammed (from the introduction to which these words are taken) the author shows scriptural parallels in this Coronation hymn of Islam to every exaggerated word of praise there attributed to the Arabian prophet. Dr. Koelle has shown in great detail[3] how Moslem authors attribute to their prophet an equality with, and even a superiority to, the Prophet of Nazareth, by ascribing to him all the glory which centres around the Christ in the New Testament. Pre-existence is ascribed to Mohammed, and his

[1] Cf. *Islam : A Challenge to Faith*, pp. 48, 49.
[2] René Basset, *La Bordah du Cheikh el Boustri*, Poeme en l'honneur de Mohammed traduit et commentée. Paris, 1894, p. xi.
[3] Koelle, *Mohammed and Mohammedanism*, pp. 242–372.

II

genealogy is traced through Abraham to Adam, as
in the case of Jesus Christ. An angel announced
Mohammed's conception and birth and the name which
he was to bear. Mohammed, like Jesus, was lost in
his childhood and found again, and at the age of
twelve he took a special journey. After the commence-
ment of his public ministry Mohammed, like Jesus,
passed through a remarkable ordeal of Satanic temptation. He, like Jesus Christ, chose twelve apostles.
His enemies were those of his own household, and he
was recognised by spirits from the unseen world more
readily than by those to whom he was sent. The
demons knew Jesus; the jinn accepted Islam at the
hands of Mohammed. The Transfiguration of Jesus
Christ is surpassed by the story of Mohammed's ascent
into heaven, where he had personal communion with
all the previous prophets, and leaving Jesus far below
in the second heaven, himself mounted to the seventh,
where, according to Moslem tradition, he ate and
drank with God.[1]

[1] The following account of this journey is given in *Miskat-ul-Misabih* :
"Whilst I was sleeping upon my side, he (Gabriel) came to me,
and cut me open from my breast to below my navel, and took out
my heart, and washed the cavity with Zam-zam water, and then
filled my heart with Faith and Science. After this a white animal
was brought for me to ride upon. Its size was between that of a
mule and an ass, and it stretched as far as the eye could see. The
name of the animal was Buraq. Then I mounted the animal,
and ascended until we arrived at the lowest heaven, and Gabriel
demanded that the door should be opened. And it was asked, 'Who
is it?' and he said, 'I am Gabriel.' And they then said, 'Who is
with you?' and he answered, 'It is Muhammad.' They said, 'Has

Koelle quotes traditions to show that, as Jesus
Christ to us, so to Moslems, Mohammed is above all
other men in worth and dignity. He was the greatest
and best of all God's messengers; his body the
true temple in which the Divine Presence dwelt.
Mohammed bore the divine seal of prophecy, and im-
parted divine benefits by laying on his hands. As a
parody of the mystery of the Lord's Supper, Mohammed

Muhammad been called to the office of a prophet?' He said, 'Yes.'
They said, 'Welcome, Muhammad; his coming is well.' Then the
door was opened; and when I arrived in the first heaven, behold, I
saw Adam. And Gabriel said to me, 'This is your father Adam,
salute him.' Then I saluted Adam, and he answered it, and said,
'You are welcome, O good son, and good Prophet!' After that
Gabriel took me above, and we reached the second heaven; and he
asked the door to be opened, and it was said, 'Who is it?' He said,
'I am Gabriel.' It was said, 'Who is with you?' He said,
'Muhammad.' It was said, 'Was he called?' He said, 'Yes.' It was
said, 'Welcome, Muhammad; his coming is well.' Then the door was
opened; and when I arrived in the second region, behold, I saw
John and Jesus (sisters' sons). And Gabriel said, 'This is John, and
this is Jesus; salute both of them.' Then I saluted them, and they
returned it. After that they said, 'Welcome, good brother and
Prophet.' . . . Then I entered the seventh heaven, and behold, I saw
Abraham. And Gabriel said, 'This is Abraham, your father, salute
him'; which I did, and he returned it, and said, 'Welcome, good
son and good Prophet.' After that I was taken up to the tree called
Sidratu' l-Muntaha; and behold, its fruits were like water-pots, and
its leaves like elephant's ears. And Gabriel said, 'This is Sidratu'
l-Muntaha.' And I saw four rivers there; two of them hidden, and
two manifest. I said to Gabriel, 'What are these?' He said,
'These two concealed rivers are in Paradise; and the two manifest
are the Nile and the Euphrates.' After that I was shown the Baitu'
l-M'amur. After that, a vessel full of wine, another full of milk,
and another of honey were brought to me, and I took the milk and
drank it. And Gabriel said, 'Milk is religion; you and your
people will be of it.'' Cf. the commentators on Surah 7 : 1.

is said to have sanctioned the drinking of his own
blood. When Malik bin Sinan sucked his wounds,
swallowing the blood, the prophet exclaimed, "Any
one whose blood touches mine, him the fire of hell shall
not destroy."

The miracles of Jesus Christ, even the fantastic
miracles given by Moslem tradition, shrink into in-
significance compared with the miracles ascribed to
Mohammed by tradition. Feeding a hungry multitude
with a handful of dates, opening the eyes of the blind,
healing the sick, turning barren lands into fruitful
fields, and raising the dead,—all these and many other
things are attributed to Mohammed.[1]

In his death as well as in his life Mohammed is
made to resemble Jesus Christ. His death was foretold; it was not unavoidable, but freely accepted by
him; he died a martyr's death, and his sufferings were
meritorious, taking away sin and helping those who
believe in him to enter paradise. "It is recorded
on the testimony of Ali that three days after his
Excellency's funeral there came an Arab, who threw
himself down upon the prince's grave, and took a
handful of earth from it, casting it on his own head,
and then called out, 'O Apostle of God, thou hast
spoken it, from thee we have heard it, thou hast
received it from God, and we have received it from

[1] Cf. Carletti, *Idhar-ul-Hak*, vol. ii. pp. 154–190: he gives forty
miracles. Also, *Two Hundred and Fifty-two Authentic Miracles of
Mohammed*, by Maulvi Mohammad Inayat Ahmad. Translated and
published by the Mohammedan Tract and Book Depôt. Lahore, 1894.

thee, and it is derived from those who came down to thee, that noble verse, "And if they have darkened their souls, let them come unto thee!" I have brought darkness on my soul: but I am come to thee as a confounded, bewildered sinner, that thou mayest ask pardon for me of the Most High.' Then there came forth a voice from that Excellency's tomb, saying three times, 'Thou hast been pardoned, thou hast been pardoned.'"[1]

Not only are all these superhuman characteristics and divine glories ascribed to Mohammed in tradition, but he is the Prophet to whom all former prophets bore witness, and concerning whose coming they testified.[2] "Wahab bin Minbeh said that the Most High sent the following revelation to the prophet Isaiah: 'I will send a prophet who is to be unlettered, and by his name I will open the ears of the deaf, and the minds of the listless; and I will clothe him with gravity, and I will make goodness his outward mark, and godliness and temperance his inward mind; and wisdom his understanding; and truth and purity his nature, and propriety his disposition; and equity his practice; and truth his law; and right guidance his leader; and Islam his people; and his name Ahmed. And through him I will show to his people the right way out of error, and the way of knowledge after ignorance; and by his name I will make the few

---

[1] Koelle, *Mohammed and Mohammedanism*, p. 373.

[2] Cf. Sayous, *Jésus Christ, etc.*, pp. 82–85.

many and the divided united; and will bring amongst the separated hearts and the antagonistic nations harmony and intimacy ; and his people shall be superior to every other; and they shall pay respect to the light of the sun, *i.e.* they shall look to the sun to know the right time for prayer.'"[1] On the same authority, God gave the following revelation to Jesus: "Declare Mohammed to be true, and believe in him; and tell also thy people that those of them who reach his time should believe in him. O thou son of the Virgin, *i.e.* O thou Jesus, know thou, that if it had not been for Mohammed, I should not have created Adam and Paradise and Hell; and the truth is, that when I made the Throne, it shook and would not stand firm till I wrote upon it, 'There is no God but Allah, and Mohammed is the Apostle of Allah,' whereupon it steadied itself and became quiet."[2]

Jesus Christ is supplanted by Mohammed not only in Moslem tradition and in the hearts of the common people who are ignorant and illiterate. He is supplanted in the hearts of *all* Moslems by Mohammed. They are jealous for his glory and resist any attempt to magnify the glory of Jesus Christ at the expense of Mohammed. When, *e.g.*, a Christmas vacation was granted in certain government schools of Egypt, the Moslem paper *El 'Alam* entered a vigorous protest,

---

[1] Koelle, *Mohammed and Mohammedanism*, p. 430.

[2] *Ibid.*, p. 431. There are numerous traditions of this character in all the later biographies of Mohammed. See, for example, *Insan-ul-Ayun, Dakaik-ul-Akhbar*, or *Kasus-ul-Anbiya*.

calling it a dangerous innovation, and stating that
Egypt was a Moslem country, and that Moslems as
such had nothing to do with the birthday of Jesus.
"Keep your feast day; we will have nothing to do
with it."[1]

"You will be interested to know," writes a missionary
from Turkey under the new régime, "that the birthday
of Mohammed is now kept, beginning with last year,
and all the schools are closed for the day. It is
reckoned the most important holiday in the year, and
we must give our Moslem boys the day off. In
Smyrna, where all Government and Custom depart-
ments observed Sunday instead of Friday as a holiday,
because this city is so largely Christian, we hear the
custom will now be reversed, and Friday established
as the weekly holiday."[2]

The new Islam does not hesitate to apply the very
name of *The Messiah* to Mohammed, as the old Islam
does His office as Mediator.[3] In a series of articles

[1] *El Alam.* Cairo, 26th December 1910.
[2] The Moslem press in Egypt is also resisting every attempt on
the part of the Copts to secure Sunday as a day of rest from
Government service. El Mueyyed (18th March 1911) in a leading
article of ten columns quoted largely from the New Testament to prove
that if any day ought to be observed it was Saturday, and that the
Copts had no right to claim Sunday, because Jesus and His apostles
did not observe the day.
[3] Sayous, *Jésus-Christ d'après Mahomét,* chap. vi: "Les passages
de l'ancient Testament sont dérobés à la gloire de Jésus-Christ pour
enrichir celle du prophète pillard et d'ailleurs l'idée même d'une
prophétie Messianique est un emprunt évident à la theologie
chrétienne."

on Islam and Socialism in a leading review of India, Mushir Hosain Kidwai speaks thus of Mohammed:—

"The time was ripe because the moral, social, religious, and political state of the whole peninsula had reached the depth of degradation. Human sacrifice to idols, the burying alive of infants, misappropriation of property and exploitation of the money of helpless orphans, forced marriages of girls and minors, cruel treatment of slaves, unrestricted polygamy and concubinage, wild despotism, vengeful blood-feuds, individualistic egotism, class and birth arrogance, and other vices, demanded from a merciful Providence the commission of a real Messiah, to clear the putrid atmosphere of Arabian society, and to save humanity, which was then in a state most susceptible to infection, from a dangerous calamity.

"Fortunately for the progress of the world, *the Messiah* did come. He came and miraculously metamorphosed the whole Arabian society by masterly introducing the principles of true Socialism in almost every phase of human life. He came and brightened the gloomy aspect of the whole world by inspiring humanity through a universal faith, with the loftiest conceptions of Divinity and purest ethics of duty. If Arabia owes its glory to Socialism, the world owes it to Islam. And Socialism and Islam both were perfected by *the Messiah*, who cured not a leper or two, but the whole leprous society; who gave a new and vigorous life not to a few dead persons, but to a whole nation; who performed not only supernatural miracles of but superstitious value in our sceptical age, but material and everlasting wonders, whose signs are manifest to this day; who ruled not only over the shifting sands that form a mirage of temporary territorial domains, but also over an ever-increasing number of living human hearts, which sing even now the same song that he set, binding them together in one chord—the Chord of God—the truest and best socialism." [1]

In the *Gospel of Barnabas*, a spurious document dating about the middle of the sixteenth century, and not referred to by Moslems until after Sale had called attention to it in his translation of the Koran, Mohammed is also called the Messiah. The *Gospel of Barnabas* was evidently written by a Christian renegade in the Middle Ages, and has for its special object the advancement of Islam, the author desiring to foist upon the world a forgery which would strengthen the claims of Mohammed and prove that Jesus Christ had foretold his coming. Every reader of the Koran knows that Jesus Christ is spoken of consistently in that book as the Messiah, yet, strange to say, this *Gospel of Barnabas* again and again gives Mohammed that title, while Jesus is made his forerunner, as John the Baptist was to Christ in the canonical Gospels. Thus in Chapter LXXXIII, where Jesus is speaking to the Samaritan women, he says,

[1] *The Hindustan Review*, March–April 1911, p. 300 (Allahabad.)

"I am indeed sent to the house of Israel as a prophet of salvation, but after me shall come the Messiah, sent of God to all the world; for whom God hath made the world."[1]　In Chapter XLIII Jesus says, "If the messenger of God whom ye call Messiah were son of David, how should David call him Lord? Believe me, for verily I say unto you that the promise was made in Ishmael, not in Isaac." And again in the following chapter: "I therefore say unto you that the messenger of God is a splendour that shall give gladness to nearly all that God hath made, for he is adorned with the spirit of understanding and of counsel, the spirit of wisdom and might, the spirit of fear and love, the spirit of prudence and temperance; he is adorned with the spirit of charity and mercy, the spirit of justice and piety, the spirit of gentleness and patience, which he hath received from God three times more than he hath given to all his creatures. O blessed time, when he shall come to the world! Believe me that I have seen him and have done him reverence, even as every prophet hath seen him; seeing that of his spirit God giveth to them prophecy. And when I saw him my soul was filled with consolation, saying: 'O Mohammed! God be with thee, and may He make me worthy to untie thy shoe-latchet, for obtaining this I shall be a great prophet and holy one of God.' And having said this, Jesus rendered his thanks to God."[2]

[1] The *Gospel of Barnabas*, p. 191.　　　　[2] *Ibid.*, p. 105.

Now although this *Gospel of Barnabas* is evidently a late forgery, it is more and more being used by Moslems as an argument against Christianity; this shows how, with the centuries, Mohammed has gradually taken the place of Jesus Christ in Moslem literature, and how even His supreme title of the Christ, or the Messiah has, both in the Middle Ages and in current periodical literature, been given to the prophet of Arabia.[1] Whether the title of Messiah is given him or not, Mohammed is for all practical purposes the Moslem Christ.

Islam is indeed the only anti-Christian religion. This world faith joins issue with everything that is vital in the Christian religion, because it joins issue in its attitude toward the Christ. By this it must stand or fall. In this respect all schools of Moslem thought are practically the same. They differ in ritual and tradition; in interpretations, broad or narrow; in going back to the old Koran or in advocating the new Islam; but whether Shiahs or Sunnis, Wahabis or followers of Seyyid Ameer Ali, their position as regards the Christ is practically the same.[2]

---

[1] Cf. Recent Moslem literature in Egypt, especially Ahmed Ali El Malyee's *Jawab 'an Su'al badh Ahl-el-kitab.*

[2] The Shiah sect also believe that Mahommed has superseded Jesus Christ, and is superior to Him in station and dignity, but they add that Ali also is in every respect not only the equal of Jesus Christ, but superior to him.   See, for example, the book entitled *Munakib al Abtal,* by Mohammed bin Ali bin Shar Ashub (Bombay), in which we are told (vol. i. p. 141) that even as Jesus Christ's miraculous birth,

"Islam," says Rev. G. Simon of Sumatra, "is not a preparation for Christianity; it is easier to build on a strange soil than first of all to tear down old buildings which are so firmly set together that they offer an unsurmountable obstacle to demolition."[1] The resolution passed by the Lucknow Conference, 1911, expressed this sentiment even more forcibly:—

"This Conference is persuaded that, in order to stem the tide of Moslem advance, it is important to strengthen the work among animistic tribes, pagan communities, and depressed classes affected by this advance; for we are clearly of opinion that adoption of the faith of Islam by the pagan people is in no sense whatever a stepping-stone towards, or a preparation for, Christianity, but exactly the reverse."

Christianity gladly admits the strength of theism as a basis of unity between Islam and Christianity. We

so was that of Ali, only in more noble degree; even as He spoke before His birth to His mother, so did Ali; even as He mastered learning in His childhood, so did Ali; even as Jesus Christ prophesied of the coming of Mohammed, so also He prophesied concerning Ali; even as He raised the dead, so did Ali; even as He opened the eyes of the blind and cured the lepers, so did Ali; even as men disagree in regard to the character of Jesus, so have they disagreed in regard to the character of Ali; so those who believe in Him give him the highest station.

Cf. the extravagant statements regarding the intercession of Husain in the *Miracle Play of Hasan and Husain*, Col. Sir Lewis Pelly (London, 1879), vol. ii. pp. 343–347, where Mohammed says: "Good tidings, O Husain! act thou according to thy will. Behold the fulfilment of God's promise. Permission has proceeded from the Judge, the gracious Creator, that I should give to thy hand this key of intercession," etc. etc.

[1] *Edinburgh Conference Report*, vol. iv. p. 147.

assert as strongly as do all Moslems that there is only
one God, *but because there is only one God there can be
only one Gospel and one Christ.* The words quoted
from Dr. James Denney at the head of this chapter
are significant in this connection. " It pleased the
Father " that in *Jesus Christ* "all fulness should
dwell "; *not* in Mohammed. " In *Him* dwelleth all
the fulness of the Godhead bodily "; *not* in Mohammed.
" In *Him* are hid all treasures of wisdom and knowledge"; *not* in Mohammed. "*He* is the Way, the
Truth, and the Life"; *not* Mohammed. This is the
issue which cannot be avoided.

The only Christianity that has a missionary message
for the Moslem world is this vital Christianity. It is
the only Christianity that can meet the deepest need
of our Moslem brethren. Our love for them is only
increased by our intolerance of their rejection of the
Christ; we cannot bear it, it pains us ; and the day is
coming when many will confess Him in the words of
a Moslem convert to a Bible-woman who was visiting
her : "*I see now that the very centre of your religion is
Christ, and I want to love and serve Him.*"

The main question even as regards the new Islam
is not how much nearer they have come to Christian
ethics and Christian civilisation in their attempts to
reform the old system, but it is the old question,
" What think ye of the Christ ? "

VIII

HOW TO PREACH CHRIST TO MOSLEMS
WHO KNOW JESUS

" Without doubt, it is no light thing to ask a man to reconsider his religious position, and see where in the light of historical fact and human reason he stands ; and it is just this demand that we make on our Muhammadan brethren. We do not come to them to try to prove that their theological dogmas are wrong, and that ours are better ; that their religious practices are tainted with the formalism against which Jesus threatened His most grievous woes. We come not to destroy, but simply to ask the educated Muhammadan to tell us what ground he has for passing by a religious faith which Muhammad himself declared to be the truth. For we maintain that what we hold, and try in spite of all the failings inherent in poor human nature to practice, is simply Christianity as Jesus taught it—in fact, the true Islam, which Muhammad and the Qur'an both witnessed to as being the Religion of God."—REV. W. R. W. GARDNER, *Christianity and Muhammadanism.*

VIII

HOW TO PREACH CHRIST TO MOSLEMS WHO KNOW JESUS

KNOWLEDGE of the Moslem Christ as portrayed in the previous chapters must awaken in every Christian heart a desire to lead our Moslem brethren from their partial, eccentric, and distorted view of our Saviour to Him in whom dwelleth all fulness and Who is the whole truth; to guide them from the twilight shadows of tradition to a full-orbed vision of the Sun of Righteousness. There is no stronger argument or plea for missions to Moslems than their conception of our Christ, and the fact that Mohammed has usurped the place of our Saviour in so many hearts. We may well voice our petitions for missions to Moslems in the words of Christ Himself, " Father, the hour has come; glorify Thy Son, that Thy Son also may glorify Thee." A passion for the glory of God, which is among the highest missionary motives, will inspire us to preach the Christ in all His fulness to those who are now following Mohammed. We think of the words of Isaiah, "Jehovah, that is My name; and My glory

12

will I not give to another, nor My praise to graven images."

In considering the practical outcome of our study of the Moslem Christ, it is first of all evident that the one message for the Moslem world and for each individual Moslem, is Jesus Christ. Their knowledge of Him is so inadequate, so distorted, so insufficient, and so utterly obscured by the glory of their own prophet, that we can only use this knowledge as a stepping-stone to higher things. "The duty seems plain," says Dr. James S. Dennis: "'Go ye into all the world, and preach the gospel to every creature.' The gospel of Christ, not of Mohammed—to *every* creature, because all need the gospel. If there were a possibility of a human substitute for the gospel, we might consider it an open question whether salvation is of Mohammed; but Christ has taught us one way of salvation for all men, and that way is through Him—through the merits of His sacrifice, and not through works or worthiness in man. I would not be understood as implying here that every Moslem is necessarily lost. If he despises and rejects Christ, and puts his sole trust in Mohammed, or even trusts in divine mercy because that mercy is his due as a Moslem, I should not feel that there was a substantial basis of hope for him. He is looking to a human saviour, or he is simply claiming the divine mercy as a subsidy to the Moslem religion. . . . . The Christian is not saved because he is a Christian. The Moslem, of course, cannot be saved because he is a Moslem. All who may be saved out-side of formal and visible connection with Christianity, will be saved because of a real and invisible connection with Christ. They will have obtained consciously, or unconsciously, by the aid of God's Spirit that attitude of humility and trust toward God which will make it consistent with His character and in harmony with His wisdom and goodness to impart to their souls the free gift of pardon through Christ's merits, and apply to them in the gladness of His love the benefits of Christ's death. It is in any case salvation by gift, received from God's mercy, and based upon Christ's atonement, and not by works or by reason of human merit. We claim, therefore, that the Mohammedan, as such, needs the knowledge of Christ, and can only be saved through Christ. He needs to be taught Christianity and brought into the light of Bible truth. He needs to recognise the dangerous errors of his religion and turn to Christianity as the true light from heaven. He needs to take a radically different and essentially new attitude towards Christ. He needs spiritual regeneration and moral reformation. In one word, he needs the Gospel. He needs all its lessons, and all its help, and all its inspiration. Here we rest the question of duty. If any class of men need the gospel, to them it should be given, and it is our mission in the world as Christians to do this."[1]

[1] Dennis, "Islam and Christian Missions" in *The Missionary Review of the World*, August 1889.

We have quoted these words at length because even
to-day there are those who doubt the expediency or
even the possibility of missions to Moslems.   While
the difficulties in the way of missionary work in some
Moslem lands may, for political and other reasons,
seem most formidable, and while the access to the
individual Moslem heart is also beset with baffling
obstacles, this does not turn away our responsibility
or our privilege.   The Church of Christ should make
use of all its opportunities to deliver the gospel message
to Moslems in full expectation that the power of the
Holy Spirit, whose special work it is to reveal the
Christ, will in God's own time lead to the triumph
of Christianity in Moslem lands and Moslem hearts.
It has been remarked with truth that Islam comes
into conflict with the doctrinal teachings of Christianity
just at those points where reason has the best vantage-
ground in opposition to faith.   The great problems of
the Incarnation, the deity of Christ, and the Trinity
are stumbling-blocks not only to the Moslem, but they
are the very problems over which Christianity herself
has pondered with amazement and awe, and with
reference to which there have been divisions in the
Church itself; but these unfathomable mysteries are
the very heart of our religion.   Without them Christianity is not differentiated from other faiths and
philosophies.

The very fact that Islam, beginning without a
mediator and with a prophet who was thoroughly

human, should in the course of centuries have ascribed to him the offices and the character of a mediator and a Messiah, can be used as an argument to prove that they need the Christ. In this also imitation is the sincerest flattery, and when we preach Christ to Moslems who know of Jesus, we are presenting to them the one thing lacking in their faith and the one unfulfilled desire in their lives. If the Cross of Christ is the missing link in their creed, then the preaching of the Cross, although it may seem to them foolishness, will yet prove among Moslems the wisdom of God and the power of God. "Just because Islam is the antithesis to the thesis of Christianity, a synthesis is possible, not by a compromise between Islam and Christianity, but by bringing to clear expression the many common features which still remain, and by showing how these common features are found in a truer form in Christianity than in Islam."[1]

Of all the common features on which we can seize as a point of vital contact with Moslems there is none superior to *the fact of the Christ*. Islam, as we have seen, admits His coming, His supernatural birth, His high office as the Bringer of a special revelation from God, His sinlessness, His compassion, and His power to work miracles. His very names afford so many points of departure to lead from the Koran and tradition to the Gospels. The contradictory accounts

[1] *Edinburgh Conference Report*, vol. iv. p. 141.

of His death, by their very contradictions and subterfuges, point to the Cross of Christ and His death for sinners as the only solution. Jesus Christ is our peace; the day He was born, the day He died, and the day He was raised again (Surah 19:34), and these three great days to which the Koran calls attention in the life of Jesus Christ are the three great holy days in the calendar of the Church—Christmas, Good Friday, and Easter. By admitting the truths which we hold in common with Moslems, by bidding them look away from their broken lights and flickering shadows to the "true Light which enlighteneth every man that cometh into the world," we can best of all help Moslems.

Just as the "Moslem conception of God is base, unholy, and to the Christian utterly repugnant,"[1] yet Mohammedan theism is a foundation on which we can build a fuller knowledge of the Godhead, of His holiness, justice, and love; so Moslems who know Jesus as a mere prophet will for this very reason welcome a larger knowledge of His character, and be led from the Koran caricature to the Gospel portrait. Our preaching should be constructive, and in this way it will most surely be destructive. We can break down false ideas of God and of Christ in Moslem theology most surely and most speedily by full proclamation of those very truths which Islam lacks. Without denying the fact that Islam is in its spirit anti-

[1] *Edinburgh Conference Report*, vol. iv. p. 141.

Christian, that it contains much that is positively
harmful in ethics, and that it is wholly deficient in
those doctrines which are the very heart of Christianity, we nevertheless admit that the acceptance
of the Old Testament prophets, the peculiar honours
paid to our Lord, and the testimony to the sacred
scriptures found in the Koran, are important prepara-
tory elements in spite of many qualifications and
denials. We must become Moslems to the Moslem
if we would gain them for Christ. We must do this
in the Pauline sense, without compromise, but with
self-sacrificing sympathy and unselfish love. The
Christian missionary should first of all thoroughly
know the religion of the people among whom he
labours; ignorance of the Koran, the traditions, the
life of Mohammed, the Moslem conception of Christ,
social beliefs and prejudices of Mohammedans, which
are the result of their religion,—ignorance of these is
the chief difficulty in work for Moslems.

The nearest way to the Moslem heart can often be
found better by subjective than by objective study.
The barrier may be in the heart of the missionary
as well as in the heart of the Moslem. He should
cultivate sympathy to the highest degree and an
appreciation of all the great fundamental truths
which we hold in common with Moslem. He should
show the superiority of Christianity both in doctrine
and life by admitting the excellences of doctrine and
life in Mohammedanism, but showing immediately

how Christianity far surpasses them. Many Moslems are at heart dissatisfied with Mohammed as an ideal of character. In spite of later tradition, the bold outline of his life and character as shown in the Koran stands out and perplexes them. The inconsistencies of his conduct are not taken away by the whitewash of tradition. His relations to women especially present a moral difficulty to many Mohammedans who are beginning to think in higher terms of ethics. Therefore, while the missionary should be careful not to offend needlessly, he should boldly challenge a comparison between the life of Mohammed and the life of Jesus Christ, even as known to Moslems from their own books. Compromise in this regard will not win the respect of Moslems. They glorify their prophet, why should we not glorify ours? A loving and yet bold presentation of the distinctive truths of our religion and of the surpassing grandeur and beauty of the character of Jesus Christ will never alienate a Moslem heart.

The heart of the Gospel and that which possesses the greatest power of appeal to Mohammedans, as to every sinner, is the union between God's mercy and God's justice manifested in the Cross of Christ. When properly presented, this doctrine is not only absolutely novel but compelling to any Mohammedan who feels a sense of sin. In order to awaken a sense of sin, which is essential in all missionary effort, the ethical standards of the Sermon on the Mount and the spotless purity of the life of Christ must be presented. It is not always wise at first to compare Mohammed and Christ. If we present the Christ as He is in the Gospel, the contrast is so evident that the comparison is made by the Mohammedan himself. We should ask every sincere Moslem inquirer to study the Gospel story and try for himself to reach a true estimate of Jesus Christ, of whom Mohammed spoke in such high terms of honour as a Prophet and an Apostle of God; to take the historical foundations of the Christian religion and examine them as critically as he pleases, and to see for himself what Jesus claimed to be, and how His claims were understood by His disciples and by the early Church. We should ask Moslems to study the Gospel in any way they like, but with only *one* object in view, "namely, that they may come face to face with Jesus Himself; that they may learn to know Him, and see how He claimed to hold a supreme position in the matter of the attitude of all men toward God, a position which none other has ever claimed."[1] In other words, we should press home the question Jesus Himself put to His disciples and to the world, "What think ye of the Christ?"

Are we not sometimes in danger of over-estimating the inward strength of Islam? The fact is that it is seamed through and through with lines of cleavage and of disintegration, which have grown wider and deeper with the centuries. Even the masses

[1] Gardner, *Christianity and Mohammedanism Compared*, p. 62.

are beginning to compare and to think. An outward show of fanatic devotion to the dogma of Islam is not always a proof of real faith in Mohammed and his teaching. When Saul redoubled his energies in persecution, his heart was already under conviction from the preaching of Stephen. Unsatisfied doubt is to-day more common than blind devotion among educated Moslems, and one has only to read recent Moslem literature to see what frantic attempts are made to save the ship of Islam by throwing overboard that which was once considered good cargo. In this connection the following words by a missionary in Burma who answers the question, "How should we preach to the Heathen?" have their lesson also as regards Islam: "We may well believe that heathen religions, so far from having arisen as some have vainly imagined out of the soil of lofty aspiration after a God unknown, are devices more or less elaborate for shutting the thought of God as He is out of the minds and hearts of men. If these various systems were the result of sincere attempts to find out God, then the farther the system is developed, the more complete in all its parts, the more open to the truth ought its devout adherents to be. But precisely the contrary is true. The more elaborate and complete the system, the less ready are its followers to yield themselves to Christ. The Gospel meets its greatest triumphs not among those who have the most finished, but among those who have the crudest systems of religion. Elaborateness, completeness, finish, here seem to be elaborateness, completeness, finish of escape from the consciousness of God."[1]

We must compel Moslems to go back to Mohammed with us; to dig beneath the rubbish of tradition and in the original foundations of Islam to see what Mohammed taught in regard to Jesus Christ, and what he himself was, on the testimony of his own book. The Moslem world is plastic and restless as it never was before. There are critical tendencies and influences at work which before were dormant. Islam, as well as the other Oriental faiths is recognising its own inadequacy and attempting to adapt itself to new conditions. In the words of Dr. Mott, "Islam is linking itself with the atheism and theism of Western lands, and is securing much protection and also added prestige by the support which it receives at the hands of officials from the West who have broken with Christianity. These men carry over to the Moslem camp all the armoury of the theistic and atheistic schools."[2]

This revival of Islam is accompanied also by a rising spiritual tide, shown in a spirit of inquiry and an unprecedented demand for the Scriptures, and the weakening hold of Moslem faith and ethics on the

[1] Rev. E. N. Harris in *The Missionary Review of the World*, April 1902, pp. 266–268.
[2] *Decisive Hour of Christian Missions*, p. 57.

educated classes, although not yet evident in numerous conversions. The investigations of the Cairo Conference and the reports of the Lucknow Conference have proved beyond the shadow of a doubt that the hour is ripe for evangelising the Moslem world.

Finally, we may well ask what Christianity itself will gain by preaching Christ to Moslems. What will be the reflex influence of a campaign for the evangelisation of the Moslem world ? What are the moral issues involved in the coming conflict between Christian and Islamic theism ? That such a conflict is inevitable the preceding chapters have abundantly proved, for, in the words of Dr. Robert E. Speer,[1] "Missions do not rest upon a maudlin erasure of all lines of distinct opinion of truth, and the purchase of good feeling by the surrender of principle to sentimental slovenliness. They involve the fierce clash of truth and error."

First of all, the Church will gain a stronger grip on the great fundamentals of the Christian faith. The doctrines of the Incarnation, the Atonement, and the Trinity will become more and more the subject of special study as we meet Moslems face to face in the battle for the truth. In reading the Gospel with and to Moslems, it will become evident more and more to every Christian that the death of Christ, which is denied in Islam, occupies the supreme place in the Gospels and in the Epistles as the very heart of God's revelation to man. The same is true in

[1] Cf. Speer, *Missionary Principles and Practice*, pp. 109–129.

regard to the nature and evidences of the resurrection of Jesus Christ, and our faith in the character of the Godhead as compared with the barren monotheism of Islam.

In the second place, the Christian Church will be forced to work out her theology experientially when in contact and conflict with unitarian, deistic Islam. In this respect the Mohammedan problem may possibly be as life from the dead to the Oriental Churches when they face its real and spiritual issues, and become conscious of the duty of evangelism. The doctrine of the Incarnation and of the Holy Spirit are not pieces of polished armoury to be kept on exhibition in proof of our orthodoxy, but are vital to the very life of the Christian. The orthodox Eastern Church will be impotent over against Islam as long as it is merely orthodox in its creed. The doctrine of the Trinity must be vitalised to become effective over against Moslem unitarianism. Rev. W. H. T. Gairdner has pointed out some of these "important moral issues involved in this conflict between trinitarian and Islamic monotheism."[1] He says, "Islam forces us to find the Trinity in our hearts, and it forces us to find the Trinity in the heart of God." After considering the solitary, in-scrutable, and characterless Sultan of heaven whom the Moslems call Allah, he asks this question: "Are

[1] See his paper on this subject at the Pan-Anglican Conference ; reprinted in *Blessed be Egypt*. Cairo, 1909.

not Moslem deism and Christian trinitarian theism between them forcing the Church to consider this problem yet once again, and in relation to the mystery of the Atonement to read a richer meaning into the great verse, 'God was in Christ reconciling the world to Himself.'"

Even as a study of the Moslem doctrine of God again and again forces from our hearts an overflow of thanksgiving and praise for the knowledge of the only true God as He is revealed in the Scriptures, so a study of the Moslem Christ and of Mohammedan substitutes for the only Mediator between God and men will lead us more than ever to a deeper knowledge and a stronger, more passionate devotion to Him "in Whom dwelleth all the fulness of the Godhead bodily," and Who, because of His sacrifice and death for sinners, is worthy to receive "power and riches and wisdom and might and honour and glory and blessing."

In the third place, it will be clearly seen that Unitarianism is *not* Christianity, when we study the Moslem doctrine of God and the Moslem doctrine of Christ. Modern Unitarianism, like Islam, begins by trying to do full justice to the humanity of Jesus, but the logical outcome of this position has been well pointed out by Dr. Duncan B. MacDonald in a remarkable address on "One phase of the doctrine of the Unity of God." He refers especially to the Unity of God according to Moslem Theology.

"The new Unitarianism seeks to carry over the

emotional content of Christianity, after abandoning the metaphysical realities which make that emotion abidingly possible. The incarnate Word is a metaphor, mythologised and misinterpreted, but it is still to declare to us the Father and to be the Light of the world. The Holy Ghost is a figurative expression, but it is still to be the abiding Comforter and the Lord and Giver of life. We are to be strict monists, and yet we are to be branches of the Vine, nourished by the mystical Vision. . . ."

"But if we are to be Unitarians as to the person of God, is all this possible? That is, if God is to be conceived as an internal as well as an external unity, how will that conception, in the ultimate working out, affect our feeling towards Him, affect our doctrine of Him? Our historical Unitarianism, as I have said, never faced that problem; or, rather, it thought that it could take the Christian conception of God, cut away from that conception the elements to which it objected and retain the rest. But you cannot take a man, if I may be allowed the parallel, cut away from him the organs of which you disapprove, and think that he will still remain a good-going and working man. The excision of a very small organ may upset the whole organism. And it is an organism with which we are dealing, and not a mechanical combination." Later in his paper, when speaking of the Moslem doctrine of God as current in early Moslem literature, he exclaims:—

" And when the thunder of the hoofs of these warriors for the greater glory of God has echoed past, what is left ? What was left for the Muslims ? What is left for us ? As I see it, only two possibilities. Either such a conception as the Christian Trinity, which breaks the awful inpassibility of the logically unified absolute, which renders possible sympathy, affection, love, trust ; which makes God knowable—that is how the Son reveals the Father to us ; which makes us the Sons of God, partakers of the divine nature, and not simply the creatures of His hand ; which finds within the Christian Church the Holy Ghost, the Comforter, the Lord and Giver of Life ; and which yet preserves God—Father, Son, and Holy Ghost—as a conscious, knowing, feeling, willing individual. Either that or Pantheism, in which the many vanish in the one, and the one vanishes in the many. . . .

" All attempts to simplify the metaphysical basis of our faith have, under the test of time and life, failed. Deists and theists have come and gone. Ethics and natural theology have claimed their own and more, have had, for a time, their claims allowed and then have vanished. In many ways the Christian Church has moved ; the guidance of the Spirit has not failed it. Its faith has seen many hypotheses, has been enfolded in many garments. But to the seeker in the great space that lies between materialism and Pantheism the presentation that still expresses most adequately the mystery behind our lives is that in the Christian Trinity, and the words that come the nearest are those of the Nicene Creed."[1]

Let a Moslem once feel the burden of his sins, and turn away from Mohammed and the Moslem Christ to the Living Saviour, the Son of God revealed in the Gospel, the Lamb of God who taketh away the sin of the world, and all his intellectual difficulties vanish like

[1] Annual Address, Hartford Seminary, September 1909. See *Hartford Seminary Record.*

the morning mist before the rising sun. Moslem converts are no longer Unitarians. They confess with heart and mouth, with the whole Church Catholic:

"I believe in one God the Father Almighty, Maker of heaven and earth, and of all things visible and invisible.

"And in one Lord Jesus Christ, the only-begotten Son of God, begotten of the Father before all worlds, God of God, Light of Light, very God of very God, begotten, not made, being of one substance with the Father; by Whom all things were made; Who, for us men and for our salvation, came down from heaven, and was incarnate by the Holy Ghost of the Virgin Mary, and was made man; and was crucified also for us under Pontius Pilate; He suffered and was buried; and the third day He rose again, according to the Scriptures; and ascended into heaven, and sitteth on the right hand of the Father; and He shall come again with glory to judge both the quick and the dead; Whose kingdom shall have no end.

"And in the Holy Ghost, the Lord and Giver of Life; who proceedeth from the Father and the Son, who with the Father and the Son together is worshipped and glorified, who spake by the prophets. . . ."

BIBLIOGRAPHY

OF WORKS REFERRED TO IN THE TEXT OR USED IN ITS PREPARATION

Ad-Damiri . . . . *Hayat - al - Hayawan.* Translation by A. S. G. Jayaker. 2 vols. London, 1906.

Ahmed Ali El Malijee. *Jawab' an Su'al Badh Ahl El Kitab.* Cairo, 1908. (A poetical attack on Christ and Christianity.)

Ameer Ali, Seyyid . *The Spirit of Islam.* Calcutta, 1902.

Basset, René . . . "La Bordah du Cheikh el Bousiri." Poème en l'honneur de Mohammed. Traduite et commentée. Paris, 1894.

Beidhawi . . . . . *Commentary on the Koran.* Cairo, A.H. 1303.

Birks, Herbert . . . *Life of Thomas Valpy French.* 2 vols. London, 1895.

Burhan ud Din Al Halibi. *Insan ul Ayoon* (A biography of Mohammed in three volumes quarto). Cairo, A.H. 1308.

Burton, Sir Richard . *Pilgrimage to el Madinah and Meccah.* 2 vols. London, 1893.

Carletti, P. V. . . . . *Idh-Har-Ul-Haqq ou manifestation de la Vérité, de el Hage Rahmat-Ullah Efendi de Delhi.* Traduit de l'arabe. 2 vols. Paris, 1880.

Caussin, De Perceval . *Essai sur l'histoire des Arabes avant l'Islamisme.* 3 vols. Paris, 1847.

Chattopadhyaya, Nishikanta.	*Christ in the Koran.* Cairo and London. (Reprint of an article by a Hindu that appeared in the *Hindustan Review* (Allahabad).)
Cheikho, P. L. . . .	*Quelques Legendes Islamiques Apocryphes.* Beirut, 1910.
Denney, James. . .	*The Death of Christ.* London, 1903.
Edinburgh Conference Report.	Vol. iv. *The Missionary Message.* Edinburgh, 1910.
Eth-Thalabi . . .	*Kusus al Anbiah.* Cairo, A.H. 1325.
Fairbairn, A. M. . .	*Christ in Modern Theology.* London, 1894.
Fairbairn, A. M. . .	*The City of God.* London, 1897.
Fluegel, G.	*Concordance to the Koran.* Leipzig, 1898.
Geiger, Abraham .	*Was hat Mohammed aus dem Judenthume aufgenommen?* Bonn, 1833.
Gerock, C. F. . . .	*Christologie des Koran.* Hamburg and Gotha, 1839.
Goldziher, Ignaz . .	*Muhammedanische Studien.* 2 vols. Halle, 1889.
Gospel of Barnabas, The.	Edited and Translated from the Italian MS. in the Imperial Library at Vienna by Lonsdale and Laura Ragg. Oxford, 1907.
Houtsma, M. Th., Arnold, T. W., Seligsohn, M., and Schaade, A.	Editors, *The Encyclopedia of Islam* : A Dictionary of the Geography, Ethnography, and Biography of the Mohammedan Peoples. London, 1910.
Hughes, Thomas P. .	*Dictionary of Islam.* London, 1885.
Ibn, Khaldoon . . .	*Mukadimet* (An introduction to his general history). Beirut edition.
Jallalain	*Commentary on the Koran.* Cairo, A.H. 1303.
Jessup, H. H. . . .	*Kamil Abdul Messiah.* Philadelphia, 1898.
Klein, F. A.. . . .	*The Religion of Islam.* London, 1906.
Koelle, S. W. . . .	*Mohammed and Mohammedanism Critically Considered.* London, 1889.

Manneval, M. . . . *La Christologie du Coran.* Toulouse, 1867. (A thesis based on the earlier work of Gerock.)

Mirkhond . . . . *Bible de l'Islam.* Paris, 1894.

Mishkat-Ul-Misabih . (Delhi Edition.) See Introduction.

Muir, Sir William . *The Beacon of Truth; or, The Testimony of the Koran to the Truth of the Christian Religion.* London, 1894.

Muir, Sir William . *The Coran.* London, 1878.

Muir, Sir William . *The Life of Mohammed.* 4 vols. London, 1857.

Nöldeke, T. . . . . *Geschichte des Qurans.* Göttingen, 1860.

Palmer, E. H. . . . *The Quran* (Sacred Books of the East). 2 vols. Oxford, 1880.

Pautz, Otto . . . . *Mohammed's Lehre von der Offenbarung.* Leipzig, 1898.

Pelly, Sir Lewis . . *The Miracle Play of Hasan and Husain.* 2 vols. London, 1879.

Pfander, Carl Gottlieb *Mizanu'l Haqq.* (The Balance of Truth.) Revised by W. St. Clair Tisdall. London, 1910.

Rice, W. A. . . . . *Crusaders of the Twentieth Century.* London, 1910.

Sayous, Edouard . . *Jésus-Christ d'après Mahomét; ou, Les Notions et les Doctrines Musulmanes sur Christianisme.* Paris, 1880.

Shah, Ahmad . . . *Concordance to the Koran.* (Miftah ul Quran). Benares, 1906.

Smith, H. P. . . . *The Bible and Islam.* London, 1898.

Sprenger, Alois . . *Life of Mohammed.* Allahabad, 1851.

Tisdall, W. St. Clair . *Mohammedan Objections to Christianity.* London, 1904.

Tisdall, W. St. Clair . *The Original Sources of the Quran.* London, 1905.

Toland, John . . . *Nazarenus; or, Jewish, Gentile, and Mahometan Christianity.* London, 1718. (Based on the Gospel of Barnabas.)

Wherry, E. M. . . . *Commentary on the Quran.* 4 vols. London, 1884.

Wright, Thomas . . *Early Christianity in Arabia.* London, 1855.

Zamakhshari . . . *Commentary on the Koran.* Cairo, A.H. 1307.

Zwemer, S. M. . . . *Islam: A Challenge to Faith.* New York, 1907.

Zwemer, S. M. . . . *The Moslem Doctrine of God.* New York and Edinburgh.

Printed by MORRISON & GIBB LIMITED, *Edinburgh*

CPSIA information can be obtained at www.ICGtesting.com
Printed in the USA
BVOW021950161212

308239BV00001B/1/P

9 780971 534643